THE FLORIDA HANDBOOK

Where to Turn, Whom to Call in Southern & Central Florida

Margo Ginsburg

Hunter Publishing, Inc.
300 Raritan Center Parkway
Edison NJ 08818
(908) 225 1900   Fax (908) 417 0482

ISBN 1-55650-649-X

© 1995 Hunter Publishing, Inc.

All rights reserved. No part of this publication may be reproduced, stored in a retrieval system, or transmitted in any form, or by any means, electronic, mechanical, photocopying, recording, or otherwise, without the written permission of the publisher.

Cover photo: MacDuff Everton/Adventure Photo

This book has been published with the purpose of providing accurate and authoritative information with respect to the subject matter covered. It is sold with the understanding that neither the publisher nor the author are engaged in rendering legal, medical or professional services. If legal or medical advice is required, the services of an attorney or physician should be sought. Every attempt has been made to provide accurate information, but neither the publisher nor the author can be held accountable for errors, omissions or changes which have occurred since this work was prepared.

Dedication

This book is dedicated to my husband, Lee, who has been my guiding light, spiritual partner, and friend throughout this project. During some frustrating moments when the book became my life, he brought humor, insight and understanding into my world. On days when the information flowed and my interviews were particularly interesting, he was there to share my sense of achievement and enthusiasm. I feel blessed to have such a wonderful husband, who is also my dearest friend.

Acknowledgments

Gathering the information and data needed to profile the cities of South and Central Florida was not an easy task. Where information was not available through printed sources, I had to rely upon many other people for assistance. In addition to my quest for factual data, I also prevailed upon many for their personal insights and descriptions. I am very grateful to all of those who shared their time and answered my many questions through telephone conversations and faxes, critical in helping to make this book possible.

I would like to thank the staff members at the various Chambers of Commerce, Economic Development Councils, and Convention and Visitors' Bureaus, who played a major role in assisting me with information.

Special thanks to the following people for going that extra distance and devoting special time and effort to this project. Whenever I ran into a stumbling block, they saved the day by providing another source or contact.

- Susan Kairalla: Naples Area Chamber of Commerce
- Casey Pilon: Sarasota Chamber of Commerce
- Stacey Rosseter: Tampa/Hillsborough Convention and Visitors' Association
- Mike Cooney: Economic Development Commission of Mid-Florida, Inc.
- Diane Reale: Public Information Office, Ft. Lauderdale
- Maria E. Llorca: Miami Convention & Visitors' Bureau

And lastly, a note of appreciation to Joel Messinger, President, Community Association Services, Deerfield Beach, who provided information for the section on *Purchasing Your Florida Home*.

Contents

INTRODUCTION	1
Facts, Symbols & Trivia	4
Laws, Licenses & Requirements	6
Establishing Residency	6
A License for Travel	7
A License for Pleasure	9
The Facts of Life	10
It's the Law	11
CITY PROFILES	12
The Palm Beaches	25
West Palm Beach	25
Boca Raton	26
Demographics	27
Taxes	28
Voting and Elections	29
Pet Registration	30
Transportation	30
Post Offices	33
Newspapers and Magazines	34
Library System	36
Health Care	38
Education	41
The Cultural Scene	46
Events and Attractions	53
Don't Miss	57
Recreation	59
Directory of Services	62
Ft. Lauderdale	66
Demographics	67
Taxes	68
Voting and Elections	69
Pet Registration	69
Transportation	70
Postal Service	73
Newspapers and Magazines	75
Library System	77

Education	80
Health Care	84
The Cultural Scene	89
Events and Attractions	95
Don't Miss	98
Recreation	99
Directory of Services	101
Miami	105
Demographics	106
Taxes	107
Voting and Elections	108
Pet Registration	108
Transportation	109
Postal Service	112
Newspapers and Magazines	112
Library System	114
Health Care	115
Education	120
The Cultural Scene	125
Events and Attractions	129
Don't Miss	135
Recreation	136
Directory of Services	139
Naples	143
Demographics	143
Taxes	144
Voting and Elections	145
Pet Registration	145
Transportation	146
Postal Service	147
Newspapers and Magazines	148
Library System	149
Health Care	150
Education	152
The Cultural Scene	155
Events and Attractions	159
Don't Miss	162
Recreation	163
Directory of Services	165
Melbourne	169
Demographics	170

Taxes	171
Voting and Elections	172
Pet Registration	173
Transportation	173
Postal Service	176
Newspapers and Magazines	177
Library System	177
Health Care	179
Education	181
The Cultural Scene	184
Events and Attractions	188
Don't Miss	191
Recreation	192
Directory of Services	195
Orlando	199
Demographics	200
Taxes	201
Voting and Elections	201
Pet Registration	202
Transportation	203
Postal Service	206
Newspapers and Magazines	208
Library System	210
Health Care	211
Education	215
The Cultural Scene	219
Events and Attractions	225
Don't Miss	227
Recreation	228
Directory of Services	230
Sarasota	234
Demographics	234
Taxes	235
Voting and Elections	236
Pet Registration	237
Transportation	237
Postal Service	240
Newspapers and Magazines	241
Library System	242
Health Care	242
Education	244
The Cultural Scene	248

Events and Attractions	253
Don't Miss	256
Recreation	256
Directory of Services	259
Tampa	263
Demographics	264
Taxes	265
Voting and Elections	265
Pet Registration	266
Transportation	267
Postal Service	269
Newspapers and Magazines	271
Library System	273
Health Care	274
Education	276
The Cultural Scene	282
Events and Attractions	287
Don't Miss	290
Recreation	291
Directory of Services	295
CONSUMER TIPS	299
Purchasing Your Florida Home	303
Helpful Hints For The Tropics	310
Auto Care	310
Farewell Snowbirds	312
Florida Pests	314
Home Security	319
Personal Care	321
Exercise	322
Pool and Spa Care	324
Storage Solutions	329
Water On Tap	332
Becoming a Part of the Community	336
Finding Your Way	335
Agencies and Free Publications	337
Great Sources Of Information	339

Introduction

Relocation is considered one of the top ten stressors in life. Even if it is a personal choice and signals a new and exciting phase of life, there are still issues which can create anxiety. People vary in their ability to tolerate change, meet new people, develop community involvements, and cope with separation from close friends, family and established support systems. One of the best ways to minimize stress is to enter into a new situation armed with enough information to make enlightened decisions.

When we decided to relocate to South Florida in 1988, we were not unfamiliar with the area. During 25 years of marriage, Florida was always a great getaway when we needed a four- or five-day vacation. As a vacationer, I adapted within minutes to the warm weather and subtropical environment. Relocating as a permanent resident, however, was quite a different experience. As we began to settle in, I realized that the differences in lifestyle, climate, and environment were significant. Being an old researcher at heart, I began to speak with people who might provide answers to questions about humidity, insects and the unpleasant taste of the water. This was the beginning of a project which evolved into the present publication. It is my hope that it will be of considerable value and benefit to new residents or the many others who are exploring different areas of Florida with relocation in mind.

The journey begins with *FLORIDA FACTS*. *Facts, Symbols & Trivia* is not only a basic introduction but is essential information if you plan to earn your "native" Floridian certificate. *Florida Laws, Licenses & Requirements* is a potpourri of practical information, such as establishing Florida residency, how to reduce your insurance premiums if you are 55 or over, and what identification you will need for a quick trip to the Bahamas.

CITY PROFILES highlights nine metropolitan areas located throughout South and Central Florida. If you are presently considering a relocation to Florida or perhaps just thinking about it for the future, the profiles offer an overview of the infrastructure and lifestyle which have become a signature of each city.

If you have recently moved to one of the cities/counties that are profiled, information about voting, library programs, transportation, education and health care should prove very helpful. City and county directories pinpoint where to turn when you have a problem or need some assistance.

If you are an oldtimer – that is, one who has lived in Florida for more than five years – it may be time to revisit Florida. One of the results of my research was the realization (and frustration) that I moved on before experiencing some of the unique places, events and attractions in our neighboring cities. The profiles highlight the cultural life and attractions in each city, such as the *French Foreign Film Festival* in Sarasota, the *Swamp Buggy Races* in Naples or the *Miami Book Fair International*.

CONSUMER TIPS explores purchasing a home and other consumer advice. After you've selected the "ideal" city for your relocation, you will have to decide on a living style which is compatible with your needs. Florida developers offer a full range of choices, from country club communities to fee simple home sites to condominium dwellings. The different types of communities are discussed with a look at some of the advantages and disadvantages of each one. Consumer Tips advises you of your rights and offers some suggestions to ensure that you maintain your Florida calm.

The next section of the book explores settling into your new environment after the initial honeymoon comes to an end. More than just a warmer climate, sandy beaches and outdoor activities, Florida is a new way of life – and, it takes some getting used to! Relocation and adjustment issues are not uncommon, but they do deserve some attention so that little frustrations do not become major problems. *HELPFUL HINTS FOR THE TROPICS* presents a series of articles related to daily living in a tropical environment. Discover how to dehumidify your closet, how to dispose of a lizard who wants to live with you, or how to maintain your automobile in the summer heat.

BECOMING A PART OF THE COMMUNITY is a guide to community resources, venues for meeting people, and other invaluable sources of information. Many veteran Floridians are unaware of the excellent free publications which are available, such as the *Automobile Insurance Shopper's Guide* printed by the Florida Dept. of Insurance or *Senior Services and Information* from the Florida Division of Consumer Services. *Outreach for Meeting People* suggests ways to engage in an area of interest as well as providing a forum to meet other people.

City-to-City Distances

	Boca Raton	Fort Lauderdale	Melbourne	Miami	Naples	Orlando	Sarasota	Tampa	West Palm Beach
Boca Raton	X	17	126	39	121	192	199	218	26
Ft. Lauderdale	17	X	144	22	105	209	201	234	43
Melbourne	126	144	X	165	201	67	171	129	101
Miami	39	22	165	X	107	228	211	245	64
Naples	121	105	201	107	X	187	105	156	147
Orlando	192	209	67	228	187	X	127	85	166
Sarasota	199	201	171	211	105	127	X	53	174
Tampa	218	234	129	245	156	85	53	X	193
West Palm Bch.	26	43	101	64	147	166	174	193	X

Facts, Symbols & Trivia

In order to become a bonafide Floridian, and not merely somebody masquerading as one, you should be acquainted with the following information and terminology. You never know when you may need to prove you're a real "Cracker."

Florida Facts

The State of Florida includes seven regions: *Southeast, Southwest, Central East, Central, Central West, Northeast and Northwest.* Its 67 counties span an area of 54,157 square miles. The distance from Key West at the southernmost tip to Pensacola in the extreme northwest is 792 miles. In 1991, Florida's population reached 13,193,432 – making it the fourth largest state in the country.

Fact, Not Fiction!

In the heart of the tropics, one of the largest and most active snow ski clubs has been in operation since 1968. The Miami Ski Club offers a variety of ski trips at discounted rates to resorts within the US and Europe as well as summer skiing in Argentina. Among the 1,200 organized ski clubs throughout the country, the Miami Club (which is a non-profit organization) has been rated in the top four. *Ph. 652-7712.*

Florida Symbols

Nickname: Sunshine State
Animal: Florida Panther
Bird: Mocking Bird
Freshwater Fish: Large Mouth Bass
Saltwater Fish: Atlantic Sail Fish
Flower: Orange Blossom
Gem: Moonstone
Marine Mammal: Manatee
Reptile: Alligator
Salt Water Mammal: Dolphin
Shell: Horse Conch or Grant Band Shell
Tree: Sabal Palm

Florida Trivia

Very few subtropical blooms have fragrant scents; Floridians might feel trapped in a perfume factory if every flower had the scent of jasmine and orange blossoms.

The expression, "Cool as a cucumber" has its roots in Florida. On a hot day, the pulp is 20 degrees cooler than the surrounding air.

The elegant *Hearts of Palm*, often served in the finest restaurants, is none other than Florida's swamp cabbage.

Florida produces more than one fourth of the watermelon crop in the United States. Color is the best test of ripeness.

Key Lime, which is native to the Florida Keys, is not a lime like any other lime; Florida's famous Key Lime Pie has a distinct yellow color rather than the traditional green.

Cantaloupe picked while it is green will not ripen; it will soften, but it will not be sweet and juicy.

When buying oranges and grapefruits, do not be deceived by the color. Be guided by the weight of the fruit; the heavier it is, the sweeter and juicier the taste.

Florida is one of the foremost producers of sweet corn, snap beans, cucumbers, eggplant, green peppers, radishes, tomatoes, squash, and escarole.

The stone crab is protected by Mother Florida. Fishermen may detach only one claw and must then return the stone crab to the water. It is able to regenerate the claw, thus maintaining the population. You can taste these delights fresh out of the Florida waters from the middle of October through mid-May.

Laws, Licenses & Requirements

Establishing Residency

Florida must be established as your legal residence to take advantage of the tax benefits. There are several ways to declare legal residency:

1. FILE A DECLARATION OF DOMICILE at the County Court House. This is an affidavit declaring Florida as your permanent and legal home. You may wish to send a copy to the tax authorities in your previous home state.

2. REGISTER TO VOTE. You must be 18 years of age, a U.S. citizen and a resident of the state of Florida (you must sign an oath). You may register at City Hall or the Court House. Voter registration closes 30 days prior to any upcoming election.

In order to keep your voter registration active, you must vote at least every two years.

3. FILE A HOMESTEAD EXEMPTION. Florida law allows homeowners a $25,000 exemption from the assessed value of their homes on property taxes. To qualify, you must be a legal resident of Florida, hold title and reside on the property as of January 1 of the year in which you apply for the exemption. Apply in person between January 1 and March 1. If the property is in joint names, each owner must present identification. Bring the following documentation: property deed, FL voter registration or declaration of domicile, driver's license and car registration. The Homestead Exemption is renewable every year. After the first year, you will be mailed an annual renewal form. Sign and return it to the office of the Property Appraiser.

Note: There are additional exemptions for senior citizens, widows and disabled individuals.

4. ENROLL YOUR CHILDREN IN SCHOOL. You will need your child's birth certificate, proof of residence, certificate of medical examination (within last 12 months), and certificate of immunization. Any child who is five years of age on or before September 1 is eligible for kindergarten.

A License for Travel

DRIVER'S LICENSE: Within 30 days after declaring yourself a resident of Florida, you must apply for a Florida driver's license. If you have a valid license from another state, you are not required to take a written exam or road test, but you must take the vision examination in order to receive a Florida license. Since a number of motor vehicle laws are different in Florida, it is beneficial to obtain a copy of the *Florida Driver's Handbook*. Your first license will be valid for 37-48 months, depending upon the month of your birth. Thereafter, it is renewed on your birthday and is valid for four years; if you have a safe driver status (no violations), it is renewed every six years.

RENEWAL: If you have not received a traffic violation, you must only take a vision test; if you have received a traffic violation within the past three years, you must also take the road sign test.

TRAFFIC VIOLATIONS: If you should get a ticket, the State of Florida will allow you to attend driving school (four hours) in lieu of points, but you still must pay the fine. You can only do this once a year, three times maximum. Always keep a copy of your certificate of completion. The State has no record that you have completed the course. If you receive more than 11 points in a year, your license is suspended for 30 days.

Note: Insurance companies may not be as forgiving as the State of Florida.

DUAL DRIVER'S LICENSE: If you want to maintain your former driver's license, you may apply for a dual license. Your Florida license may only be used in the state of Florida. The dual license is useful for people who are still maintaining a residence in another state.

In addition to your local driver's license bureau, the Department of Highway Safety and Motor Vehicles can answer your questions. *Ph. 904-488-0250*

LICENSE PLATES: As soon as you become a legal resident or gain employment, you must register your car in Florida. To obtain a license plate, you will need your automobile title, registration and proof of automobile insurance as well as a notarized affidavit certifying your Vehicle Identification Number (VIN) and current odometer reading. You must renew your tags annually in the month of your birthday. You may apply 30 days before – while you're still a year younger!

If your automobile is leased, you will need to request a copy of the title from the lease holder. Leased vehicles are always renewed in June.

Note: New residents must pay a hefty registration fee, ranging from $450 to $500, for the privilege of driving in Florida.

MOTOR VEHICLE INSPECTION PROGRAM: If you reside in Broward, Dade, Duval, Hillsborough, Palm Beach or Pinellas County, your automobile must pass an annual emissions inspection, if it is a 1975 or newer model. The cost is $10 (cash only). This must be completed within 90 days of your registration renewal. After your auto has passed the test, mail the tear-off portion of the inspection form to the tax collector or bring it to a tag office to obtain your new sticker.

Note: The different inspection locations and hours of operation are listed on your registration renewal form.

FLORIDA INSURANCE: All drivers must carry proof of automobile insurance (Personal Injury Protection and Property Damage Liability). Non-residents must also carry this insurance if they drive a car more than 90 days a year in Florida.

Note: There is a "55 Alive/Mature Driving Program" (offered by AARP). Senior drivers may enroll in an eight-hour refresher program which discusses age-related physical changes and reviews rules of the road. According to State law, insurance companies must reduce premiums for three years to all drivers 55 years and older who complete this course.

BOATS: You must show title and register your power boat (or any boat that has an engine) with the County Tax Collector. The craft size determines the fees. Title certificates are issued yearly, beginning July 1. You must always have it on board with you. There is no mandatory instruction, license or age minimum required of the boat owner or individual steering the boat through Florida waters.

Note: The Marine Industries Association of South Florida offers a hotline for boat owners and water sport enthusiasts. If they cannot answer your questions, they will refer you to the proper source. *Ph. 800-BOAT-001.*

PASSPORTS: If you need a passport for travel, contact your county courthouse or the main branch of your post office for an application. For identification, you will need either an original birth certificate with the official seal or an expired passport as well as two two-inch passport photos. Allow three-four weeks for processing. If you need one in a hurry, contact the Passport Agency in Miami.

If you are planning to cruise to the Bahamas or one of our neighboring islands, you will need proof of citizenship – either a passport or other documentation. In lieu of a passport, you may use a birth certificate (the original with raised seal), notarized birth certificate, voter's registration card, or certificate of naturalization. Photocopies are not accepted. Photo ID must accompany any of these documents. Mexico prefers passport identification, but will accept any of the above as proof of citizenship.

A License for Pleasure

HUNTING is permitted in Florida's National Forests. Deer, quail, duck, and wildcat are hunted game, but the seasons may vary for each from year to year. Raccoon and rabbit are usually hunted year round. Licenses (and a copy of the game laws) are issued at the Court House and several sport shops. Contact the Florida Game and Freshwater Fish Commission for more information.

FRESHWATER FISHING licenses are required of all persons over 15 and under 65 years of age. License fees differ for residents and non-residents. They are valid for one year, beginning July 1. Licenses can be purchased from the County Tax Collector's office or from various bait dealers and some sporting goods stores. Freshwater fishing has an open year-round season with 24 different species of game fish.

Contact the Florida Fisheries Division for freshwater fish site information and restrictions. *Ph. 813-648-3202.*

SALT WATER FISHING licenses are now required for the sports fisherman, with the exception of those over 65 or under 16 years of age. If fishing from piers, bridges or shoreline, you are not required to purchase a license. Charter boat patrons, fishing for the day, are also exempt – but boat owners are not.

Closed Seasons
Bay Scallops – Season is closed from April 1 to June 30.
Oysters – Season is closed from June 1 to September 1.
Stone Crab Claws – Season is closed from May 15 to October 15.

Contact the FL Marine Patrol for more information. *Ph. 800-342-5367.*

The Facts of Life

FLORIDA TAXES: The Florida state constitution prohibits a personal income tax (as well as an inheritance tax). The state, counties and municipalities are supported by some of the following taxes: 6% *Sales Tax*; *Property Taxes*; *Intangible Personal Property Tax* (stocks, bonds, mutual funds, trusts, notes, etc.); *Documentary Stamp Tax* (registration of promissory notes, deeds or any recorded financial obligation with the state); and *State Utility Tax* (gross receipts tax). Other taxes include *corporate, business,* and *personal use taxes,* such as those levied on beverages, cigarettes and gasoline.

Note: If you have questions regarding Florida taxes, it is best to call the Taxpayer's Assistance Line (FL Dept. of Revenue). *Ph. 800-872-9909.*

FLORIDA WILLS: Since Florida has no inheritance tax, it is a good idea for new residents to execute a revised will. If your will was prepared in your former state, that state may claim you as a resident and demand its share of taxes from your estate. Even if they do not succeed, they may legally delay the disposition of your assets for a long period of time.

If your will is to be probated in Florida, there are certain legal stipulations which must be followed. Florida requires that a Personal Representative be named as the executor of your estate. This person may be a spouse, related through a blood relationship, or if a non-relative, a legal resident of Florida. If a financial institution is elected as your Personal Representative, it must be located in Florida. Without a will, the State has a legal formula which specifies who gets what! Seek out a Florida attorney who specializes in estates and trusts.

Living Will
Florida residents can document their wishes regarding the use of life-prolonging procedures and apparatus should they become terminally ill. You can obtain this legal declaration at an attorney's office or through the social service department of your community medical center. It must be signed by two witnesses. Copies should be given to your physician and nearest of kin.

It's the Law

DRIVING UNDER THE INFLUENCE is a serious matter and Florida's DUI laws are very stringent. First-time offenders are subject to a fine of $250-$1,000; six months to one year revocation of their driver's license; a minimum of 50 hours of community service; and mandatory attendance at a substance abuse education program.

It is also unlawful for a driver or passenger to possess an open bottle of alcohol while in an operating vehicle (except for licensed chauffeured vehicles).

FLORIDA SEAT BELT LAW: Anyone, six years or older, must wear seat belts while sitting in the front seat of a moving vehicle. Anywhere in the vehicle, children three years or younger must be in federally approved separate safety seats. Children four-five years of age must either be in safety seats or wearing seat belts.

If you will need a child safety seat for only a brief time, contact the National Safety Council within your county regarding their Loan-A-Seat Program.

WHEN IT RAINS, drivers must turn on headlights.

HANDICAPPED PARKING: Fines for parking in designated handicapped spaces are serious, ranging from $100 minimum to $250 maximum.

City Profiles

Introduction

The society of years ago saw generations of families spending a lifetime in the same city in which they were born and raised. Families became uprooted primarily as a result of a job change. People advancing in age did not think of disassociating themselves from their community, family and lifelong friendships. Today, millions of people are planning for their second careers and retirement years in communities other than where they spent their formative years. Mobility is on the rise as people search for quality of life and opportunity.

Although Florida is one of the prime spots for retirees, many young people and families are moving there as well for lifestyle reasons while still in their working years. From 1980 to 1992, Florida's population increased by 38.4%.

Unfortunately, many people approach the issue of relocation in a less than systematic way. It is critical to develop a set of criteria and prioritize the importance of each need. If you enjoy rolling hills in your physical environment (and perhaps you never gave it a moment's thought), South Florida isn't the place! However, there are many other areas in Florida which do have hilly terrain. If you enjoy outdoor tennis year round but equally dislike long months of humidity, be aware that South Florida offers both in abundance. Once you've explored your lifestyle choices and requirements, you need to discover which city or community will satisfy those that are most important.

This section is dedicated to sharing my information and research on nine cities in South and Central Florida. Since the state covers such a large area, I decided to profile cities which share similar climates. The nine cities selected either support large populations or are among the fastest growing in the state. Each profile explores 14 areas of daily life, such as transportation, education, health care, cultural pleasures and leisure activities. In order to present the special vitality and heartbeat of each city, I had to make some difficult choices. I have described many – but certainly not all – of the universities, hospitals, newspapers and magazines, cultural events, attractions, and leisure activities within each city and its surrounding area. It is my hope that you will continue the research which I have started and contact the various Chambers of Commerce for a full and complete listing.

The framework used to profile the cities is presented below, along with general information which pertains to all.

◆ DEMOGRAPHICS

This section includes data on the size, population, age and climate in the county and city. Age breakdowns reflect the diversity of the population and the appeal to various age groups. Larger cities have a larger workforce, bigger tax base, and a broader support system for higher education, cultural and medical institutions. They also tend to be more bureaucratic, more impersonal and more likely to have too much traffic on the major roads!

In considering a move to Florida, one must look at the projected growth of an area, not just its present population. Many areas are in a high growth mode, anticipating more residents, more services and more opportunities. *Table A* on page 22 shows the growth of the nine counties over the past ten years as well as that projected for the year 2000.

Incorporated and Unincorporated Areas

In presenting demographic information, data is provided for both incorporated and unincorporated areas within the county. "Incorporated" refers to any area that is geographically and legally part of a municipality; the residents pay municipal taxes, vote for municipal legislators and receive municipal services. In unincorporated areas – those not within city boundaries – residents receive needed services through the county. For example, the county sheriff's office, not a municipal police department, provides unincorporated residents with police protection.

◆ CLIMATE

Florida's climate ranges from temperate in the north to subtropical in central and southern areas, and reaches tropical conditions in the Keys.

Winters in South Florida are warm, with average temperatures ranging from the upper 70s to the mid 60s in January. Central Florida has cooler winters, but still mild, with January temperatures ranging from the mid-to-low 70s to the mid 50s. Some of the cold fronts, which come through to Central Florida causing chilly days and nights, do not reach South Florida. The summer season in both regions is hot and humid with intermittent flash storms and rain.

South and Central Florida do not experience four distinct seasonal climate changes. There are basically only two seasons: dry and wet. Winter's dry season begins in November and continues through April. The summer begins in May with constant humidity through October.

If you are moving from the Northeast, with its wintertime chill factor, to sunny Florida, you must now contend with a heat index. A 90° day with 90% humidity generates a heat index of 122°.

◆ TAXES

This section covers both property taxes and sales tax. Millage rate information is provided for each city and unincorporated area of the county. Discounts are given as rewards for early payment. According to Florida statute, all counties may discount property taxes 4% if paid in November; 3% if paid in December; 2% if paid in January; and 1% if paid in February. Property taxes are due by March 31st. The state sales tax is 6%. Some counties levy an additional 1/2%-1% for county use. Groceries (food items), prescription drugs, and over-the-counter drugs are tax exempt.

Note: Although the State of Florida has a very humanistic approach to animals, pet food is not tax exempt.

◆ VOTING AND ELECTIONS

According to Florida Statute, state and county elections are held during the general election on the first Tuesday after the first Monday in November. The first primaries are held on the first Tuesday nine weeks prior to the general election in November. If no one candidate receives a majority of the vote (50% plus one), a second primary or "run-off" is held between the two candidates who placed first and second in the first primary. It is scheduled on the first Tuesday five weeks prior to the general election.

The books close for new registration and party changes 30 days before the first primary. If you are too late for the primaries, you may register 30 days before the general election to vote in the November elections.

◆ PET REGISTRATION

Each county has it own jurisdiction regarding pet registration and vaccination. If you are bringing a dog or cat from another state or intending to purchase one when you get settled, you will need to know the registration and inoculation requirements. In order to avoid any citations, it is also important to be aware of pooper-scooper laws, whether your pet must be leashed, or can even accompany you to the beach for the day. Many of the county and city ordinances are described in this section.

The Florida State Animal Control Association, located in Orlando, is a central agency which prepares and sponsors animal welfare legislation for passage at the state level. *Ph. 407-282-9600.*

Florida Statutes
If you are planning to adopt a pet, according to state law all dogs and cats sheltered by a humane society or animal welfare agency must be sterilized before they are adopted. Statute 828.29 states that pet stores, breeders or anybody selling an animal must present a health certificate and proof of inoculations at the time of sale. The new owner must have the pet examined by a veterinarian within 30 days, if it is to be used to document the health status of the animal.

◆ TRANSPORTATION

Air Travel
Table B on page 22 presents a listing of toll free airline numbers which you can access from any city.

Highway Information
For travel and highway information, contact the Florida Dept. of Transportation (Public Information). There are regional offices throughout the state which can offer assistance. They will answer questions regarding expressway directions, highway interchanges, mileage and tolls on any of the state or federal roads.

County		
Dade	Miami Office	305-470-5349
Collier	Ft. Myers Office	813-338-2341
Sarasota	Bartow Office	813-533-8161
Hillsborough	Tampa Office	813-975-6060
Orange	Deland Office	904-943-5479
Brevard	Deland Office	904-943-5479
Broward	Ft. Lauderdale Office	305-477-4090
Palm Beach	Ft. Lauderdale Office	800-932-3368

Getting Around The City
Pockets of unincorporated areas, zig-zag boundaries and streets which dead end can lead you into the State of Confusion. Getting around a new city can be an exhausting process, especially if you are one of those who cannot ask for directions. In addition to keeping a good city map in the car, the best guidelines are the zero ("0") lines: the streets which divide many of the cities into North/South and East/West quadrants. The street numbers ascend as you travel north, south, east or west from the "0" line. Contact the department of urban planning or engineering at city hall for the streets and locations of the dividing lines.

◆ POSTAL SERVICE

Postal sub-stations or contract stations were established by an Act of Congress as early as 1847. Today, they are a major consumer convenience and provide more options for customer service. They frequently serve as an outreach in rural districts as well as providing extra locations in the more populated areas. Since some contract stations may not provide all postal services, such as overseas parcel processing, it is best to call ahead and find out specific services and hours of operation. The contract stations, which are regulated by the United States Postal Service, are usually located within retail stores and many have Saturday hours of operation. They are a great alternative to the long lines found in many post offices, especially during the holiday season.

For your convenience, you can purchase stamps by mail. Ask your carrier for a postage paid envelope or call 800-STAMP 24.

Leaving Town
If you plan to be away from home for any extended time, notify your post office. To forward mail temporarily or to file a permanent change of address, use form #3575. File this form, in person, at the post office serving your zip code. The nearest facility is not necessarily the station responsible for your mail delivery. Filing three-five days in advance will ensure that your instructions become effective on the requested date. The amount of time mail will be held is based on guidelines established by the local postmaster.

If you do not inform the post office of your plans, mail will be delivered for ten days and then returned to sender as unclaimed.

◆ NEWSPAPERS AND MAGAZINES

One of the best ways to learn about a new city is through its local newspapers and magazines. The investment is small and the rewards are great. You may want to review several newspapers or magazines prior to selecting the one or two that are most suited to your particular interests. Information about the real estate market, employment opportunities, local news and issues, social and cultural events, and a community calendar of meetings/events can provide a wealth of information about the area.

◆ LIBRARY SYSTEM

The library of old has matured and no longer has the sole function of lending books and providing reference materials for term papers. Today's county library systems are actively involved with the community through:

- Activities for children designed to excite them about reading at an early age.
- Collections which include not only books, but also music, videos, and computer resources.
- Multimedia events which showcase ethnic cultures and promote community understanding.
- Special programs which include film series, lectures, book reviews, seminars and workshops.
- Efforts to increase the literacy levels of both native and immigrant populations.
- Services tailored to the special needs of the disabled, impaired and homebound.
- A call-in reference desk to research questions on the spot.
- Meeting rooms which are open to civic groups for forums and seminars.

◆ HEALTH CARE

Hospitals often have a variety of outreach programs for the community. After you are settled into your new home, call the various hospitals in your community for a calendar of events. Many different programs may be offered, such as health-related seminars, resources for seniors, or support groups. Some hospitals have instituted an Ask-A-Nurse Program, which is a 24-hour hotline for health related problems. It is wise to become familiar with your local hospitals, in case you have to choose one at a moment's notice in an emergency.

◆ EDUCATION

Even though the state has specific educational objectives, counties, nevertheless, do vary in their educational focus, level of community support and available resources. In this section, highlights of each county's educational system are described with an emphasis on their special programs and achievements. Two tables are presented for analysis and comparison. Per pupil spending in each county is shown in *Table C* on page 23. Countywide student performance, as measured by 10th grade math and communications scores, is shown in *Table D* on page 24.

The colleges and universities situated in each of the cities add a significant dimension to the community. In addition to providing opportunities for higher level education, they enrich the cultural life of area residents through a variety of campus lectures, concerts, college theater, and a selection of adult continuing education courses.

College Tuition and Residency Status

To be eligible for in-state tuition status at any of the ten state universities within the University of South Florida system or any of Florida's 28 community colleges, a student must present proof of residency issued 12 months prior to enrollment.

At least two or three of the following documents are necessary to show proof of residency:

- Proof of purchase of a permanent home in Florida
- Declaration of Domicile
- Florida driver's license
- Florida voter's registration
- Florida vehicle registration
- Florida vehicle title
- Professional/occupational license in Florida
- Florida incorporation or other evidence of legal residence
- Letter from employer on company letterhead stating full-time and permanent employment

Rent receipts, leases, tax returns, school or college records are not acceptable for documenting proof of Florida residency, although they can be used as supporting evidence.

If declared as a dependent, a student must show documentation of Florida residency of his/her parents or legal guardian. If a student is not declared as a dependent, proof of income must be established. For more detailed information, contact the USF Office of the Registrar. *Ph. 813-974-3350.*

◆ CULTURAL SCENE

Each of the cities profiled has an active cultural life which includes the performing and visual arts. Florida is no longer a sleeper or cultural wasteland. Since the mid-1980's, many of the major cities in Florida have constructed state-of-the-art, acoustically engineered performing arts centers. These new elegant concert halls can accommodate Broadway scale musicals, international dance troupes and transmit the clarity of sound of symphonic orchestras. Many small theaters have also appeared on the scene. Call the local Arts Council and ask for a calendar of cultural programs in your community.

◆ EVENTS AND ATTRACTIONS

To liven up lazy weekends, each city has an array of events and attractions to suit almost any interest. Some of these are similar, but many are quite unique, reflecting the personality of the area. Outdoor summer concerts, fall visits to botanical gardens and zoos, winter tree lighting festivals and Christmas boat parades offer residents year round activities.

◆ DON'T MISS

There are often treasures in our own backyards that are all too often missed. It can be as simple as taking an evening stroll along Ft. Lauderdale's New River, observing a spectacular sunset at the Naples Pier, or visiting a quaint antique village outside of Orlando. If you want to hasten the acculturation process after you relocate, ask the natives about special places to visit or things to do that most tourists and newcomers never hear about!

◆ RECREATION

Leisure activities play an important role in the Florida lifestyle. Many people relocate to Florida's year round tropical climate to indulge their undeniable affection for golf, tennis, boating, water sports and the beach. Others enjoy the physical pleasure of walking, jogging and exercising under the warmth of the sun.

In Florida, the Department of Parks and Recreation operates the parks and playgrounds as well as sponsoring a wide variety of recreational activities, such as athletic (tennis, golf, swimming, boating) and physical fitness programs (aerobics, exercise and dance). There are athletics and team sports for children and adults; some have programs for the physically disabled. If you want to know where to jog, hike or camp, they have a complete listing of parks, as well as information about public golf courses, tennis courts, marinas, fishing holes and other sporting locations.

◆ FLORIDA BEACHES AND OCEANFRONT

Blue skies and a good weather report may lead you to the beach, but ocean conditions and sea pests may keep you out of the water. A blue flag signifies the presence of the Portuguese man-of-war; this flag, used in conjunction with either a red or a yellow one, indicates safety conditions for swimmers.

Sea Pests

Man-of-war. They are most prevalent during the winter months, from November through April; they are found in tropical waters and float up the Eastern Seaboard from the Gulf Stream. The Portuguese man-of-war is a cousin to the jellyfish. In water or on shore, leave them alone; do not puncture their bubble, which contains a harmful gas. The tentacles have poisonous stingers, which can be extremely painful.

Jellyfish. They are often found on both coasts of Florida from late summer through mid-October.

Sea Lice. This is the commonly used name for a species of jellyfish larvae which release a toxin. The sea lice season usually begins in April and may extend into September. Some people experience a slight prickling sensation before red welts or blotches appear under swim suits and underarms. Itching usually lasts two-four days. If there are ocean reports of sea lice, do not remain in a wet bathing suit. After bathing, shower (if possible), or immediately towel dry and change into dry clothes. The Palm Beach County Health Unit suggests a topical 0.5 cortisone cream and an oral antihistamine for mild cases. If you have a more serious reaction, contact your physician immediately.

Red Tide. These microscopic, single-celled plants usually appear in late summer and early fall, but not necessarily every year. In high concentration, they cause a reddish-brown tinge in the gulf waters. This particular species is endemic to the Gulf of Mexico, from St. Petersburg to Naples. Sunbathers may feel the effects of red tide from winds which blow the toxins, making them airborne. Individuals may experience a respiratory irritation, coughing, and/or cold-like symptoms. Red tide is usually short lived and may only last from a day or two to a week before it is washed away by currents.

During red tide occurrences, bivalve shell fish, such as clams, oysters and muscles, digest the plant organisms and accumulate toxins. As a precautionary measure, shell fish beds are not open for recreational fishing during these times. Crabs, shrimp and lobster are not affected since they are not part of the bivalve shellfish family.

The designated months and time periods for the appearance of sea pests are only guidelines since variable meteorological conditions, hydraulic currents and mother nature play an important role. There are years when sea pests are minimal and do not impose any significant problem to bathers.

Parking Permits
If you plan to make regular visits to the beach, many of the ocean-side cities offer annual beach parking permits. The reduced cost as well as the parking convenience is well worth the trip to the City Department of Parks and Recreation. Many (but not all) of the county beaches provide free public parking lots.

◆ CLOSING THOUGHTS
The nine cities profiled are within an easy drive of each other, and there is much to enjoy in each one. Once you relocate to Florida, the choice is yours! You can comfortably settle into a community, become thoroughly absorbed in a routine of golf, tennis, shopping, cinema and restaurants and never stray too far from home. Or, you can spread your wings and experience the wealth of colorful and engaging activities, attractions and events in neighboring cities. If you have recently moved to Florida, I hope that you will read all of the profiles. The Convention and Visitor's Bureau will be happy to send you a full calendar of events scheduled for each city.

Tables

A. Population Growth, 1980-91

Florida County Comparisons

	1991	% Change 1980-1991	Population Projection Year 2000	% Change 1991-2010
Brevard	409,370	49.97	502,587	44.30
Broward	1,277,677	25.48	1,467,554	28.69
Collier	161,600	87.97	210,298	61.13
Dade	1,961,570	20.67	2,183,841	21.62
Hillsborough	843,059	30.32	979,172	30.52
Orange	701,096	48.90	857,921	44.28
Palm Beach	883,034	53.10	1,104,136	48.27
Sarasota	283,140	39.99	341,024	39.34

Source: Florida County Comparisons 1992
Florida Department of Commerce
Division of Economic Development

B. Airlines

Aeromexico	(800) 237-6639
Aeropostal	(800) 468-9419
Air Canada	(800) 422-6232
Air Jamiaca	(800) 523-5585
Air Sunshine (Provides Commuter Service)	(800) 435-8900
Airways (Provides Commuter Service)	(305) 526-3852
Air France	(800) 237-2747
All Nippon Airways ANA (Japan)	(800) 235-9262
American	(800) 443-7300
American Eagle (Provides Commuter Service)	(800) 433-7300
American West	(800) 247-5692
American Trans Air	(800) 225-9920
Bahamas Air	(800) 222-4262
Braniff International	(800) 272-6433
British Airways	(800) 247-9297
BWIA	(800) 327-7401
Chalk/Paradise Island Airlines (Has Seaplane Svce)	(800) 432-8807
Canadian Airlines	(800) 426-7000
Carnival	(800) 222-7466

Cayman Airways	(800) 422-9626
Comair	(305) 763-2211
(Provides Commuter Service)	
Continental	(800) 525-0280
Delta	(800) 221-1212
Iberia	(800) 221-9741
Icelandair	(800) 223-5500
Laker Airways	(305) 653-9471
(Provides Service to Freeport)	
Lufthansa	(800) 645-3880
Martinair Holland	(800) 366-4655
Mexicana Airlines	(800) 531-7921
Midwest Express	(800) 452-2022
Northwest	(800) 225-2525
Sun Country (Provides Commuter Service)	(800) 359-5786
TransBrasil	(800) 872-3153
TWA	(800) 221-2000
USAir	(800) 428-4322
USAir Express (Provides Commuter Service)	(305) 526-6237
United	(800) 241-6522
Virgin Atlantic Airlines	(800) 862-8621

Note: Commuter Flights provide service to Florida cities, the Keys and the Bahama Islands. Check to find out who goes where.

C. Revenue for Education*

Includes Federal, State and Local Revenue Sources for 1990-1991

	Revenue $
FLORIDA	5,198
Brevard	4,949
Broward	5,470
Collier	6,007
Dade	4,978
Hillsborough	5,249
Orange	4,954
Palm Beach	6,059
Sarasota	6,277

* Per FTE (full-time equivalent – represents the equivalent of one full-time student)

Source: Florida County Comparisons 1992
Florida Department of Commerce
Division of Economic Development

D. State Student Assessment Test*

Percent of 10th Grade Students Passing the SSAT- 3/11/91

	Mathematics	Communications
FLORIDA	75%	86%
Brevard	77%	90%
Broward	79%	89%
Collier	78%	85%
Dade	62%	76%
Hillsborough	84%	92%
Orange	77%	89%
Palm Beach	78%	86%
Sarasota	86%	92%

* The State Student Assessment Test-Part 11 measures the application of basic skills in reading, writing and mathematics to practical, everyday problems. A passing score on the SSAT-11 was made a graduation requirement by the 1976 Florida Legislature.

Source: Florida County Comparisons 1992
Florida Department of Commerce
Division of Economic Development

The Palm Beaches

West Palm Beach

Palm Beach County welcomed its first visitors when a Spanish vessel en route from Trinidad to Spain was shipwrecked along the coast. A rich cargo of wine and coconuts washed ashore, bringing settlers to the beach for the first "TGIF" (Thank God, It's Florida) party. The nuts were planted with little knowledge that palm trees would follow.

Henry Morrison Flagler, a partner of John D. Rockefeller at Standard Oil, infused life into the area when he extended his railway to the Palm Beaches. Recognizing the potential draw of the sun, beaches and coastal blue waters, he opened the Royal Poinciana Hotel. It accommodated close to 2,000 guests, most of whom were seeking relief from the harsh northern winters.

Flagler's organization chartered the town of West Palm Beach in 1893. Its original settlers were workmen who built the luxurious estates of Palm Beach, but lived across the water in the more modest homes they constructed for themselves. The town was incorporated in 1894. West Palm flourished as new businesses were established in the community. The rich and famous of Palm Beach continued to draw upon the services and servants from its sister city. By 1920, the city housed half the county population of 18,654. Growth was slowed by a fire which destroyed the original Breakers Hotel, a hurricane of monstrous proportion in 1928, and the depression of the 1930s. Since World War II, the area has again prospered, continuing to attract residents by the thousands.

Today, West Palm Beach is a city where business is conducted and residents confront the issues of health, education, and day-to-day living. Many consider West Palm Beach, which is the county seat, the hub of the county's business life. It is a city of neighborhoods – both wealthy and poor, government offices and new development. During the early '90s, residents saw the opening of a performing arts center and a new judicial complex.

Boca Raton

Boca Raton anchors the southern part of Palm Beach County. Although the Spanish never settled in Boca, old Spanish maps indicate that ships passed through, anchored, or were shipwrecked there, beginning in the mid 1500s. The name Boca de Ratones, which translates to mouth of the rat, refers to the shape of the sand bar at the north side of the inlet.

The first property to be developed was a simple house built by a civil engineer in 1895. With the completion of Flagler's Florida East Coast Railway in 1896, a small community of settlers arrived and sustained themselves by growing fruits and vegetables, which were then shipped north. While food was plentiful, the early pioneers became weary and frustrated by hurricanes, crop failures, infestation and ill-timed freezes. Even Richards, the civil engineer, decided to head north. Boca Raton would have been barren once again, except for the vision of a Japanese businessman. He sent word to others in Japan and when they arrived, the Yamato colony was formed as a farming community. One of the original settlers was George Morikami, who became a citizen at the age of 82. Throughout the years, he accumulated 150 acres of land which he later donated to the county in memory of the Japanese community.

Boca Raton was eventually incorporated in 1925. Investors began to purchase oceanfront property. One of them, well-known society architect Addison Mizner, established the Mizner Development Corporation with the purpose of realizing his architectural visions in this emerging city. In addition to the many homes he designed, he is perhaps best known for the $1.25 million Spanish-style Old Cloister Inn which had its grand opening in 1927. Subsequently renovated, it is now known as the Boca Raton Resort and Country Club. Although his company went bankrupt, Mizner's contributions made a strong impact on the development of the city. His Mediterranean Revival style can be seen in much of the local architecture. World War II actually stimulated the growth of the area with the location of a large airbase and facilities for 20,000 troops. Today, Boca Raton is home to many Fortune 500 companies, including IBM, WR Grace, Siemens-Nixdorf, Sony Professional Products, and Pepsi Cola, Latin American Division. The expansion of Florida Atlantic University's Research Center, favorable tax rates, and available commercial property continue to make Boca Raton an ideal corporate center. The city's rapid growth has seen an explosion of malls, boutiques, restaurants, and recreational facilities. Boca Raton is an upscale community with a blend of old wealth and new glitz. Five miles of beachfront, a tropical lifestyle and a multitude of new residential villages continue to lure people from far and wide.

Demographics

◆ Size

Palm Beach County occupies 1,993 square miles with approximately 45 miles of coastline. From east to west, it is about 40 miles wide. Since Palm Beach initially developed in a north/south direction with considerable distance between the two, many use the designations of North County and South County. The two profiled cities are situated at each end.

The 37 municipalities within Palm Beach County occupy 186 square miles; the unincorporated areas total 1,807 square miles. Boca Raton spans 27.11 square miles. West Palm Beach is 46 square miles in area.

Population. The population of Palm Beach County was 896,970 as of 1992.

Municipalities. All of the municipalities below, whether they are classified as villages, towns or cities, are self-governing entities and levy taxes to provide municipal services.

	Classification	Population
North County		
Juno Beach	Town	2,121
Jupiter	Town	28,500
Lake Park	Town	7,000
North Palm Beach	Village	18,000
Palm Beach	Town	40,000
Palm Beach Gardens	City	25,000
Riviera Beach	City	27,639
Royal Palm Beach	Village	16,500
South Palm Beach	Town	1,480
Tequestra	Village	4,500
West Palm Beach	City	68,270

Note: The population in the Town of Palm Beach decreases considerably out of season.

Central County

Atlantis	City	1,653
Boynton Beach	City	46,000
Greenacres City	City	18,680
Lake Clarke Shores	Town	36,000
Lake Worth	City	28,560
Lantana	Town	8,300
Manalapan	Town	375
Ocean Ridge	Town	2,500
Palm Springs	Village	10,192

South County

Boca Raton	City	63,224
Delray Beach	City	46,860
Gulf Stream	Town	1,000
Highland Beach	Town	3,209

Note: In a recent vote, the residents of West Boca chose to remain unincorporated. It has a population of 96,000 people.

◆ Age Demographics

Under 18	21.5%
18-44	38.3%
45-64	20.5%
Over 65	25.6%
Median Age	39.9 years

◆ Climate

Elevation: 20 feet
Annual Rainfall: 59.44 inches
Average Summer Temperature: 81.7 degrees
Average Winter Temperature: 67.2 degrees

Taxes

◆ Property Taxes

Property taxes are one of the major sources of revenue to local governments outside of federal and state revenue sharing. The unincorporated areas within Palm Beach County have millage rates which range from 17.4571 to 20.2029 per $1,000 of assessed property value.

The City of West Palm Beach has a total millage rate of 27.3479 or 27.4493, depending upon the area of the city. If your property is located in the drainage district of West Palm Beach, the millage rate jumps to 29.3479.

The City of Boca Raton has a total millage rate of 21.8074 or 21.8362, depending upon the location of the property within the city.

◆ Sales and Use Taxes

The county does not levy any additional sales tax other than the Florida state tax of 6%.

Voting and Elections

County Government Center
301 N. Olive Avenue
West Palm Beach
Ph. 355-2040

Palm Beach County is governed by a board of county commissioners who are elected from seven single-member districts to serve a four-year term. Elections are held every two years. The even numbered districts vote in November of 1994 and 1998 and the odd numbered districts vote in 1996 and 2000. A county administrator is appointed by the board of commissioners.

West Palm Beach
City Hall
200 Second Street
Ph. 659-8000

In 1991, voters changed the city charter to provide for the election of a full time mayor to administer the city's policies and directives. The mayor can hold office for no more than two consecutive four-year terms and must be a resident of the city. The city commission consists of five commissioners elected at-large for a two-year term. Elections are held on the second Tuesday in March.

Boca Raton
201 W. Palmetto Park Road
Ph. 393-7708

The city is governed by five council members, including the mayor, for a two-year term of office. Two council seats become available every year while the mayor's seat is up for election every odd year.

Elections are held on the second Tuesday in March. The council appoints a city manager as the administrative head to oversee the operations of city services.

Pet Registration

Cats and dogs are required to have a rabies vaccination at the age of four months, be licensed with the county, and tagged. Under four months of age, the county requires juvenile tags. In lieu of tags, cats may be tattooed in the right ear, but must have their numbers registered with Animal Care and Control. The rabies vaccination is effective for either one or three years while all tags must be renewed annually. Leash laws are in effect throughout the county. Leashes may not be longer than six feet in length. Pooper-scooper laws are enforced by the individual cities.

In Boca Raton and West Palm Beach, dogs are not permitted entry into the city parks. Boca Raton does not welcome pets on its beaches either. County-operated parks, however, do permit dogs if they're on a leash. In certain parks, there are places where dogs are not permitted, such as jogging trails, but signs are posted indicating restricted areas. Dogs may visit the beach parks, but not the beaches.

The Humane Society of Palm Beach was established in June of 1993. Its primary objectives are to educate the public about the necessity of spaying and neutering pets and to function as an adoption center for unwanted animals. *Ph. 338-9414.*

Transportation

Air Travel

PALM BEACH INTERNATIONAL AIRPORT
West of I-95, between Southern Blvd. and Belvedere Rd.
Communications Center - *24 Hr. Ph. 471-7420*
Passenger Page Service: *Ph. 471-7400*
Parking Authority: *Ph. 471-7459*

Although Palm Beach International Airport underwent a considerable expansion in 1988, it still maintains a very manageable scale and tropical essence. The airport has a three-level terminal with three concourses leading to the 24 gateways. As an international airport, there are charter flights to and from Canada and the Caribbean as well as regularly scheduled service to the Bahamas. A new state-of-the-art customs facility is situated at the main terminal. The airport served close to five million passengers in 1992.

The interior space is light and airy, enhanced by 30 major works of art in different media. As part of the Art in Public Places endowment, a $300,000 fund was allocated for art purchases. En route to concourse C, take a few moments to enjoy the wonderful mobiles hanging from the ceiling. If time allows, visit the two exhibition areas for rotating works of art. Very Special Arts, headquartered in Washington, DC, promotes the work of handicapped artists in public places, such as airports. Local artists also have the opportunity to exhibit their work on a rotating bimonthly-monthly basis.

Palm Beach International Airport is approximately 25 miles from downtown Boca Raton and three miles from West Palm Beach

Amenities. Scott Business and Travel has a business center located at the airport with small conference rooms, fax and copy services, postage and lottery tickets, and travel service. Currency exchange is only available for conversion of foreign currency into dollars. An ATM machine is adjacent to the business center on the mezzanine level.

A new entertainment center, also designed as a passenger lounge, can accommodate approximately 35 people. During the season, PBI presents a variety of musical programs with invited choral groups and musicians. If the timing is right, travelers awaiting flights may be entertained by a live concert in the new lounge. Future plans include a large screen TV. It is located across from the business center.

For hungry travelers, an attractively decorated restaurant and several walk-in eateries offer some tasty selections.

PBI also has amenities for handicapped travelers, including special ramps, parking close to the terminal, and a TDD communications system for the hearing impaired.

Parking. There is sheltered parking in both the long term and short term garages. Parking facilities can accommodate 3,400 cars, but places are difficult to find during peak season. Visitors can park at metered spots opposite the baggage claim.

Ground Transportation. Airport transportation is provided to and from any of the cities and communities in the Palm Beaches through private limousine, taxi, and airport shuttle services. They are listed in the telephone directory. Limousine services can also be arranged on-site at the airport.

Public Transit. Tri-Rail offers train service to/from Palm Beach; buses are scheduled to meet the trains at the designated airport station and shuttle passengers to the main terminal. Call for schedules.

Major Airlines include:
American
Continental
Delta
Northwest
TWA
United
USAir

Commuter Airlines include:
Airways International
American Eagle
Bahamas Air
Comair
Henson
Paradise Island

Local Transportation

Buses. CoTran (Palm Beach County Transportation Authority) provides public bus service from Jupiter to Boca Raton. It is an intracounty system and does not operate in either Broward or Martin counties, although there are intercounty connections. Forty-six buses, which are wheelchair equipped, travel along 18 fixed routes. Feeder buses also service the six Tri-Rail stations, transporting passengers to business, government, education, and shopping centers. Buses run six days a week; no service is provided on Sundays or major holidays. Hours of operation are from 5:30 am until 8:30 pm. Special fares are available for seniors, handicapped, and students. Regular commuters can purchase monthly passes. The *Shopper Hopper*, a Saturday special, is an express service which takes shoppers from mall to mall. For route information and schedules contact CoTran. *Ph. 233-1111; Ph. 996-4372.*

Train. Tri-Rail transports passengers from West Palm Beach to Hialeah, making 15 stops during its 1 hour and 35 minute journey. There are six stations in Palm Beach County. Weekly and monthly passes are available. Tri-Rail also provides service to the three major airports, Joe Robbie Stadium, and the Orange Bowl through a network of shuttle buses. It operates seven days a week, year round, but not on Thanksgiving or Christmas. *Ph. 800-Tri-Rail.*

Special Transportation. SpecTran operates a Dial-A-Ride program providing door-to-door service for disabled individuals who need transportation in order to get to work. Mae Volen Senior Center (servicing Boca Raton and South County) and DOSS, Division of Senior Services for Palm Beach County, assist senior citizens with special transportation needs. Contact CoTran for a full listing of agencies which provide these special services.

Post Offices

From time to time, full service post offices change their hours of operation to coincide with demand. Hours of operation may vary during major holidays.

West Palm Beach: Full Service

General Mail Facility Main Station	3200 Summit Blvd. Monday-Friday: 7:30 am -6:00 pm Saturday: 9:00 am -1:00 pm	697-2027

Hours of service for stations and branches: Monday-Friday: 8:30 am - 5:00 pm

Downtown Station	434 Clematis Street	659-6114
Lake Park Branch	900 10th Street	844-7277
N. Palm Beach Branch	643 US Hwy. 1	842-1881
Northwood Station	516 Northwood Road	655-1144
Palm Beach Gardens Branch	3330 Fairchild Gardens Avenue	622-1447
Palm Beach Gardens Mall Station	3101 PGA Blvd.	
Riviera Branch	1905 Blue Heron Blvd.	844-4226
Royal Palm Beach Village Hall Station	1050 Royal Palm Beach Blvd.	
South Boro Station	5007 S. Dixie Hwy.	585-3722

34   The Palm Beaches

Wellington Station   12794 W. Forest Hill Blvd.   697-2027

Postal Contract Stations

Eckerd Drugs	721 Village Blvd.	684-4626
Eckerd Drugs	5335 N. Military Trail	697-5170
Eckerd Drugs	11936 Forest Hill Blvd.	793-2126
Eckerd Drugs	11586 US Hwy. #1	622-0703
Bealls Dept. Store	10201 Southern Blvd.	790-1725
Eckerd Drugs	6064 Okeechobee Blvd.	683-9665
Eckerd Drugs	6358 Forest Hill Blvd.	964-1702

Boca Raton: Full Service

Woodlands Branch Main Branch	604 Banyon Trail Monday and Friday: 8:00 am - 5:30 pm Tuesday-Thursday: 8:00 am - 5:00 pm	997-1619
Downtown Branch	170 NE 2nd Street Monday: 8:00 am - 5:00 pm Tuesday-Friday: 8:30 am - 5:00 pm Saturday: 9:30 am - 12:30 pm	395-4733
Palmetto Park Branch	1275 W. Palmetto Park Rd. Monday-Friday: 7:30 am - 5:00 pm	368-3920

Postal Contract Stations

Spanish River Hardware	275 NE Spanish River Blvd.	392-0180
Eckerd Drugs	9108 Glades Road	487-1943
Camino Cards	221 W. Camino Real	392-1511
Sandalfoot Cove Gift Shop	9850 Sandalfoot Blvd.	482-4565
Regency Court Station	3003-C8 Yamato Road	241-2442
Highland Beach Community Station	3612 S. Ocean Blvd.	278-1448

Newspapers and Magazines

THE NEWS, a Knight-Ridder publication, is a daily local paper for Boca Raton and Delray Beach residents. Its format, with stylized sections and use of color graphics, was designed to be reader-friendly. In addition to international and national coverage, a local news section gives full attention to community happenings. The classified sections are laid out in tabular form, allowing the reader to quickly identify items for sale. Condominiums, for example, are classified by price, location, development, size of unit, and additional descriptive comments. Automobiles are classified by make, model, year, owner's comments, price, and phone number in the same easy-to-read fashion. In the entertainment guide, movies are listed alphabetically in the first column, followed by the theaters, times of showings, and locations. Special sections include *Business Monday; Parent/Child* on Wednesday; *Food* on Thursday; and *Weekend Review* on Friday. *Ph. 368-9400.*

The SUN SENTINEL, the second largest newspaper of the Tribune Company, is an innovative and informative provider of local, state and international news and entertainment. It is published in Ft. Lauderdale, but does have two Palm Beach news bureaus. The editorial staff is direct, often blunt and sometimes humorous. Feature sections include Lifestyle, Sports, Business, and Entertainment. The Palm Beach editions cover items of local interest. *Ph. 832-2223.*

The PALM BEACH POST has the largest newspaper circulation in the county. In addition to its international, national and local emphasis, it also presents weekly sections on business, food & dining, and entertainment. *Ph. 820-4663.*

Many of the monthly special sections feature what-to-do-in-Florida information:

February: *The Fact Book; Guide to Southern Palm Beach County; Baseball Spring Training.*
April, July and November: *Guide to the Northern Palm Beaches.*
May: *Discover Florida.*
June and October: *Guide to the Western Communities.*
October: *Discover the Treasure Coast.*
November: *R & R* (guide to area fun).

◆ Magazines

There are several magazines which present articles and features of local interest.

BOCA RATON MAGAZINE: *Ph. 997-8683*
PALM BEACH ILLUSTRATED MAGAZINE: *Ph. 659-0210*
PALM BEACH LIFE: *Ph. 820-4751*
PALM BEACH TODAY: *Ph. 655-8667*

Library System

Central Library
3650 Summit Boulevard
West Palm Beach
Ph. 233- 2600 (WPB)
Ph. 930-5115 (toll free from Boca Raton)

The Palm Beach County Library System includes Central Library, 11 branches, and an Annex which houses the Bookmobile. With a collection of more than 590,000 books, magazines and newspapers, plus a varied selection of audio-visual materials, the library is able to meet the needs of students, residents and the business community. The county system serves residents of the library taxing district in the unincorporated areas as well as most municipalities which have a city library. Many independent municipal libraries belong to the Library Cooperative, permitting residents access to the county system. If you live within a city which does not participate in the cooperative, you may purchase a county library card.

The library houses the MacArthur Foundation collection of great classics and the PBS series on medicine, health, and astronomy. Some of the special offerings include films with an educational focus, travelogues, classics, and popular selections. How-to video cassettes and free VCR movies may also available for loan. Special programs are offered for the disabled, impaired, and homebound. A recent federal grant will be used to purchase television magnifiers for the visually impaired.

The Palm Beach County Library System has many monthly activities for children, such as story hours, reading programs and movie matinees. *Children's Story Hour* feature stories, songs, fingerplays, films, and arts and crafts for different ages. The *Homework Express* is a help workshop which discusses the resources available at the library.

Poetry programs, Great Books discussion groups and seminars are held at various library locations for the adult population.

For Job Seekers: Central Library subscribes to a national service that compiles weekly job opportunities from Help Wanted Ads in 64 cities around the country and stores them on microfiche.

Reference Section: Renovations are underway to accommodate the shift to a more electronic reference section.

- Use of the compact disc (CD-ROM) to store local and national newspaper articles and magazines provides fast and user friendly access to information. Health reference information as well as business data and articles are available by entering only a key word or phrase.
- *PhoneDisc USA* enables users to access residential addresses and phone numbers anywhere in the US by typing in the person's name. Using the system, a nationwide search can be done by name. Home computer operators can directly access the catalogue system.
- Future applications will expand to phone-in books.

Focus, a monthly newsletter, features the various library programs and a calendar of events.

West Palm Beach Municipal Library
100 Clematis Street
Ph. 659-8010

The city library, which dates to 1921, has a collection of 125,000 volumes. It is also part of the Library Cooperative Network which entitles residents to county privileges free of charge. Located downtown, the municipal library includes a large variety of business and medical references for the layperson, cookbooks, and children's books. For history buffs, there is a collection of books and references on the local history of West Palm Beach. It also houses the State Document Depository for Palm Beach County.

Boca Raton Public Library
200 NW Boca Raton Blvd.
Ph. 393-7852

The city library does not have a cooperative arrangement with the county system. Those living outside city limits must pay a $35 fee to belong. The library offers residents a choice from among 112,000 books; 450 periodicals; more than 5,250 video cassettes; 3,100 compact discs; and 1,800 audio cassettes, the majority of which are books-on-tape. The Youth Services Department offers a variety of programs for children of all ages on an on-going basis.

Southwest County Regional
20701 95th Avenue S.
Boca Raton
Ph. 482-4554

For residents living in unincorporated Boca Raton, the Southwest County Regional library branch is at their disposal. Library patrons can access all of the county's programs and services.

Health Care

◆ West Palm Beach

St. Mary's Hospital
901 45th Street
West Palm Beach
Ph. 844-6300

The largest hospital in Palm Beach County, St. Mary's is a nonprofit, 430-bed, acute care medical/surgical facility. It is on a 100-acre campus and has a 550-member medical staff. Special services include neonatal and pediatric intensive care; single-room maternity care; orthopedics; and cardiac care which includes a coronary unit. With a trauma-equipped Emergency Department, St. Mary's is the designated Trauma Center for northern Palm Beach County.

Its health services have been augmented by a Child Development Center; Cystic Fibrosis Center; and the operation of a Women's Health Service. The hospital offers a Community Cancer Program and other innovative outreach offerings, ranging from bicycle safety, educational seminars, prenatal medical care, and a variety of medical screenings. A new Outpatient Surgery Center will feature 12 surgical suites in which patients requiring endoscopic surgery, laser surgery, plastic surgery, breast biopsies, hernia repairs, and other procedures can benefit from "one-stop treatment."

Good Samaritan Medical Center
N. Flagler Drive and Palm Beach Lakes Blvd.
West Palm Beach
Ph. 835-2348

This acute care 341-bed medical facility provides a broad range of both inpatient and outpatient treatment programs. Its ER Department has staff physicians specially trained in pediatric emergency medicine to deal with child injuries and trauma. An outpatient Laser Center provides the latest technology in surgical procedures. Good Samaritan has a Neonatal Intensive Care Unit and single room maternity service. Other special programs include a sleep disorder program and a sports medicine clinic for weekend athletes. Preventive medicine is offered through its Health and Wellness Center which works with patients through individualized exercise programs.

Humana Hospital Of The Palm Beaches

2201 45th Street
West Palm Beach
Ph. 842-6141

An acute care facility with 250 beds, Humana provides a complete range of medical and surgical services. It has 24-hour Emergency Room, Outpatient Treatment, and Cardiac Care Units. Its managed care programs include educational programs to ensure wellness among its members.

JFK Medical Center

5301 S. Congress Avenue
Atlantis
Ph. 642-3633

JFK is a private, 369-bed, acute care medical facility. It has over 350 physicians representing all fields of specialization on its staff and is very community-focused. It takes special pride in its Heart Institute, Cancer Center, and Diagnostic Imaging Breast Center. It also has a program for alcohol and chemical dependency. Playing an active role in the community, the hospital sponsors health fairs, screenings, lecture series, and support groups in its efforts to promote wellness.

Glenbeigh Hospital Of The Palm Beaches

1950 Benoist Farms Road
West Palm Beach
Ph. 848-5500

Glenbeigh, a subsidiary of Glenbeigh Health Sources, is a private hospital specializing in the treatment of chemical dependency, eating disorders, sexual abuse, and other psychological and behavioral problems. Providing health care service to the community for more than 20 years, it is a fully accredited hospital, highly recognized for its treatment of addictive diseases.

◆ Boca Raton
Boca Raton Community Hospital
800 Meadows Road
Boca Raton
Ph. 395-7100

Built and supported by community donations, the Boca Raton Community Hospital was established in 1967 as a non-profit facility. An acute care, medical/surgical hospital accommodating 394 beds, it has been awarded many honors for the quality of its medical care and personalized service. The largest hospital in south Palm Beach, it is staffed by more than 350 physicians providing health care in 48 specialties. A 24-hour walk-in Emergency Room provides medical care for acute illness as well as minor injuries requring immediate attention. Boca Community's specialties include the Lynn Regional Cancer Center; a $3.1 million Cardiac Catherization Lab; a Diagnostic Radiological Center with a 2.4 million MRI scanner; Boca Back Center; Pain Management Center; SurgiCenter Plus, an outpatient surgical facility; and a new Maternity Unit. The hospital is highly visible in the health care education of the community, offering lectures and discussions on preventive medicine and alternative treatment options.

Boca Raton Community Hospital Women's Center focusses on the special concerns of women: mammography, breast biopsies, and osteoporosis screening. Education is stressed and a large volunteer program assists in its community outreach. *Ph. 393-4098.*

Lynn Regional Cancer Center
(of Boca Raton Community Hospital)

Lynn Regional Cancer Center is the only cancer care facility in the area. Boca Raton Community Hospital's cancer program has earned the designation as an Approved Cancer Center by the American College of Surgeons' Commission on Cancer. From diagnosis of the disease to medical/surgical interventions, radiation therapy, and ongoing support, the Center has been recognized for its high quality of patient treatment by the American Cancer Society. A state-of-the-art facility was recently opened in Delray Beach. *Ph. 637-7200.*

West Boca Medical Center
21644 State Road 7
West Boca
Ph. 488-8000

Located a few miles outside the city limits, West Boca Medical Center is a private, acute care facility providing treatment to residents living within both incorporated and unincorporated areas. The Medical Center, which opened in 1986, has 185 beds for medical and surgical care, along with a walk-in Emergency Center. It provides both inpatient and outpatient diagnostic and surgical procedures. Specialized facilities include the Florida Laser Center; the Sinus Therapeutic Laser Center; and the Family Birthcare Pavilion, staffed by 25 obstetricians, four midwives, and 14 neonatologists; a Neonatal Intensive Care Unit and a Pediatric Intensive Care Unit. West Boca is proud of its Child Life Program which deals with children's concerns, including their fears of being in a hospital.

Education

PALM BEACH COUNTY SCHOOL DISTRICT
3300 Forest Hill Blvd.
West Palm Beach, FL 33406
Public Affairs Office: *Ph. 434-8228*

Palm Beach County has the 15th largest school system in the country and the fourth largest in the state. There are 75 elementary schools, 19 middle schools, and 17 high schools within the school district. Six special/alternative centers and three vocational/technical facilities in the county provide additional services to various student populations.

◆ Special Programs
Computers and Technology. There are more than 11,700 computers available to students – and the number keeps growing. High schools have at least two computer labs and middle and elementary schools have a minimum of one. Each classroom in grades 2-5 is equipped with four computers. Satellite and cable telecommuni-

cations bring instructional programming into every classroom; instruction in specialized and advanced courses is channeled through a video network which accesses remote college and high school studios.

Academy and Magnet Programs. There are 12 schools in the school district. In addition to providing a strong academic program, students have a unique opportunity to receive instruction in areas of strong interest to them.

- The High Technology (HT) Program, at Suncoast Community High School in Riviera Beach, focuses on computer science and engineering.
- The Academy of Finance, at William T. Dwyer Community High School in Palm Beach Gardens, emphasizes the world of finance and different careers in the financial sector.
- Academy of Engineering and Technology, at Forest Hill High School in West Palm Beach, teaches academic, vocational and technical skills.
- Computer Technology Academy, at John I. Leonard High in Lake Worth, has been designated as one of the five model technology schools in the State of Florida. With special funding for computer equipment and technology as well as teacher training, the Academy has over 500 computers for classroom use, nine computer labs and electronic communications technology.
- Aerospace Science, Medicine and Criminal Justice magnet programs are offered at Lake Worth Community High School.
- South Florida Life Magnet, at Palm Beach Gardens Community High School, focuses on travel and tourism, global business and entrepreneurship, and sports management & recreation.
- The Teacher Academy, at Palm Beach Lakes High School in West Palm Beach, exposes students to the teaching profession. Current instructional methods and applications of technology to assist in the learning process are emphasized.
- Environmental Research and Field Studies Academy, at Jupiter High School, specializes in environmental studies and the earth sciences.
- High Technology Program, at Suncoast Community High School in Riviera Beach, teaches computer programming, computer graphics, and computer hardware design.
- International Baccalaureate Program, at Atlantic Community High School in Delray Beach, is a rigorous academic program for highly motivated students.

- Montessori Program, at S.D. Spady Elementary School in Delray Beach, is a magnet school for children in pre-K through 6th grades. It is based on providing learning experiences which are suited to each child's developmental needs.
- Palm Beach County School of the Arts, a magnet school in West Palm Beach, is dedicated to the visual/performing arts and communications arts. Students are enrolled from the 6th through the 12th grades.

Dual Enrollment Programs. Special programs also include college level learning opportunities offered to students in 11th and 12th grades with a B average or better. They can enroll in classes at either Palm Beach Community College or Florida Atlantic University and receive college credits.

Business Internships. Many in the business community have become partners in education and provide internships and resources to the school system.

Exceptional Student Education (ESE) Programs

- Programs for gifted students are located throughout the school system. Gifted centers are located within 13 elementary schools; all middle and high schools have gifted classes.
- Alternative schools offer students who have not fared well in the traditional system, and are at risk of dropping out, smaller classes for more individualized attention.
- Three Severe Emotionally Handicapped (SEH) Centers focus on students with psychological dysfunction.
- Royal Palm, a pre-K through 12th grade school, has programs designed for students with multiple handicaps. An on-site physical therapist is part of the multidisciplinary approach; special equipment and medical attention is available as needed.

Adult Community Education Programs are located in 23 schools throughout the county, serving approximately 250,000 people.

The **Homework Assistance Program** provides help in completing homework assignments through the services of certified teachers. *Ph. 800-548-0245.*

Child Care Programs for children who are alone before or after school hours are sponsored by the school district at various elementary schools.

Note: Palm Beach County has more than 100 private schools. For information about them, contact the Association of Independent Schools of Florida. *Ph. 305-666-1856.*

COLLEGES AND UNIVERSITIES

Florida Atlantic University has six campuses located within Broward, Palm Beach and St. Lucie counties. Its 850-acre main campus, with more than 11,000 students, is in a park-like setting in Boca Raton. Its nine colleges – Arts and Humanities, Business, Engineering, Science, Social Science, Nursing, Urban and Public Affairs, Education, and Liberal Arts – offer 53 areas of study leading to baccalaureate degrees. There are 43 master's degree programs and 14 Ph.D. degree programs. For the non-matriculated community, FAU's Department of Continuing Education provides a wealth of courses appealing to many different interests. *Ph. 367-3000 (Boca Raton); 624-6925 (North Campus).*

FAU has received recognition for the following special programs:

- An Ocean Engineering Program, initiated in 1964, was the first of its kind in the country. The State of Florida has designated it as a "Program of Distinction." Every other year, FAU hosts the International Human Powered Submarine Contest, races between human powered, two-person submarines.
- Dr. Scott Kelso, a renowned scientist, directs the Center for Complex Systems, a multidisciplinary research facility for brain sciences which focuses on the relationship between the brain and behavior.
- Dr. William Glenn, the world authority on high definition television, heads the research program and laboratory at FAU.
- The University Theater is available as a venue for students enrolled in the performing arts. The Dorothy F. Schmidt Center for the Arts and Humanities is under construction.
- The FAU library has seating capacity for 1,400 students, 500,000 books, 1.5 million microforms, and 4,000 subscription periodicals. Its noteworthy collections include publications on Florida, taxation, economics, business, women's studies, ocean engineering and Judaica.
- The Jay Raddock Chair for the Study of the Holocaust has recently been endowed. It has the largest collection of Holocaust materials and Judaica in Florida.
- The Lifetime Learning Society, with more than 12,000 members, offers courses, seminars and workshops for seniors 55 years and older.

Lynn University, formerly the College of Boca Raton, is a four-year, private college with a diverse population of more than 1,400 students representing 40 states and 38 countries. It is situated on 123 acres with beautifully landscaped grounds, dormitories and athletic fields. Lynn's Bachelor of Arts program includes aviation management, fashion design, behavior science, hotel/restaurant management, tourism and travel administration. Although it has a strong focus on career programs, a student may also earn a Bachelor of Arts degree in liberal arts studies. Graduate degrees are offered in hospitality services, healthcare administration, and international management. The Continuing Education Department offers courses on Saturdays and during weekday evening hours.

The University has plans to expand its present facilities to house new dormitories, more classrooms, a new library, a conference center, a gymnasium and athletic facilities. With the completion of all construction, it forecasts a student enrollment of 2,350 by the year 2004. *Ph. 994-0770.*

Barry University has a satellite facility in Boca Raton which offers programs leading to a Bachelor of Professional Studies degree and a Bachelor of Liberal Studies degree. Adult students returning to college are eligible for credits for previous work and life experiences. *Ph. 487-9230.*

Palm Beach Community College, founded in 1933, was the first public community college in Florida. It has four campuses: Central campus in Lake Worth; North campus in Palm Beach Gardens; South campus in Boca Raton; and Glades campus in Belle Glades. PBCC has a population of over 20,000 students at its four campuses, with approximately 16,000 students enrolled in its degree programs. All full-time faculty have advanced degrees. There are 50 different programs which lead to an AA degree, including a liberal arts degree for transfer to a four-year institution. Thirty areas of study lead to an AS degree. Its Center for Business and Industry includes the Motorola Center for Innovation and Technology. Students studying computer-integrated manufacturing gain practical experience at the Motorola Center, which integrates robotics in its manufacturing process.

The Continuing Education Studies Program at PBCC offers more than 400 courses during the year in personal and human development, computer courses, how-to courses, business seminars, career development, and liberal arts studies. The Institute of New Dimensions serves seniors 55 years and older with a superb variety of programs. *Ph. 439-8000.*

The Cultural Scene

Kravis Center For The Performing Arts

Sitting atop 5.4 acres along Okeechobee Road, the Kravis Center for the Performing Arts had its grand opening on November 28, 1992 – long-time dream of many Palm Beach residents. A large share ($40 million) of the $55 million construction cost came from private contributions.

The Kravis Center has been described as a little modern, a little art deco, and a little old world European. The elegant multi-level entrance lobby, a blend of glass, marble and steel, is supported by towering columns and lit by canister sconces. The grand marble staircase provides a majestic element. The Dreyfoos Concert Hall, which is the main theater, seats 2,200. Deep maroon upholstery, white and gold pillars, a dome-style ceiling, and balconies that wrap around the concert hall create the appearance of a European opera house. The theater's acoustics were designed by the famed Russell Johnson. A full-balanced acoustical environment was created to enhance the differing sounds of symphonic music, recitals, operas and contemporary music.

Two other performance halls at the Kravis include a 2,000-seat multipurpose outdoor amphitheater and a 300-seat black box playhouse.

The Kravis Center is home to the Palm Beach Opera Company, Miami City Ballet, Ballet Florida, and the Florida Philharmonic Orchestra. During the year, it presents an outstanding season of performances by world acclaimed classical and opera virtuosos and companies, dance troupes, pop, jazz and comedy celebrities, and Broadway theater and musicals.

In addition to its evening performances, the Kravis Center for the Performing Arts presents afternoon programs for retired and senior citizens. Low prices and a diverse array of productions featuring name entertainers make the Adults at Leisure Series a special one. The Center's educational outreach efforts include a Students & Teachers Arts Resource Series, featuring high caliber artists performing on the Dreyfoos stage. In its first season, 12,000 children were admitted free of charge. *701 Okeechobee Blvd., West Palm Beach. Ph. 833-8300.*

Ballet Florida

The Ballet Florida, a professional company, was established in 1986. Each season, it presents four major productions at the Kravis Center. With a troupe of 22 dancers under the direction of Marie Hale, a repertoire of classical and contemporary ballet is performed. In addition to engagements in Palm Beach, the Ballet Florida performs on tour during the fall and spring. Dedicated to educating young students and introducing them to the art of the ballet, it presents many performances of Peter and the Wolf in schools and theaters whenever it is in town.

The Ballet Florida also offers instruction for children, beginning at four years of age, and adults. Classes are held in ballet, tap, jazz and modern dance. *500 Fern Street, West Palm Beach. Ph. 659-1212.*

Caldwell Theater Company

Performances by an excellent group of professional actors, well designed and constructed sets, and a selection of plays ranging from drama and comedy to small scale musicals create a wonderful evening of theater. Attributed to a consistent level of quality, sell-outs are frequent during the October through May season. The five or six productions usually include several innovative premieres which are mixed with the more familiar ones. The summer showcase includes two or three theatrical productions. The Caldwell Company performs in a newly-designed intimate theater which accommodates 305 patrons. *7873 N. Federal Highway, Boca Raton. Ph. 241-7432.*

Norton Gallery

The Norton Gallery is not really a gallery, but rather a museum of fine art with 10 galleries and more than 4,000 works in its permanent collection. It has been recognized for its fine collection of Impressionist and Post-Impressionist artists such as Gauguin, Monet, Pissaro, Renoir, Matisse, and Picasso, among others. Works by O'Keefe, Hopper, Sheeler, and Pollack contribute to making the American Collection a memorable experience. Norton Gallery also possesses a significant collection of Chinese antiquities in jade, bronze and ceramics from the Shang Period through the early 20th century. During the year, Norton Gallery hosts 10 major traveling exhibitions and curates six exhibits which are on loan to other museums. The outside courtyard has beautifully landscaped gardens, fountains and sculptures by Rodin, Moore, and Brancusi.

There is something going on at Norton every Sunday. *Sundays at Norton* enhance leisure time through programs, such as artist lectures, musical performances, dance recitals, jazz on the lawn, gallery tours and family activities. During the year, there are special lectures, workshops and demonstrations. Exhibiting artists are invited to speak about their art and share their perspectives with guests. Well-informed docents provide daily gallery tours at 2 pm throughout the year.

Outreach programs are focused in the Belle Glades area where there is a high population of students at-risk. After-school art projects have been developed and coordinated by the Norton Gallery in conjunction with Belle Glades community centers and the school system. At the end of the school year, students are invited to exhibit their work at the Norton Gallery. *1451 S. Olive Ave., West Palm Beach. Ph. 832-5194.*

The Morikami Museum and Japanese Gardens

In a secluded setting in South Palm Beach, almost a century-old connection to a Japanese community continues to thrive. During the early 1900s, a group of Japanese young men and women emigrated to Boca Raton and formed a farming community which they called the Yamato Colony. One of its members, George Morikami, willed his personal land holdings to Palm Beach County for the creation of a park in memory of the Yamato Colony. In his honor, the Morikami Museum was opened in 1977, dedicated to the culture and understanding of Japanese life. Limited gallery space, however, resulted in the opening of a larger museum in 1993. The new facility incorporates exhibition galleries with changing exhibits of Japanese arts, crafts and artifacts; the Infotrom Gallery, housing a multimedia touch-screen computer system with information, music and video on Japanese life, past and present; a library and reading room; a 225-seat theater; an authentic Tea House, demonstrating the art of the Japanese tea ceremony; and the Cornell Cafe, offering homestyle Japanese cooking. Part of the Japanese tour includes the original museum, Yamato-kan. Styled after a Japanese residence, it is decorated to reflect contemporary Japanese life and includes a boy's room, tea ceremony room, and bathing room.

During the year, the Morikami Museum features a full calendar of activities which focus on Japanese life and culture. It hosts traveling exhibitions of folk craft, textiles, and fine art; demonstrations of Japanese crafts; floral and horticulture shows; international films and lecture series; Japanese folk dances and music; and even some off-the-beaten-path events, such as a salute to Samurai baseball.

Surrounding the Museum is a 200-acre park with Japanese gardens. Here you stroll through pine forests, watch waterfalls, and gaze at the golden koi (carp) swimming in the lakes, while a nature trail awaits the more active guests. The Bonsai gardens display a rare collection of miniature native Florida trees cut and trimmed in Japanese style. *4000 Morakami Park Road, Delray Beach. Ph. 495-0233.*

The Pope Theater Company

The Theater Company is committed to presenting contemporary plays by new and upcoming playwrights. A majority of the plays are Florida or South Florida premieres. The emphasis is on character-driven, issue-centered works to elevate the audience's consciousness. Five plays, mostly dramas, are performed in the 258-seat Lois Pope Theater during the October-through-May season. On Friday and Sunday evenings as well as Wednesday matinees, *Talk Back* invites the audience to remain after the play and engage in a question and answer session with the director and actors. During the summer season, two or three lighter-themed plays are usually performed.

The Pope Theater Company also presents the *New Voices Series*, a Monday evening play reading program. Actors sit on stage and read the scripted play to see how it works and solicit audience reaction. The playwright and actors engage in a dialogue with the audience after the work is performed. *Monday Night Movies* is another program hosted by the Pope Theater Company. International art films, mostly contemporary with a few classics, are featured during the series. After the screening, a professor from FAU's film department leads a discussion about the film.

As part of its commitment to education, the Pope Theater Company has a school-based touring program, the *Learning Stage*. Local playwrights are commissioned to write plays which are issue-oriented for students. One-act plays, with fully costumed actors and stage sets are presented at the schools. Study guides, workshops and question and answer sessions supplement classroom learning.

The Lois Pope Theater is across from the Ritz Carlton Hotel, south of Palm Beach. *262 South Ocean Blvd., Manalapan. Ph. 585-3404.*

Henry Morrison Flagler Museum

The Museum is the restored private home of Henry Morrison Flagler, a pioneer in the development of Palm Beach. The 55-room mansion was constructed in 1901 at a cost of $4 million. The Flaglers used the Palm Beach residence only two months during the year. In 1925, 12 years after his death, it was converted to a luxury hotel for the rich and famous. His granddaughter purchased the property in 1959 for $1.5 million, after learning that the property was on the market, with plans to either sell or demolish the hotel. She subsequently donated it to Palm Beach and the State of Florida.

Its permanent collections include Victorian furniture, paintings, china, glass, and dolls along with displays of costumes and lace. A one-hour guided tour highlights the treasures and history of the Flagler estate. His famous private railway car, located on the grounds, is also available for viewing. *1 Whitehall Way, Palm Beach. Ph. 655-2833.*

Duncan Theater (Professional Guest Artist Series)

Situated on the campus of Palm Beach Community College in Lake Worth, the Duncan Theater presents a diverse program of drama, dance, and chamber music. Each series can be purchased as a set or for singular performances. With an emphasis on dance, the series of seven may include as many as five dance programs and two theatrical productions. National and international touring companies of considerable artistic acclaim perform. Although the season's subscription series is from November through April, summer highlights feature dance performances and popular music concerts. Children's programs are also brought to the stage during the year.

During the year, students enrolled in the music and theater departments at Palm Beach Community College also perform at the Duncan. Call the box office for the upcoming performance schedule at the theater. *4200 Congress Avenue, Lake Worth. Ph. 439-8141.*

Boca Raton Museum Of Art

In September, 1993, the Boca Museum of Art purchased a new site. Eleven acres of land and a building which spans an area of four football fields will be home to a new Museum Center, a multi-functional cultural complex. Moshe Safdie, world renowned architect and designer of the National Gallery of Canada in Ottawa, has been commissioned to redesign the present space. The Museum Center will accommodate 50,000 square feet of art, craft and photography galleries; a community art school; an art library; sculpture gardens; a 100-seat "turn of the century" restaurant; a 700-seat theater; a vintage automobile museum; and a Great Gallery capable of accommodating very large exhibitions or formal affairs for 1,000 people.

Permanent collections of the museum include African Art, featuring masks, statuary, ritual and fetish objects; Pre-Columbian Art with a collection of pieces from the Mayan, Aztec and Inca cultures; photography, which includes more than 1000 works from 1840 to the present; the Dr. and Mrs. John J. Mayers Collection, an assemblage of works by the modern masters from the late 19th-early 20th century. The museum also has a collection of outstanding works by Florida artists which will be exhibited when the Museum Center opens in the fall of 1995.

Continuous educational activities have been very popular. The museum hosts two lecture series. The evening program features nine lectures by renowned artists and critics; the *Lunch and Learn* program is a series of 12 lectures which focus on current exhibitions within the museum. *Children's Days*, held on Saturdays, begin with guided tours of museum exhibitions, followed by arts and crafts. The *Art School*, which has been a part of the Museum for more than 25 years, offers a large selection of classes and studio workshops. Professional instructors teach classes in painting, drawing, sculpture, ceramics, photography, jewelry making and many specialty crafts. There are studio classes for all ages and ability levels. Contact the Museum for a schedule of events and exhibitions. *801 West Palmetto Park Road, Boca Raton. Ph. 392-2500.*

Boca Pops

The Boca Pops, a 75-member orchestra, has been delighting Palm Beach audiences for many years. Its repertoire includes a wide range of music? ₃, ₎res, from light classical to Broadway medleys, from Disney tu₋:ᵤs to international folk music, and from Big Band to Billy Joel. The Voices of the Pops, a 12-member choral group, sometimes accompany the orchestra with their stunning musical harmonies. Under the artistic d⁻ ⁻tion of Maestro Derek Stannard, the Pops performs at the FAU ₋nter Auditorium. It presents 20 performances during the season, which begins in November and continues through April. During special holiday times, the Pops performs free outdoor concerts for the community at Mizner Park,

Royal Palm Plaza and on the FAU campus. As part of a community outreach program, it auditions outstanding instrumentalists, pianists and vocalists for several musical scholarship awards. Winners are given the opportunity to perform with the Boca Pops. *100 NE. 1st Avenue, Boca Raton. Ph. 391-6777.*

Jupiter Theater

The Jupiter Theater, established in 1979 by Burt Reynolds, is now owned and operated as a dinner theater by Richard Aikins. It seats 428 people for acts I & II – dinner and performance. Its diversified menu and high quality cuisine has been cited for excellence by the National Dinner Theater Association. In addition to the mainstage theater, a preferred dining room is available for those who wish to dine in a separate room; after dinner they are reseated in the first six rows of the theater. Three sky boxes which can accommodate a party of six are available for special nights out. Each box has its own chef and waiter service for personalized dining prior to the performance.

Top Broadway shows and actors headline the year-round schedule of musicals, comedies, and star attractions. Eight to 10 shows are staged each year in addition to performances by well-known popular artists. Subscription seats can be purchased for the mainstage theater productions. *AudioLink*, which magnifies sound through headphones, is available for the hearing impaired.

The Jupiter Children's Theater produces youth-oriented popular classics, such as *Jack and the Beanstalk* and *Sleeping Beauty* for the Palm Beach County School System. Students have an opportunity to experience live theater in a state-of-the-art theatrical setting. *1001 East Indiantown Road, Jupiter. Ph. 746-5566.*

South Florida Science Museum

The South Florida Science Museum has been stimulating and entertaining visitors since 1959. The *Gibson Observatory* houses one of the largest and most powerful telescopes in the state. The *Planetarium* treats travelers to a voyage through the universe and a galaxy of educational entertainment in the form of sky shows, with meteor and laser displays. The Aquarium features antique diving equipment and aquaria food web models, as well as a touch tank experience for children. The *Light and Sight Hall* has exhibits demonstrating illusions, color blindness, and other visual phenomena. The *Native Plant Center* showcases the lush plant life of the tropics. A winding path leads to a hidden pond in a secluded setting.

Docent tours are available in addition to numerous special hands-on educational workshops. If you are looking for something interesting to do on a Friday evening, visit the museum for the Friday night laser show. *4801 Dreher Trail North, West Palm Beach. Ph. 832-1988.*

Events and Attractions

South Florida Fair

Distinguished as the county's largest and oldest event, the South Florida Fair dates back to 1912. Keeping with tradition, it is not surprising that the livestock and agricultural exhibits have a special place at the fair. Carnival rides and games, sunset parades starring the Clydesdale Budweiser horses, celebrity entertainment, and musical performances featuring country & western, jazz, big band, folk, gospel and pop provide non-stop activities. The Exposition Center showcases a different part of the world each year through incredible exhibits which make the journey entertaining, exciting and educational. *Yesteryear Village* is the site of restored historic Florida buildings. Working artisans, equipment and machinery gives visitors a view of early Florida. The Fair is a 17-day event held during the second half of January. It is worthwhile to obtain a schedule of events before going to the fairgrounds. *Southern Blvd., 7 miles west of I-95, West Palm Beach. Ph. 793-0333.*

Boca Museum Of Art Juried Art Show

This premier art festival, considered by many to be among the best in South Florida, is held annually in February at Crocker Center. The Harris Rhodes Report has designated it as one of the top 20 outdoor festivals in the country. More than 1,500 world-wide artists and craftspeople participate in the juried process, but only 200 are selected to exhibit their work. Approximately 50,000 visitors attend during the two-day show. A variety of media is represented in the exhibition and awards are presented to the "best of the show." Live concerts provide musical entertainment as people meander or just sit and relax. Gourmet food vendors display their particular artistry and cook up their specialties. *At Crocker Center, off Military Trail, Boca Raton. Ph. 392-2500.*

Sunfest

SunFest, billed as Florida's largest jazz, art and water events festival, is held during the first weekend in May, from Wednesday through Sunday.

- *Music:* Its two main stages present a musical lineup featuring 30 national recording artists in jazz, pop, blues, and World Beat music. In addition to star attractions, three other stages showcase local and regional talent, rock 'n' roll bands and jazz clinics.

- *Art:* A variety of international hand-made art, crafts, collectibles, jewelry and toys are exhibited in the Miami Herald Marketplace. The Sunbank juried art show features more than 120 artists working in a variety of media.

- *Water Events:* Visitors line up along the Intracoastal to watch the parasailing demonstrations, powerboat races, wave runner exhibitions and water ski shows. Water ski professionals in full costume perform extravaganzas on skis, including barefoot tricks and free-style jumping.

The Nationsbank Youth Park entertains youngsters with puppet and magic shows, lip sync contests, high school jazz bands and games. Cellular One's fireworks display, one of the largest on the East Coast, is held on Friday evening. Whatever day you decide to attend Sunfest, don't eat beforehand. More than 60 vendors prepare an international menu to please any palate, including specialties from some of the leading restaurants in the area. *Flagler Drive, bordering the Intracoastal Waterway, from Banyan Street to Lakeview Avenue, West Palm Beach. Ph. 659-5980.*

Boca Festival Days

The Boca Festival has become an annual event in August which wakes up the entire city during those doggy days of summer. The festival provides an avenue to raise money for charities, promote local businesses, showcase local talent and generate some good, old fashioned fun. The premier event is Wine and All That Jazz, a wine tasting festival held at the Boca Raton Resort and Club. *Boca Expo*, a large trade show, provides visibility for businesses in the community. Many look forward to *Gallery Go-Round*, a trolley tour of the local galleries. Other events include softball games, fishing tournaments, art shows, amateur photography contests, an antique car show, concerts, talent shows and many other events.

Contact the Boca Chamber of Commerce in mid-July for a listing of events and locations. *Ph. 395-4433.*

Fiesta On Flagler

Latin jazz, hot foods, Flamenco dancers, and folk art & crafts highlight this wonderful, colorful ethnic festival which celebrates the Hispanic heritage. The fiesta spirit of this three-day weekend takes over Flagler at the beginning of November. In addition to a line up of performers, an equestrian show is one of the special events. *West Palm Beach. Ph. 582-3514.*

ArtiGras

The ArtiGras festival, under the auspices of the Northern Palm Beaches Chamber of Commerce, is an annual three-day event held during President's weekend in February. Local, regional and national artists submit slides to a panel of jurors. Two hundred artists and one hundred crafts people are selected to showcase their work. There is also a *Celebrity Art Pavilion* with work from well known personalities. Along with the silent auction, a number of works are auctioned publicly during Sunday afternoon.

In addition to considerable community support, area schools are encouraged to participate in ArtiGras. Elementary schools are asked to select two student paintings to display in the *Future Celebrity Pavilion and Competition*. The artist of the award-winning work receives a prize and the school receives a $500 grant. The *Sand Sculpting Competition* invites elementary, middle and high school students to demonstrate their artistic talents with sand. Prizes are awarded for first and second places. The *Art Wall*, covered with one foot squares of paper, appeals to the artist in adults as well as children. For two dollars, you can draw whatever you wish on the wall. The proceeds from the 600 squares are used to fund high school senior scholarships. In the youth area, children's activities include face painting, sidewalk art, and sheet painting. On stage, there are plays, puppet shows and magicians. *Gardens of the Palm Beaches Mall, Kew Gardens Blvd. and The Gardens Pkwy., Palm Beach Gardens. Ph. 694-2300.*

Annual Palm Beach Home and Garden Show

Products and services for the home and garden attract over 35,000 people to this four-day event over Labor Day Weekend, from Friday through Monday. Showcasing more than 100 exhibitors, it provides an excellent source of ideas for anyone ininterested in decorating or remodeling a home. Home demonstrations and seminars are scheduled during the four days. *West Palm Beach Auditorium, Palm Beach Lakes Blvd. & Congress Avenue, West Palm Beach. Ph. 683-6012.*

Dreher Park Zoo
The Dreher Park Zoo is home to more than 500 animals, mostly from South America, Australia, Africa – and Florida. Its 22-acre site provides a natural habitat for its residents, including a simulated rain forest for certain South American species. Except for the Reptile House, all of the animals in the zoo live outdoors. Beautiful peacocks, pelicans and herons roam freely through the grounds. A new butterfly house and garden, cultivated with plants known to nourish butterflies, attracts many different and colorful species.

Dreher Park provides a safe home and nursing care for many endangered species or those who have suffered injuries. The zoo's primary goals are rehabilitation, species protection, conservation and education – in addition to offering many hours of enjoyment to visitors. A 1/4-mile boardwalk and nature trail circle the domicile for injured native Florida wildlife.

Zoo personnel encourage visitors to attend even in light, drizzly rain – a time when the animals and birds are at their chattiest! *I-95 and Summit Blvd., West Palm Beach. Ph. 533-0887.*

Gumbo Limbo Nature Center
Gumbo Limbo, a 67-acre park, was built to protect the largest tropical coastal hammock between South Palm Beach and Dade Counties. The hammock, comprised of trees commonly found within Central and South America, is truly a tropical environment. A 1/3-mile elevated boardwalk passes through a hardwood hammock and mangrove community while a 40-foot-high observation tower offers views of native flora and fauna. The Nature Center houses exhibits of birds, live snakes and an observation bee hive. The Ocean Engineering Research Building, an FAU research facility, is open to the public. Four outdoor 20-foot-wide aquariums contain sea turtles and other marine life. Indoor and outdoor classrooms provide hands-on educational experiences for school children and adults. There are many adult programs that explore the unique wonders of nature through seminars, workshops and interpretive field trips. *1801 North Ocean Blvd., Boca Raton. Ph. 338-1473.*

Lion Country Safari

Africa comes alive in South Florida as visitors drive along eight miles of paved roads in a wildlife preserve while 1,300 wild animals roam free and gander at their visitors. Some of the animals are very curious by nature and will walk up to your car for a good look, while others may ignore you or even sleep through your visit. All are interesting to watch, photograph, and enjoy – but do not get out of your car. At the completion of the journey, an amusement park, petting zoo and paddle boat rides offer tamer activities. *Southern Blvd. West of I-95. Ph. 793-1084.*

Moroso Motorsports Park

For a change of pace and a little excitement, Moroso Motorsports Park offers competitive bracket racing every Saturday evening on an NHRA (National Hot Rod Assoc.)-sanctioned quarter-mile drag strip.

Special Events

The *All Chevy Show*, held at the end of March, is a two-day extravaganza with classic model judging, drag racing and a car corral for used automobiles and parts as well as new products.

The *Pepsi Jet Car Nationals*, held in September, feature the largest jet car race in the South. Nitrous oxide fuels the cars, which run at 290 miles an hour. The "Original Jet Truck" is quite a vision as it takes a run down the track.

The *Pepsi Citrus Nationals* are held at the end of November. Alcohol dragsters, funny cars, and jet cars are the highlights of this winter drag racing event.

Events for sports cars and vintage models are also held at Moroso's Motorsports Park. The *National Roadway Race*, sponsored by the Sports Car Club of America, is a 2.25-mile 10-turn road course held in January. The *SVRA Vintage Road Race*, featuring old museum quality vintage cars in competition on the road course, takes place in March. *17047 Beeline Hwy., Palm Beach Gardens. Ph. 622-1400.*

Don't Miss

Exercise Along A1A. Jogging, walking, bicycling along AIA on a spring, winter, or fall morning. It is not only great exercise, but an exhilarating visual experience. Ocean scenery, views of the Intracoastal, beautiful homes, and interesting looking people (also exercising) are among sights along the way.

Weekends At Mizner. A Friday or Saturday evening at Mizner Park in Boca Raton is the place to see and to be seen. Residents and visitors dress up (and down) to stroll, window-shop, people-watch, and dine in one of the many outdoor restaurants nestled in this architecturally unique setting.

Keeping Cool, The Boca Way. On a hot day (or evening), people gravitate to Town Center Mall in Boca Raton for some relief! For some reason, one forgets about the heat in this air conditioned shopping mecca. Every important department store is represented, together with hundreds of boutiques, chain stores, galleries and a wonderful food court. Try the Boardwalk French fries, if your cholesterol count is low.

The Road Of The Wanabees. Drive along AIA from Boca Raton to Palm Beach – in a convertible, of course. As you pass some of the luxurious oceanfront estates, magnificent views, and lush tropical foliage, you cannot help but think that it doesn't get much better than this!

Worth While. Spend an afternoon on Worth Avenue in Palm Beach. This is where the rich and famous shop, so leave your wallet at home. You won't be able to afford the prices, but you will have fun. Although there are many Rolls Royces to attract your attention, explore the winding courtyards in between the shops, have lunch, marvel at the architecture, plantings, and art.

Turtle Watch. Between May and September, thousands of turtles lay eggs on South Florida beaches. During June and July, turtle walks are organized by local environmental groups. Gumbo Limbo in Boca Raton has guide-directed walks at 9 pm, Monday through Thursday, during this period. *Ph. 338-1473.*

Holiday Boat Parade. Watch the holiday boat parades in December. Each community along the Intracoastal has a festival to celebrate Christmas. Residents line the bridges to watch the gala parade of boats decorated in vibrant colors, banners, and lights.

Recreation

Football

The Miami Dolphins play their home games in Ft. Lauderdale's Joe Robbie Stadium, only 20 miles from Boca Raton, and not more than an hour's drive from West Palm Beach. *Ph. 800-255-3094.*

Baseball

According to some, South Florida only came of age with the debut of a major league baseball team. The Florida Marlins play their season in Joe Robbie Stadium. Spring training brings the national pastime even closer. From late February to March, the Montreal Expos and Atlanta Braves practice and play other teams in West Palm Beach's Municipal Stadium. Seats are scarce and fans are plentiful. Call in advance for tickets. *Ph. 684-6801 (Expos), 395-4433 (Braves).*

Minor league excitement for the entire family is offered by the Class A West Palm Beach Expos, who play their entire home season at Municipal Stadium. Prices are reasonable and the fans are close to the action from mid-April through September. *Ph. 684-6801.*

Basketball

The Miami Heat, an NBA team, is within easy access by auto, bus or Tri-Rail. *Ph. 305-577-4328.* In addition, an exciting collegiate basketball tournament, the Holiday Classic, is played in the West Palm Beach Auditorium in December.

Golf

Palm Beach County has more than 145 golf courses.

West Palm Beach
Emerald Dunes Golf Course
2100 Emerald Dunes Drive
An 18-hole, 7,006-yard course with par 72. Facilities include a driving range, lessons, and pro shop. *Ph. 684-4653.*

Palm Beach Lakes Golf Club
1100 N. Congress Avenue
An 18-hole, 5,421-yard course with par 70.

Facilities include a driving range, club rentals, lessons, and pro shop. *Ph. 683-2701.*

Boca Raton
Municipal Golf Course
8111 Golf Course Rd., 1/2 mile west of the Turnpike at Glades Rd.

Two public courses: an 18-hole, 6,593-yard course with par 72 and an executive nine-hole, par-3 course. Facilities include a driving range, putting green and club rentals. *Ph. 483-6317.*

Red Reef Executive Golf Course
111 N. Ocean Blvd.
An executive nine-hole, 1,628-yard course with par 3 is situated adjacent to the ocean. It is not quite Pebble Beach since you have to caddie yourself! Club rentals are available. *Ph. 391-5014.*

Southwinds Golf Course
19557 Lyons Road
An 18-hole, 5,800-yard course with par 70. Facilities include a driving range, large putting green, golf instruction and club rentals. *Ph. 483-1305.*

Polo

Players and horses become one in this fast paced "sport of kings." Every Sunday afternoon polo matches are played in the Polo Stadium in Wellington. These weekly contests begin in the latter part of December and continue through April. The Polo Stadium also hosts the World Cup tournament. *Ph. 793-1440.*

In South Palm Beach, polo enthusiasts should visit the Royal Palm Polo Club, which has been hosting polo matches for more than 60 years. *6300 Clint Moore Road, Boca Raton. Ph. 994-1876.*

Tennis

The Palm Beaches have over 1,100 tennis courts. Many professionals call South Florida home. The Virginia Slims tournament is played in Delray Beach in March, just prior to the Lipton Classic in Key Biscayne.

Fishing

Salt and freshwater fishing is available year-round in the Palm Beaches. Sailfish in winter, blue marlin in spring, and dolphin and wahoo in summer present challenges to all levels of enthusiasts. Keep in mind that recreational saltwater licenses are required. Many daily charter firms can be found at local marinas, captained by experts in finding the best offshore spots.

Beaches

West Palm Beach
Beach Conditions: *Ph. 624-0065*
County Dept. of Parks & Recreation: *Ph. 966-6600*
West Palm Beach Dept. of Leisure Services: *Ph. 659-8077*

The residents of West Palm Beach cross the Intracoastal to nearby coastal communities in order to enjoy the sand and surf.

Lake Worth Municipal Beach, Lake Ave., east of AIA, *Ph. 533-7367*
Amenities: Fishing pier; public swimming pool overlooking the ocean; playground; surfing area south of the pier; picnic facilities; snack bar; cabana rentals; metered parking.

R.G. Kreusler Park, 2695 S. Ocean Blvd., Lake Worth, *Ph. 586-0489*
Amenities: Large grassy areas for sunbathing; John G's restaurant is close-by; metered parking. Undesignated surfing area north of Kreusler Beach. Kreusler Park is a county beach, north of Lake Worth Municipal Beach.

Phipps Park, S. Ocean Blvd., Lake Worth, *Ph. 586-0489*
Amenities: Grassy areas; playground; tiki huts along dunes; snorkeling along rock ledge; picnic facilities; metered parking. Phipps Park is a county beach, 1 1/2 miles from the Lake Worth pier.

Midtown Public Beach, Gulf Stream Rd. & A1A, Town of Palm Beach
Amenities: Walkway adjacent to beach; Charlie's Crab is across A1A. Metered parking, but may be difficult in season.

Riviera Municipal Beach, Blue Heron Bridge to A1A, Singer Island, *Ph. 845-4070*
Amenities: Raft rentals; snorkeling; restaurants & shops nearby; snack bar; cabana rentals; free and metered parking.

Boca Raton
Daily Beach Conditions: *Ph. 393-7989*
Municipal Dept. of Parks & Recreation: *Ph. 393-7811*

South Beach Park, Palmetto Park Road & A1A, *Ph. 393-7973*
Amenities: Elevated pavilion overlooks the beachfront; several walkways leading to the beach span the dune. A small beach with simple charm. Convenience stores on Palmetto Park Rd. Parking lot and parking along Palmetto Park Rd. (if available).

Red Reef Park, 1/2 mile north of Palmetto Park Rd. & A1A, *Ph. 393-7974*
Amenities: Elevated boardwalk for strolling, lit until 10 pm; pavilion overlooks the ocean; snorkeling reef; play area and grills in shaded areas; parking lot.

Spanish River Park, South of Spanish River Blvd. & A1A, *Ph. 393-7877*
Amenities: Wide stretch of sandy beach is connected by tunnels to the municipal park. Park has grills; pavilions; shaded areas; playground; nature trail; observation tower; parking lot and parking along Spanish River Blvd. (if available).

Directory of Services

9-1-1 Emergency Only	POLICE • SHERIFF• FIRE• MEDICAL•RESCUE	
AGENCY	**DESCRIPTION**	**PALM BEACH (407)**
ALCOHOL & DRUG ABUSE	Intervention & Referral	800-253-8770 845-8600
CRISIS HOTLINE	24 Hour Help Line *North County* *South County*	 547-1000 243-1000
ABUSE CENTER: AID TO VICTIMS	Women in Distress; Shelter for Abused Women	265-2900
POISON CONTROL & INFORMATION CENTER		800-282-3171 650-6333
SENIOR SUPPORT *SUNSHINE SERVICE*	Telephone Reassurance & Support *North County* *South County*	 547-1000 243-1000
TEEN HOTLINE	*North County* *South County*	547-TEEN 243-TEEN
TELEPHONE SUPPORT FOR LATCH KEY CHILDREN: *PHONE FRIEND*	Telephone Companionship For Children Home Alone *North County* *South County*	 547-1000 243-1000

Directory of Services   63

U.S. COASTGUARD	Search & Rescue Ocean/Intracoastal	844-4470
TIME/TEMPERATURE & WEATHER		832-3801

County Services

AGENCY	DESCRIPTION	PALM BEACH (407)
GOVERNMENT CENTER	301 N. Olive Avenue	355-2040
		355-3623
PUBLIC INFORMATION	Information & Referral	355-2754
ANIMAL CONTROL		233-1200
BOARD OF EDUCATION		278-0366
COUNTY COOPERATIVE EXTENSION SERVICE		233-1700
COUNTY COURTHOUSE		355-2996
EMERGENCY MGMNT	Disaster Readiness Training & Evacuation Information	233-3500
FIRE PREVENTION		233-0050
FL. HIGHWAY PATROL	All Interstate Roads & Turnpikes	540-1145
GARBAGE COLLECTION		697-2700
LIBRARY		233-2600
	South County Number	930-5115
LICENSES	Auto Tag	355-2264
	Parking Permit - Handicapped	355-2622
	Boating Registration	355-2622
	Fishing & Hunting	355-2622
MASS TRANSIT	Bus Route Information	233-1111
	TRI-RAIL	800-874-7245
PARKS AND RECREATION		966-6600
PASSPORT INFORMATION		697-2028
PROPERTY APPRAISER		355-3230
SHERIFF		688-3000
TAX COLLECTOR		355-2264
TRAFFIC VIOLATION INFORMATION		355-2994

VOTER REGISTRATION		355-2650
WATER/SEWER		686-2656
Emergency/After Hours		686-2656

Human Services

AGENCY	DESCRIPTION	PALM BEACH (407)
AMERICAN ASSOC. OF RETIRED PERSONS	Florida State Headquarters; Provides source for local contact	813-576-1155
AMERICAN RED CROSS	Hurricane Shelter Information, Disaster Relief, Blood Banks	833-7711
CHILD CARE RESOURCE & REFERRAL	Information & Referrals on Licensed Child Care Centers & Registered Family Care Providers	265-2423
CRISIS LINE OF PALM BEACH	Connects You with the Appropriate Person or Agency Who Can Answer Your Question or Assist You With A Particular Need	547-1000 (No. County) 243-1000 (So. County)
HANDICAPPED/DISABLED SERVICES		355-4883
HEALTH DEPARTMENT		840-4500
I R S	Location & Hours of Local Offices Tax Information Tax Forms	800-829-1040 904-354-1760 800-829-3676
NEWCOMERS CLUBS Boca Raton	Contact Chamber of Commerce	395-4433
West Palm Beach	Information Not Available	
SENIOR CITIZEN SERVICES	Information/Assistance Programs for Seniors	355-4746
SOCIAL SECURITY		800-772-1213
SOCIAL SERVICE TRANSPORTATION	Reduced Fares, Dial-A-Ride for Seniors & Special Groups	930-8747
UNITED WAY	An Excellent Resource for Community Information	832-7300
VETERAN'S ASSISTANCE		355-4761
VOLUNTEER CENTER	A Clearinghouse for Volunteer Positions	820-2550

RETIRED SENIOR VOLUNTEER PROGRAM (RSVP)		820-2550
WOMEN'S RESOURCE CTR WOMEN'S HORIZONS	Sponsored by the Jr. League of the Palm Beaches	689-7590

City Numbers

	BOCA RATON	WEST PALM
GOVERNMENT CENTER	City Hall	City Hall
	201 W. Palmetto Park Road	200 2nd St
	393-7700	659-8000
CITY CLERK	393-7740	659-8020
POLICE (Non-Emergency)	338-1234	837-4000
FIRE (Non-Emergency)	395-9290	835-2900
DRIVER'S LICENSE	994-0440	640-6180
ELECTRICAL SERVICE FL Power & Light	395-8700	697-8000
GARBAGE COLLECTION	393-7867	659-8047
LIBRARY	393-7852	659-8068
PARKS & RECREATION	393-7995	688-6300
TELEPHONE COMPANY Southern Bell	780-2355	780-2355
VOTER'S REGISTRATION	393-7742	355-2650
WATER AND SEWER	338-7300	659-8080
Emergency/After Hours	338-7300	659-8090

Civic Organizations

Greater Boca Raton Chamber of Commerce	395-4433
Chamber of Commerce of the Palm Beaches	833-3711
Palm Beach County Convention & Visitor's Bureau	471-3995
Economic Council of Palm Beach County	684-1551
Business Development Board	684-2401

Ft. Lauderdale

The Ft. Lauderdale of old, a spirited gathering place and playground for college students on Spring Break, has matured and evolved into a worldly, sophisticated city. During the mid-1980's, a new identity began to take root. Although the city continues to attract tourists, it has also developed a more serious cosmopolitan image. The Ft. Lauderdale community has actively endorsed this effort and demonstrated its commitment to growth through its support of bond issues and personal involvement.

A major development which the city has fervently endorsed is the New River Project in the heart of downtown Ft. Lauderdale. Riverwalk, a linear park and urban waterfront, features a Performing Arts Center, museums, parks, marinas and restaurants. A new and exciting entertainment and shopping district, which would include movie theaters, restaurants, night life, and interesting boutiques, is presently on the drawing board for 1995. Riverwalk is evolving into a gathering place for friends, cultural activities, entertainment and leisure.

Perhaps it is only fitting that Ft. Lauderdale should return to its roots at the New River. The Seminole Indians inhabited the property along the river until Major William Lauderdale, a resident of Tennessee and close supporter of Andrew Jackson, organized troops to fight the Second Seminole War. The troops arrived at the New River in 1838, constructed a fort and subsequently named the site after Major Lauderdale. Stranahan House, the first trading post in the area, also functioned as a way station for commerce along the New River and a school house. Ft. Lauderdale was incorporated in 1911 and selected as the county seat in 1915 when Broward County was formed.

Today Ft. Lauderdale is the fifth largest city in Florida. Named the "Yachting Capital of the World" with its 165 miles of coastal waterways, it continues to attract people who enjoy boating along the coastal waters and canals. While offering a variety of leisure activities, Ft. Lauderdale also has a vital business community. It is headquarters to many national and international corporations, which actively support the city's cultural institutions and events. A new Convention Center, which debuted in 1991, hosts national and international trade shows in a state-of-the-art facility. Port

Everglades, the second largest cruise ship port in the world, is also a port of call to military vessels and cargo.

Ft. Lauderdale is still in the process of dynamic growth. Its downtown has become a hub of business, culture and entertainment. At the core of the city's ongoing development is a community with a shared vision.

Demographics

Broward County lies on the east coast of Florida, between Palm Beach County to the north and Dade County to the south. The City of Ft. Lauderdale is approximately equidistant from West Palm Beach and Miami. Broward County encompasses 28 municipalities.

◆ Size

Broward County spans 1,197 square miles which includes 23 miles of beachfront along the Atlantic Ocean. Three hundred miles of navigable waterways have given rise to the nickname, "Venice of America." The Everglades, to the west, occupies about 2/3 of the county. The city of Ft. Lauderdale contains 31.65 square miles.

◆ Population

In 1993, Broward County had a population of 1,317,406 people. Unincorporated Broward contains 152,227 residents.

NORTH BROWARD
Coconut Creek	NW	32,000
Coral Springs	NW	83,974
Deerfield Beach	NE	46,997
Hillsboro Beach	NE	1,748
Lighthouse Point	NE	10,500
Margate	NW	43,563
North Lauderdale	NW	26,506
Parkland	NW	6,000
Pompano Beach	NE	72,458
Sea Ranch Lakes	NE	619
Tamarac	NW	45,000

CENTRAL
Ft. Lauderdale	CE	150,631
Lauderdale-By-The-Sea	CE	33,308
Lauderdale Lakes	CW	27,341

Ft. Lauderdale

Lauderhill	CW	50,052
Lazy Lakes	CE	33
Oakland Park	CE	26,590
Plantation	CW	69,250
Sunrise	CW	64,400
Wilton Manors	CE	13,500

SOUTH BROWARD

Cooper City	SW	22,108
Dania	SE	13,024
Davie	SW	43,382
Hallandale	SE	30,997
Hollywood	SE	125,000
Miramar	SW	41,719
Pembroke Pk.	SW	4,933
Pembroke Pines	SW	72,600
Weston*	SW	9,500

*Weston, developed in the mid 1980's, is a large residential community in southwest Broward, not a municipality.

Oceanside Municipalities: Dania, Deerfield Beach, Fort Lauderdale, Hallandale, Hillsboro Beach, Hollywood, Lauderdale-By-The-Sea, Lighthouse Point, Pompano Beach and Sea Ranch Lakes.

◆ Age Demographics

	Broward County	Ft. Lauderdale
0-20	24%	22%
21-44	37%	40%
45-59	14%	15%
60+	25%	23%

The median age in Broward County is 37.7; in Ft. Lauderdale, it is 37.3.

◆ Climate

Elevation: 8 feet
Annual Rainfall: 65.9 inches
Average Summer Temperature: 82 degrees
Average Winter Temperature: 68.6 degrees

Taxes

◆ Property Taxes

Unincorporated Broward, which receives services from the county, has a millage rate ranging from 22.2406 to 22.6693. Ft. Lauderdale has a millage rate of 26.4459. Other municipalities have rates which range from 22.2406 to 28.2629 per $1,000 of assessed property value.

◆ **Sales and Use Tax**
Broward County collects a 6% sales tax levied by the State of Florida.

Voting and Elections

Broward County elects seven commissioners for a four-year term. They are elected by the district in which they reside, but serve the interests of the entire county. A chair and vice-chair are elected by fellow commissioners every year. Every two years, either three or four of the district seats are up for election.

Ft. Lauderdale elects four commissioners by district and a mayor, who is elected at-large, to serve a three-year term of office. The primary is held on the second Tuesday of February and the general election takes place on the second Tuesday of March. Elections for commissioners are not staggered; five seats become available every three years (1994; 1997; and 2000). A city manager, appointed by the commission, is responsible for the day-to-day operations of the government. *Ph. 761-5006.*

Supervisor Of Elections: Broward County, 115 S. Andrews Avenue, Ft. Lauderdale, FL 33301. *Ph. 357-7050.*

Pet Registration

All dogs and cats must be vaccinated and licensed when they reach four months of age. Broward County enforces nuisance and leash laws with fines. Owners are held responsible for pets which spoil public property. Animal Control operates an adoption center for stray and unwanted pets; they are medically evaluated and sterilized prior to adoption. The Center extends an open invitation to people who are looking for a special pet to take home.

The Humane Society of Broward County also offers adoption services for unwanted animals who are brought in by their owners. Euthanasia is a special service available to pet owners who need to put their pets to sleep. An active volunteer organization provides direct care for the animals in the kennels & cattery and offers adoption counseling services. The Society sponsors a variety of events throughout the year. The *Pets for People Showdown* features a pet photo contest; a dog wash; a dog show with categories such as the happiest dog and best buddies; and a cat show which offers a prize for the "coolest cat." The *Humane Society News* is a quarterly newsletter which features animal services, volunteer needs and upcoming events. *Ph. 463-4870.*

Transportation

Air Travel

FT. LAUDERDALE/HOLLYWOOD INTERNATIONAL AIRPORT
100-300 Terminal Drive
Ft. Lauderdale, FL 33315
Main Number: *Ph. 359-6100*
Control Center - 24 Hr. *Ph. 359-1200*
Passenger Page Service: Each airline has its own paging number which can be accessed through the Control Center.
Parking Information: *Ph. 359-0206*
Administration: *Ph. 359-6116*

Today's Ft. Lauderdale/Hollywood International Airport, with its lush tropical plantings and graceful palm trees, covers two square miles of land. Since its modest beginnings and the start-up of passenger service in 1953, the airport has grown into a major transportation facility. During the early 1980's, the airport underwent a reconstruction effort. Architects designed the new facility in the shape of a horseshoe, with terminals along the rim and a multi-story parking garage situated in the center. It is only a hop, skip and a jump from the garage to any one of the entrances. Modern, spacious terminals, an efficient design, and a network of highways to and from the airport make it a particularly user-friendly airport. Within a short distance from Broward County communities, easy highway travel from South Palm Beach and North Dade have also made it a convenient airport to access from neighboring counties.

At its three terminals, 18 scheduled and 14 charter airlines provide service to destinations around the world, including nonstop service to Europe.

Major Airlines include:

American	Icelandair
American Trans Air	Midwest Express
Carnival	Northwest
Chalk Int'l	Paradise Island
Comair	TWA
Continental	United
Delta	USAir

Commuter Airlines within Florida:

Air Sunshine	Continental
Comair	USAir Florida Shuttle

Commuter Airlines to the Bahamas:
Airways Int'l
Island Express
Laker Airways

Amenities. Paintings and works of art are on display in the *Lee Wagener Gallery* in Terminal 2 of the airport. Changing exhibitions showcase the work of talented Broward artists; the *Alamo Student Art Gallery* focuses on the work of Broward's younger artists. Don't miss Duane Hanson's sculpture, *Vendor with Walkman* in Terminal 2. It is easy to be mesmerized by its life-like resemblance.

Business Centers are conveniently located in each of the three terminals. A small conference room, fax machine, copier, foreign currency exchange, and baggage storage are available in Terminals 1 and 2; in addition, the Terminal 2 facility is equipped with an ATM and credit card money machine; the Terminal 3 center has mostly automated services. An Information Center is located in Terminal 2.

The airport provides user-friendly services for the handicapped traveler. It also offers the TDD communications system in all terminals for the hearing impaired.

Ground Transportation. Broward County Transit bus service is available to and from the airport via the #1 bus which travels to and from three hub sites: Broward Terminal (for northern destinations); Hollywood's Young Circle and Aventura Mall in North Miami Beach (for destinations southward). Buses from the airport operate every 20 minutes, Monday through Friday and every 30 minutes on the weekends. From each of the hubs, one can reach most locations within Broward County as well as connect to buses which travel into Palm Beach or Dade counties. Call the Customer Service Center for more information. *Ph. 357-8400.*

Free shuttle bus service connects the airport and the Tri-Rail system. Buses meet the Tri-Rail train at the Ft. Lauderdale/Airport station, beginning at 5:54 am and continuing until 7:20 pm, during the week. Shuttles depart from the airport at Terminals 1 and 3 en route to the Tri-Rail station, from 6:35 am until 7:21 pm, on weekdays. Call Tri-Rail for weekend schedules and to verify weekday schedules. *Ph. 728-8445.*

Various limousine companies, van lines and taxis also service the airport. Look for the rate comparison charts posted at each dispatch station outside the terminal.

If you wish to rent a car, there are five on-site agencies at the airport: Avis, Budget, Dollar, Hertz and National.

Local Transportation

Broward County Transit: BCT operates approximately 200 buses per day over 30 routes covering 300 square miles in Broward County. The system runs from city to city. Commuters from Margate and neighboring Coral Springs may drive to one of the Park 'n Ride facilities and board a bus to downtown Ft. Lauderdale. BCT is also an intercounty system with service which extends from Boca Raton to North Miami Beach, where connections can be made for continued service within Palm Beach or Dade County respectively. Bus service is available seven days a week, with more limited service on Sundays and holidays. Regular service hours are approximately 5:30 am until 10 pm, depending upon the route. Call for information regarding routes and schedules. *Ph. 357-8400.*

Weekly and monthly transpasses may be purchased at the Broward Central Terminal, County Libraries and the Mass Transit Office, located at 3201 W. Copans Rd., Pompano Beach. Apply in person or by mail. There are special fares for the handicapped, seniors and students. Call to verify necessary documentation.

Tri-Rail: A tri-county commuter train, which spans 67 miles, services 15 stations from West Palm Beach to Miami/Hialeah. There are six Broward stations with stops at Deerfield Beach, Pompano Beach, Cypress Creek, Ft. Lauderdale, Ft. Lauderdale Airport and Hollywood. Tri-Rail also provides transportation to the Miami

Arena for Heat games and Joe Robbie Stadium for most Dolphin games and special events.

Free shuttle buses at Tri-Rail stations connect to the airport, shopping and business districts. Call to find out their drop off locations.

The Trolley: The Downtown Fort Lauderdale Trolley System offers free service during weekdays to the heart of downtown Ft. Lauderdale. The Red Line (Courthouse) travels the downtown area in a north/south direction, from 7:30 am to 5:30 pm. It passes downtown's government center and office buildings en route to the shops and restaurants along Las Olas Blvd. The Green Line (Las Olas) travels east/west, from 11:30 am to 2:30 pm. The Blue Line, a special lunch trolley, travels south of the river, crossing Riverwalk to Las Olas, from 11:30 am to 2:30 pm. The three trolleys converge at Las Olas Blvd. and SE 3rd Avenue. Call for schedule and routing information. *Ph. 463-6574.*

Postal Service

Post Offices

Main Office	1900 W. Oakland Pk. Blvd. Monday-Friday: 7:30-7:00 Saturday: 8:30-2:00	527-2010
Colle Station	1404 E. Las Olas Blvd. Monday-Friday: 8:30-5:00	764-5931
Coral Ridge Station	3296 N. Federal Hwy. Monday-Friday: 8:30-5:00	563-3339
Gateway Station	1776 E. Sunrise Blvd. Monday-Friday: 8:30-5:00 Saturday: 8:00-noon	463-6776
New River Station	330 SW 2nd St. Monday-Friday: 7:30-6:00 Saturday: 8:30-2:00	761-1173
Southside Station	2801 S. Federal Hwy. Monday-Friday: 7:30-6:00 Saturday: 8:30-2:00	761-1198
Andrews Ave. Annex	3400 N. Andrews Ave. Monday-Friday: 7:30-4:30	568-1325

Ft. Lauderdale

Contract Stations

Contract Stations perform most postal services. Call for hours.

Party Basket TOWNE MALL #1	6915 W. Broward Blvd.	583-5350
Plantation LTD FASHION MALL	321 N. University Dr.	370-1884
National Parcel STADIUM STATION	5313 N. State Road 7	484-8700
United Postal INTRACOASTAL BRANCH	3032 E. Commercial Blvd.	351-9551
Sailor's Canteen PORT EVERGLADES	State Road 84	524-1467
City of Sunrise CITY OF SUNRISE	2260 NW 68th Ave.	572-2409
P.K.G.'s N. OCEAN BLVD.	3556 N. Ocean Blvd.	561-9231
Harbor Pharmacy STATION 9	2210 SE 17th Street	524-3700
Ward's City PROSPECT RD. #5	169 NW 44th Street	776-5040
Debbie's App. STATION 10	5223 W. Broward Blvd.	581-1761
Plantation Print STATION 15	1639 S. University Dr.	475-0774
Postal Services MIDWAY	8281 W. Sunrise Blvd.	424-8660
Eckerd Drugs WOODMONT	8233 NW 88 Ave.	722-2634
Books Unlimited PINE RIDGE	8966 State Road 84	474-4330
Eckerd Drugs WEST END	1120 Weston Road	384-7667

Newspapers and Magazines

The SUN-SENTINEL has been in the Ft. Lauderdale community since 1911. It was not until 1953, however, that the first Sunday morning edition was printed. Ten years later, it was purchased by the Tribune Company of Chicago, which publishes six daily newspapers, owns seven television and six radio stations. The Sun-Sentinel provides international, national and local news coverage throughout Broward and South Palm Beach counties. The metropolitan news section, however, is different for each of the two counties. Six zoned supplements featuring community happenings in different areas of Broward are published several times a week. *Ph. 356-4000.*

- *Showtime*, published on Friday, provides a comprehensive guide to entertainment and activities scheduled for the weekend and upcoming week. Restaurants, theater, film, music, art, and festivals are listed and reviewed.

- *Weekly Business* is published every Monday and features business trends and news in South Florida as well as articles on personal finance. The *Business Calendar* lists seminars, meetings and events. Other sections include *What's New in Business* and *People in Business*.

- *XS* is an award-winning alternative weekly publication for non-traditional readers in Broward and South Palm Beach counties. Directed towards active young adults, it features a wealth of leisure activities and entertaining stories. As a guide to concerts, plays, lectures, sporting events nightclubs, shows and restaurants it details weekly events. *Ph. 356-4943.*

THE MIAMI HERALD, which dates back to 1910, is a daily publication with circulation in Dade, Broward, and Palm Beach counties. It presents international, national and local news coverage. *Neighbors*, published twice weekly, brings community news about local people, places, business, and events to five different zones in Broward. Weekly sections include *Business Monday*, featuring local and national business happenings and trends; *Living And Learning* (Friday), information about kids' activities, education, & healthcare; *Weekend* (Friday), a guide and calendar of attractions, events, performances, dining and restaurant reviews; *Tropic* (Sunday), a magazine format featuring stories about people and places, current issues and lifestyles in South Florida. There are also special sections published monthly throughout the year, which include *Florida Outlook* (January); *How To Buy A Home* (March); *Where To Dine In South Florida* (April); *Destinations* (April); *Discover The Gulf* (May); *Neighborhoods* (October); *Season Of The Arts* (November). Call for their *Special Section Calendar*. *Ph. 527-8940.*

◆ Special Interest Publications

WATERFRONT NEWS, published monthly, covers waterfront issues, communities, and people. There are also feature articles on travel, sports and recreation as well as restaurant reviews and a calendar of events. *Ph. 524-9450.*

WATERWAY TIMES, a monthly magazine, specializes in boating and marine activities. Human interest stories; environmental issues and concerns; scientific articles; and industry news, hints and tips are featured. *Ph. 761-1937.*

◆ Business and Financial Publications

SOUTH FLORIDA BUSINESS JOURNAL is a weekly newspaper covering Dade, Broward and Palm Beach counties. The paper, part of a chain owned by American City Business Journals Inc., features business news articles with an emphasis on real estate, tourism, hospitality, retail, media, marketing, technology, education, banking, finance, health-care and sports. *Ph. 359-2100.*

BROWARD DAILY BUSINESS REVIEW. Published in three counties. For an overview of subject matter and coverage, refer to Miami's Newspapers and Magazines: Miami Daily Business Review. *Ph. 468-2600.*

GOLD COAST, an upscale arts and culture publication, presents stories on local celebrities in the arts; features on architecture, interior design, theater and books; and a detailed calendar of cultural happenings. Charitable events and the people involved in making them successful are also featured in each issue. Elegant, artistic photographs complement the interesting stories. *Ph. 764-1952.*

SOUTH FLORIDA MAGAZINE focuses on Florida lifestyles along the Gold Coast. For more information, refer to Miami's Newspapers and Magazines. *Ph. 445-4500.*

ACTIVITY LINE, a telephone communications network, provides a comprehensive portfolio of daytime activities, nighttime entertainment, restaurants, community information, services and religious listings in six languages – English, Spanish, German, French Swedish and Portuguese. *Ph. 964-3836.*

Library System

The Broward County Library System includes the Main Library, two regional and 28 branch libraries. Three additional branches are scheduled for completion in the near future. The Main Library is also a research facility for Florida Atlantic University and Florida International University. It has four major departments: Business, Science and Technology; Fine Arts; Humanities; and Government Documents.

The Main Library was designed with a six-story center atrium. The north facade, which is glass, overlooks a plaza and a lovely park. A European-style cafeteria within the library serves a menu of quality fresh food. A choice of seating is available in the cafe or on the terrace overlooking the plaza. Frequent noontime concerts enhance the delightful ambiance. The library also houses an interesting gift shop, for browsing or buying. Its greeting cards, designed by local artists, are especially noteworthy!

Broward County Main Library
100 South Andrews Avenue
Ph. 357-7444

Special Programs
Florida Center For The Book, established in 1984, has the distinction of being the first affiliate of the Center for the Book in the Library of Congress. The Center's mission is to spread the good word about books; enrich literary experiences; expand the reading population; and develop awareness of the library's offerings and multiple activities in the community. A sampling of past programs which the Center has supported include:

- Let's Talk About It – What America Reads.
- Rediscovering the 1930's: the WPA and the Federal Writer's Project.
- Raise A Reader kits for new parents and babies statewide to generate new participants for the Year of the Young Reader.
- Banned Books Week, featuring programs with Malcolm Boyd, Norma Klein and Dave Barry.

- Evenings with the Author Programs; Literary Seminars; and Book Fairs.

Library Edition, also under the aegis of the Florida Center for the Book, is a weekly cable television program. Well known authors, new writers on the scene, publishers, literary agents, editors, and critics discuss books, writing, and publishing trends.

Day Of Literary Lectures and Night Of Literary Feasts. The Day of Literary Lectures presents panel discussions throughout the day with an assemblage of well known and best selling authors. The Night of Literary Feasts features an elegant evening with authors and friends at the homes of Broward's elite residents.

Antiquarian Book Fair offers old, rare and out-of-print books; maps; and prints.

Children's Reading Festival, scheduled during a weekend in mid-April, is dedicated to children who enjoy reading as well as creating a cadre of new readers. Music, mime, and children's productions of favorite tales, presented on the various stages in and around the library, provide entertainment while continuous performances by national and local storytellers captivate young imaginations. Other highlights include face-to-face discussions with authors and illustrators, workshops, arts and crafts, and a parade of costumed characters.

The Broward County Library System celebrates the cultural diversity of its communities through the vast holdings of literary resources in its ethnic collections. The Main Library subscribes to newspapers and magazines published in Spanish, French, German, Italian, Russian, Hebrew and Arabic. The West Regional Library houses a collection of books in more than a dozen foreign languages and 350 foreign language audio cassettes and records.

Ethnic Collections
- *Jewish:* The West Regional Library houses a collection of 500 books and 100 videos on Jewish culture; Hallandale has 500 volumes and Lauderdale Lakes offers a large Holocaust section. The Main Library offers the Writings of Isaac Mayer Wise in its research collection.
- *African-American:* The Main Library houses the United Negro College Fund Archives; Black Biographical Dictionaries 1700-1950; the papers of the NAACP on microfilm; and Black Heri-

tage films and videos. The Von D. Mizell branch has 6000 Black Heritage materials and an authentic African Hut on permanent display. Most of the branches have the "Coretta Scott King Award Books" for children and young adults.
- *Spanish:* South Regional/BCC Library has more than 700 books in Spanish and a collection of Spanish-language videos for children; the Main Library has dozens of films on Spanish culture; the Riverland branch has a variety of materials in Spanish.

The **Main Library Video Collection** is there for the asking! One of the largest video libraries, there are 2,000 feature films, 2,000 children's videos and 8,000 educational and documentary videos. In the latter collection, there are films on art and architecture, business, dance, education, history, law, music, photography, recreation, religion, sales/marketing, science, social issues, sports, theater, travel and technology.

The **College Video Center**, on the sixth floor of the Main Library, houses a collection of 800 video tapes of colleges and universities from around the country, including all of the major schools. Visit different colleges on these guided tours of the campus. Many of the videos have filmed segments of classroom instruction, campus life and social activities.

The **Music Collection** at the Main Library has received the highest praise from music buffs. Its comprehensive holdings include 4800 CDs, 7800 audio cassettes, 7700 LPs and more than 10,000 videos. The collection contains standard classical works as well as rare and remarkable operas, symphonies, concertos, and compositions for piano and violin. For those who enjoy other types of music, the library also circulates holdings from its pop, jazz, folk and country and western collections. You can check out four recordings at a time for 28 days or listen to them in the library on CD, cassette or LP players.

Dial-a-Story presents children's tales which are narrated over the phone. These four-minute stories are available seven days a week, during day and evening hours. The stories are changed twice weekly. *Ph.* 357-7777.

Community Information. SEFLIN Free-Net, a dramatic new communication process, is being developed by SEFLIN, the Southeast Florida Library Information Network. Free-Net will offer a free network of community information with files on government agencies, civic groups, schools, businesses or other organizations. You will be able to access Free-Net 24 hours a day, using a home computer and modem to enter the system. The pilot program is scheduled for 1994. Future plans for Free-Net include linking South Florida with a national network of information.

Education

SCHOOL BOARD OF BROWARD COUNTY
600 Southeast 3rd Avenue
Ft. Lauderdale, FL 33301
Ph. 305-765-6000

Broward County has one of the largest accredited school systems in the country, serving more than 180,000 students. There are 113 elementary, 31 middle and 22 high schools. To accommodate different student needs, there are three full-time vocational/technical centers, two community/adult schools, nine exceptional student centers, and two alternative centers.

Propelled by the district's capital improvement plan, classroom equipment and facilities are continually updated – from the remodeling of science laboratories to purchasing a computer system for every school.

◆ Partnership Programs
The Career Education Department conducts biannual surveys of businesses in Broward County to update their knowledge regarding the critical skills which businesses are seeking and the projected job opportunities for upcoming graduates.

The Academy of Finance offers a two-year honor's program in financial services as part of the curriculum at six high schools. The program is a partnership between the School District, the National Academy Foundation and local businesses.

The Academy of Travel and Tourism offers a two-year program of preparatory skills for the tourism industry. These courses can be taken as part of the curriculum at four high schools. The program is a partnership between the School District, the National Academy Foundation and the local travel and tourism industry.

Partners in Excellence is a collaborative effort between the Greater Ft. Lauderdale Chamber of Commerce and the School Board to enhance student experiences. More than 200 businesses in collaboration with the school system have made a commitment to generate a better prepared workforce.

◆ Magnet Programs

Twenty-one magnet school programs offer concentrated study in the performing arts, science, computers, high technology, international studies and liberal arts.

The *Dillard School of the Arts* has a highly acclaimed training program for talented students. Classes which are offered include study in the visual arts; dance; theater performance; production and design; vocal, instrumental and high technology music; and TV and mass media. As part of the high school curriculum, students must complete all academic requirements. In their chosen areas of study, students participate in intensive classroom instruction, studio experience and different performing venues. Guest artists and instructors enhance the program and share their experiences. DSA has state-of-the-art performing facilities, equipment and technology.

◆ Special Programs and Services

- *Instructional Television Center* (ITV) produces more than 200 instructional programs for support and enhancement of the classroom curriculum.
- *Computer Instructional Programs* have a student/computer ratio of 9:1, a notably good ratio for such a large school district.
- *Broward's Music Program* has received acclaim for its high tech musical instruments and electronic equipment.
- *Saturday Screening Programs* focus on early detection of skill deficiencies and developmental needs of kindergarten students.
- The *Multicultural Educational Department* provides programs for foreign born and potentially English proficient (PEP) students. There are also multicultural outreach services to assist students and their families. PEP students represent 103 countries.

Note: There are 50 accredited private schools in Broward County. For information on the focus and educational programs at each school, contact the Broward County Nonpublic School Association. *Ph.* 966-7995.

UNIVERSITIES AND COLLEGES

Nova University, established in 1964, is situated on a sprawling 200-acre residential campus in the community of Davie, southwest of Fort Lauderdale. Offering undergraduate and graduate study, it is the second largest doctoral degree-granting private university in the State of Florida. Approximately 12,000 students attend classes. The University's Schools and Centers offer specialized studies in oceanography; law; computer and information science; business; social and systemic studies; education; psychology; educational and therapeutic resources for families; and undergraduate studies. The Farquhar Center for Undergraduate Studies has courses in 19 majors. The Hospitality Center has educational programs related to the travel, cruise, hotel and restaurant industries.

Nova University's Business School, located in Fort Lauderdale on a 10-acre campus, offers programs leading to the MBA and Ph.D. The Oceanographic Center, on a 10-acre site in Dania, near Port Everglades, also offers graduate studies in marine biology and oceanography. The Abraham S. Fischler Center for the Advancement of Education, which confers Master's, Doctoral and Educational Specialist degrees, is the largest graduate school of education in the country. *Ph. 475-7300.*

Broward Community College, which has been serving Broward residents since 1960, is the oldest institution of higher education in the county. During its first year, BCC attracted an enrollment of 701 students; today, it serves more than 60,000 residents annually at its three campus locations and three educational centers. BCC offers 55 career programs; 54 university transfer degree programs; and 11 one-year certificate programs. Students may enroll in a liberal arts curriculum and prepare for university transfer at any one of the campuses. A wide selection of non-credit courses is also available through the continuing education department. *Ph. 761-7465.*

Campus Highlights:
- *The North Campus* (Coconut Creek) is the host campus for Electronic/Engineering Technology, Acting and Drama, and Liberal Arts.
- *The South Campus* has a renowned Aviation curriculum with three programs in aviation: Airline Maintenance, Professional Pilot and Aviation Administration. Office Systems Technology trains office managers and staff in state-of-the art equipment and technology.

- *The Central Campus* (Davie) offers a curriculum in Health Sciences, Performing Arts, Hospitality Management, Criminal Justice, and Liberal Arts.
- *The Fort Lauderdale Center* (home of the administrative offices), attracts residents working in the downtown area who are interested in pursuing a general academic program.
- *The Center for Economic Development* (Ft. Lauderdale) provides business classes and seminars geared to the needs of the business community. The Ropes Challenge Course uses an experiential approach to teach teamwork and communication.
- *The Center for Health Science Education* (Davie Campus) offers pre-professional training and technical degrees in the Health Sciences. A wide variety of programs are available including nursing, medical assisting and hospital technologies.

Florida Atlantic University is part of Florida's State University system. It enrolled its first class of students in 1966 at the Boca Raton main campus. It presently has 16,500 students in attendance at its four campuses: Boca Raton, North Palm Beach, Davie and Ft. Lauderdale. It offers 13 Ph.D. programs, more than 45 Master's degree programs, and a large variety of undergraduate studies.

- *FAU Davie* is situated on the BCC Davie campus. It is an upper division college for students who have completed the first two years at another institution. Many students graduating from BCC continue their studies at FAU. Baccalaureate degrees are awarded in liberal arts, business, education and social sciences. A Master's degree is offered in educational leadership. FAU Davie has an enrollment of 3,500 students attending both day and evening classes. *Ph. 476-4500.*
- *FAU University Tower* is a graduate facility located in Fort Lauderdale. The College of Urban and Public Affairs offers a Master's degree in Public Administration as well as Urban and Regional Planning. A Doctoral degree is awarded in Public Administration. Courses in business administration leading towards an MBA are also available in the accelerated weekend MBA Program. *Ph. 355-5247.*
- *FAU's Life Long Learning Society* is a continuing education enrichment program. Its seminars in history, music, psychology, politics and health are taught by experienced leaders in the field. Each class meets for eight weeks, beginning in mid-October. Classes are held at the South Beach Community Center in Hollywood.

Fort Lauderdale College, founded in 1940, is a business school offering both two- and four-year curriculums in business administration, international business, management, accounting, marketing, computer science, and hospitality management. A two-year paralegal program is also available. *Ph. 568-1600.*

Art Institute Of Fort Lauderdale, established in 1968, offers associate and bachelor's degrees in the visual and practical arts. *Ph. 463-3000.*

Health Care

There are 23 licensed public and private hospitals in Broward County. Within the public sector, there are seven hospitals which are under the administration of the North and South Broward Hospital Districts. The 16 private hospitals are either independent or part of a larger hospital system.

The North Broward Hospital District, which services the northern two-thirds of Broward County, consists of four medical centers: Broward General Medical Center, Imperial Pointe Medical Center, North Broward Medical Center and Coral Springs Medical Center. Although each one operates as a community hospital, together they have the advantage of shared resources. Broward General Medical Center and Imperial Pointe Medical Center serve the Ft. Lauderdale community.

Broward General Medical Center

1625 SE 3rd Avenue
Ph. 355-4400

Broward General, which opened in 1938, is a veteran of the Florida health care system. It is a 744-bed facility offering a diverse range of medical/surgical services. Some of its prominent health care services and specialties:

- Broward General Heart Institute, a leading facility in cardiac medicine, offers the most advanced care and treatment for a full range of heart problems ranging from diagnosis, catherization, surgery, intensive care to physical fitness and modification programs.

- *PET Scan Center,* an acronym for Positron Emission Tomography, is a non-invasive new scanning procedure which can detect coronary artery disease before a heart attack strikes.
- *Neonatal Intensive Care Unit* has a dedicated wing with 63 beds for premature babies or seriously ill newborns. Recognized specialists and highly trained nurses provide quality care and round-the-clock monitoring.
- *Kidney Stone Center of South Florida,* located on the BGMC campus, offers lithotripsy, a non-surgical procedure which pulverizes the stones.
- *Sleep Disorder Laboratory* diagnoses sleep disorders through monitored sleep studies.
- *Cancer Helplink* offers a free telephone information service for people who have concerns about cancer. *Ph.355-4888.* BGMC also has a highly recognized cancer program, approved by the American College of Surgeon's Commission on Cancer.

The "Garden Suites" are Broward General's premium, private rooms with many extra personal touches for added comfort. Patients may even dine from a special gourmet menu... if your doctor approves.

Imperial Point Medical Center
6401 North Federal Hwy.
Ph. 776-8500

Imperial Pointe Medical Center, which opened in 1972, has 204 licensed beds. It has become a major medical/surgical center. During recent years, it has also developed areas of specialization which include the following:

- *Comprehensive Cardiology Services* offers patients state-of-the-art technology, such as cardiac ultrasound imaging, nuclear cardiology studies, diagnostic stress testing, computerized electrocardiograms and cardiac catherization. Imperial Point also provides 24-hour ambulatory monitoring of heart patients.
- *An Adult Fitness Program* is a medically supervised program tailored to each individual's health and fitness level. Beginning with health screenings, a personalized exercise program is prescribed and monitored by medical specialists.
- *A Mental Health Unit,* tending to 47 beds, is a 'hospital within a hospital' dedicated to helping patients receive quality therapy from mental health professionals in a medically supported setting.

- *Community Outreach Programs,* such as the monthly series of public seminars, provide information on various health issues.
- *A 24-hour Emergency Department* with a Chest Pain Emergency Unit offers immediate medical attention.
- *Chronic Pain Management Programs* for acute or chronic sufferers offer relief through medical treatment and learned strategies.

Premium Private Rooms in the 'Imperial Wing' have upgraded furnishings and decor as well as a special menu. If well enough to eat, you can dine like royalty.

Cleveland Clinic Florida

3000 West Cypress Creek Road
Ph. 978-5107

The Cleveland Clinic is a not-for-profit, multi-specialty group practice which provides a team approach to medical care. It offers a full spectrum of adult specialties and coordinated medical services within a single facility. A collaborative approach provides patients access to the appropriate physician in even difficult-to-diagnose medical situations. Although Florida's Cleveland Clinic opened its doors in 1988, the Cleveland Clinic Foundation has a well known legacy in medical circles. Cleveland Clinic has a commitment to research, education and advanced medical care. Through pioneering efforts, they have achieved many medical breakthroughs, such as:

- The discovery of cardiac catherization and angiography.
- The development and refinement of bypass surgery.
- The implementation of new surgical techniques to treat cancer of the breast and the digestive system.
- The invention and refinement of artificial organs and assist devices including the artificial heart, kidney, liver and pancreas.
- Major innovations in the management and control of high blood pressure and cholesterol.
- An integrated approach to the diagnosis and treatment of stroke and degenerative neurological disorders.

Many of the Cleveland Clinic physicians are recognized in their fields and all are either board certified or board eligible in one or more specialties.

Cleveland Clinic Hospital
2835 North Ocean Blvd.
Ph. 568-1000

Formerly the North Beach Hospital, it was purchased by the Cleveland Clinic Foundation network in 1990. The hospital underwent a restoration and refurbishing process and emerged as a modern facility. A not-for-profit, 153-bed hospital, physicians from Cleveland Clinic Florida as well as community physicians in 30 different specialties are on staff providing a variety of health care services to the community.

- A new surgical wing and recovery area incorporate advanced technology. Laproscopic and laser equipment permit sophisticated procedures which are performed by the surgical staff. Some of the specialties offered include colorectal surgery; neurosurgery; ophthalmology; orthopedics; plastic/reconstructive & aesthetic surgery; urology; and vascular surgery. The hospital hosts the only accredited residency program in colorectal surgery in South Florida.
- New and modern endoscopy suites are also available for endoscopy procedures.
- A full range of cardiac diagnostic studies and pulmonary procedures to diagnose and treat respiratory disorders use the most modern technology.
- An expanded Emergency Department includes a new Chest Pain Center for people experiencing early signs of heart attack.
- In radiology, a new high tech CT scanner completes studies in minutes and speaks to patients in seven languages.
- Rehabilitation services include physical therapy; speech therapy; and therapeutic interventions for sports-related injuries.
- A Wellness Center is offered to community residents. A staff of certified physiologists develop exercise programs suited to each individual's level of fitness.
- The *Med Take Bedside Computer System* allows nurses to chart medications and patient progress quickly and efficiently; this frees up additional time to spend with patients. Physicians have access to patient information and updates at any time, day or night. Hard copies are printed out at the nursing station for the permanent record.
- *Community Outreach Programs* offer free weekly lectures by staff physicians; the hospital also sponsors a Seniority Program, designed for people 55 and over.

Holy Cross Hospital

4723 North Federal Hwy.
Ph. 771-8000

Holy Cross Hospital is a major full service, medical/surgical, 587-bed facility. As a Catholic hospital sponsored by the Sisters of Mercy, it is strongly associated with Christianity's spiritual values. A major contributor in the health care system, Holy Cross provides a considerable number of special services to the community.

- A Comprehensive Cancer Center, which opened in 1991, is a 34,000-square-foot facility. It employs the most sophisticated technology and equipment for diagnostics and therapeutic treatment. The Center has been certified by the National Cancer Institute to participate in research studies.
- *Cardiac care* is a specialty at Holy Cross. Specialists perform highly intricate heart surgery, catherizations, and other cardiovascular procedures. Holy Cross is also involved in research of arrhythmia and 'transvenous defribrillators' to prevent cardiac arrest.
- The *Maternity Center* provides comprehensive services, beginning with a four-week prenatal education program for expectant parents. It presents information about what to expect during pregnancy, the birth process and post delivery. A *Pregnacise Class* offers an exercise and fitness program for mom and baby. A *Sibling Education Program* is conducted for children three years of age and older. Hands-on instruction teaches how to hold, diaper and feed a newborn brother or sister. The one-hour session also includes a film, "Big Kids and Babies." During the birthing process which takes place in one room – a labor/delivery/recovery suite – the immediate family is welcome to share in the experience. The Maternity Center also includes a *Neonatal Intensive Unit* for newborns who need critical care and monitoring.
- *Neurosurgery procedures,* utilizing advanced technology including all types of laser neurosurgery, are performed on both adult and pediatric populations.
- The *Center for Diabetes* has both inpatient and outpatient care. Programs to help manage and control diabetes are offered through a multidisciplinary team approach of medicine, diet, exercise, education and counseling.
- An *Intensive Rehabilitation Unit,* overseeing 43 beds, provides therapeutic programs to patients recovering from illness, such as stroke, neuromuscular disorders, spinal cord injuries, and

orthopedic disorders. At the *Living Skills Center*, patients relearn how to perform daily tasks within a simulated and safe environment.
- *Community Outreach Programs* are scheduled on a regular basis. A lecture series is presented by staff physicians every Wednesday evening. Holy Cross also sponsors a start-up cancer support group three times a year. Contact the hospital for their calendar of events and other community offerings.
- *Classic Suites* are luxurious private rooms with special amenities and provisions, such as rooming-in accommodations for family members. *A La Carte Services* include a visit from a manicurist, massage, special gourmet meals or secretarial services.

The Cultural Scene

Florida Philharmonic

The Florida Philharmonic is the largest cultural organization in the state and the second largest orchestra in the southeastern U.S. Weekly radio concerts broadcast its classical sounds to more than 40 cities. Created through the marriage of the Fort Lauderdale and Boca Raton Symphonies in 1984, it has gained a prestigious reputation for its young age. As a regional orchestra, it performs for the tri-county areas of Dade, Broward and Palm Beach. It also provides the musical accompaniment to the Greater Miami Opera Association.

Under the musical leadership of British conductor, James Judd, the 85-piece symphony performs 150 concerts each year, including three different series of musical selections. The 10-concert "Celebrity" series features a repertoire of classical selections highlighted by different celebrity soloists. The four concert "Proms" series showcases the works of well known composers. The audience hears familiar compositions and is also introduced to lesser known works. The third series, "Peter Nero and Pops at the Philharmonic," is a four-concert program of popular musical sounds spanning the different eras of music. In addition to the subscription concerts, the Florida Philharmonic performs free outdoor concerts at Mizner Park in Boca Raton and Bayfront Park in Miami.

Before the performances, informal lectures are usually presented to discuss the elements of the music the audience is about to experience. Open rehearsals also welcome visitors who want to learn more about symphonic music. In addition to a busy performance schedule, it upholds a strong commitment to educating young audiences; children are introduced to symphonic music through Kinder Concerts and a stimulating educational program. *3401 NW 9th Avenue. Ph. 561-2997.*

Broward Center For The Performing Arts

At the heart of the new Arts and Science District and Riverwalk, the Broward Center for the Performing Arts sits majestically on a hill overlooking the New River. The scenic waterfront, pathways, fountains, tropical gardens and foliage are part of the spectacular setting and breathtaking view. The gracefully designed and acoustically engineered building houses the 2700-seat Au-Rene Theater and the 595-seat Amaturo Theater. Award-winning architect, Benjamin Thompson created a rich and elegant facility in the tradition of some of the opera houses of Europe. In keeping with a contemporary, tropical context, its design incorporates an open airy flow, curvilinear spaces and multi-level lobbies. Prior to the performance and during intermission, theater patrons enjoy the open air courtyard which offers a dazzling view of the city at night. The Broward Center for the Performing Arts, which made its debut in February, 1991, presents a wide range of entertainment including Broadway musicals, plays, symphonic concerts, dance and pop artists in concert. It is home to the Ft. Lauderdale Opera, Miami City Ballet, the Florida Philharmonic, Concert Association of Florida, and Sinfonia Virtuosi & Chorus. *201 SW 5th Avenue. Ph. 522-5334.*

The Miami City Ballet

The Miami City Ballet is a young, yet sophisticated classical ballet company which had its premier performance in October, 1986. The 39 dancers were selected from major dance companies around the world. Edward Villella, a principal dancer with the New York City Ballet for more than 30 years, has served as its artistic director, sharing the neo-classical vision and style of his mentor, George Balanchine. The company presents a series of four programs; three to four ballets, some of which are world premiers, are performed during each program. The season begins in October and extends until April. The Nutcracker Suite is traditionally performed before the Christmas holidays. *Bailey Hall & The Broward Center for the Performing Arts; Ph. 532-4880 (Miami Office).* Note: For more detailed information, refer to Miami's Cultural Scene.

Brian C. Smith's Off Broadway Theater

Opened in 1988, Brian C. Smith's theater is well-known to locals for its quality performances. Contemporary drama, comedy and musicals are produced from a selection which includes original plays, South Florida premieres and Broadway hits. A cast of professional actors are selected for each show from open auditions. Originally an old Florida movie house, it has been refurbished with comfortable seating for 300 theater-goers. *1444 NE 26th Street. Ph. 566-0554.*

Coral Ridge Concert Series

Started in 1972 to provide more dimension to the cultural life in Ft. Lauderdale, the Coral Ridge Concert Series presents an eclectic selection of musical programs from October through May. The musical diversity of the 17 concerts, which includes gospel, pop, classical, country, sacred and choral, is unique to the area. Dynamic, well-known musical artists, an in-house choral choir and a 55-member professional orchestra perform during the season. An annual highlight is *The Many Moods of Christmas* concert. *Coral Ridge Presbyterian Church, 5555 N. Federal Hwy. Ph. 491-1103.*

Drama Center

The Drama Center, an equity theater, had its premiere performance in 1989. Its focus is on producing contemporary, innovative and original works. The theater, which only seats 120 people, encourages a close connection between the actors and audience. The fine selection of dramas and comedies combined with high quality performances produce a memorable evening of theater. Four plays, many with a Jewish theme, are presented during the season which begins in October. The Drama Center also offers acting classes for children ages 6-16. *2345 W. Hillsboro Blvd., Deerfield Beach. Ph. 570-9115.*

Sun Bank Sunday Jazz Brunch

The Sunday Jazz Brunch, a lively upbeat weekend affair, is held the first Sunday of each month at Riverwalk's Bubier Park. Jazz musicians and vocalists perform on three stages, as listeners relax on chairs and blankets or stroll the banks of the river. Restaurants set up booths and serve a gourmet brunch from 11 am to 2 pm. *Andrews Ave. & Las Olas Blvd. Ph. 761-5703.*

Bailey Hall

Bailey Hall, with a 1200-seat capacity, is a major stage for presenting a variety of professional performances. From October through

March, Bailey Hall hosts national touring companies performing Broadway musicals, professional dance companies and well known vocalists. Broward's Friends of Chamber Music use Bailey Hall as a venue for presenting a series of concerts by internationally renowned chamber musicians. The Florida Philharmonic and the Miami Ballet are the two resident companies which perform during season. *Broward Community College, 3501 SW Davie Road, Davie. Ph. 475-6884.*

Parker Playhouse

Parker Playhouse is a 1,200-seat theater which presents a series of Broadway shows. Touring Broadway companies perform there from November through April. *707 NE 8th Street. Ph. 764-0700.*

Sinfonia Virtuosi & Chorus

The Sinfonia and Chorus present a series of five performances of classical masterpieces. The musical arrangements selected are designed for small symphonies, choral accompaniment and ensembles. Renowned international guest artists are invited to perform with the Sinfonia for an evening of exceptional music. During the Summer Music Festival, the Sinfonia hosts a major orchestra from another country for two weeks, presenting them to South Florida audiences. Maestro Brooks-Bruzzese, the Sinfonia's artistic director, has performed in many of Europe's concert halls. He was honored with an invitation to conduct the Hungarian Virtuosi in Budapest for a PBS documentary, which was filmed on location. *Broward Center for the Performing Arts. Ph. 561-5883.*

The Ft. Lauderdale Museum Of Art

The Museum of Art, founded in 1958, is recognized as a major cultural institution by the State of Florida. In 1985, the museum moved into a new, modern and spacious facility of 63,800 square feet, situated in downtown Ft. Lauderdale.

The museum has an impressive permanent collection of over 5,000 works of art. A major focus is directed towards 20th Century European and American art. The various galleries include works by Pablo Picasso, Henri Matisse, Alexander Calder, Henry Moore, Salvadore Dali and Andy Warhol. The museum also holds many noteworthy works by William Glackens, a well-known American Impressionist painter. The Glackens Collection includes his oils, watercolors, drawings and graphics. The museum's holdings of CoBrA art, an acronym for Copenhagen, Brussels, Amsterdam, is considered to be the largest in the Western Hemisphere. CoBrA, a Northern European Expressionist movement after WW II, has been compared to American Abstract Expressionism. Other galleries in the museum include outstanding collections of African, South Pacific, Pre-Columbian and American Indian art and artifacts.

During the year, the museum hosts a variety of special events and programs. The season begins with the *Annual Hort Competition and Exhibition* in September. M. Allen Hort was an early benefactor who believed that local artists should be encouraged and recognized by their community. The Hort Competition invites artists from Broward, Dade, Palm Beach and Monroe counties to participate in this juried fine art event. *Art a la Carte*, which presents an evening of fine dining in the main gallery, is the season's social opener. Leading restaurants in the area compete with one another in their presentations of gourmet delights, featuring hors d'oeuvres and desserts. The *Festival of Trees*, the museum's celebration of the winter holiday, begins on the last Monday in November and continues for a week. A Gingerbread Village, decorated Christmas trees, wreaths, menorahs, and handicrafts are displayed in the main gallery. During the opening night party, guests demonstrate their auction savvy as they bid on the live Christmas trees. A special highlight of the festival are the *designer vignettes*, an exhibition of designer rooms within the galleries, furnished and appointed in various periods and styles.

Art lectures by the museum's curator, guest lecturers, and exhibiting artists highlight the different exhibitions during the season. Docent-guided tours are available on Tuesday, Thursday and Friday at 1 pm. Call the Museum of Art for information on membership, volunteer programs, and calendar of scheduled exhibitions and events. *One East Las Olas Boulevard. Ph. 763-6464 (Event Hotline); 525-5500 (Administration).*

Museum Of Discovery & Science

The Museum of Discovery & Science opened in November of 1992 to rave reviews and community excitement. Its mission is to provide interactive learning experiences in an atmosphere of fun. As a science museum, it seeks to increase the science literacy of adults and children throughout South Florida. Its simulated habitats, hands-on experiences, scientific experiments, graphic panels, videos, computer interactions, and challenging games make learning about the environment and how things work easy and enjoyable. MODS is often described as a "playground for the mind."

The museum houses seven exhibition areas. *Florida Ecoscapes* explores Florida's ecology with exhibits which include a Beach, Living Reef, Underwater Grotto, Barrier Islands Habitat, Mangrove Estuary, Sloughs and Swamp, Sinkhole, and Scrub Habitat. If you are not familiar with each of these terms, a visit to MODS is a must! *Sound* examines the physical properties of sound, current technology, as well as a look into the future technology of sound and recorded music. *Space Base* reenacts the development of rocketry, space flight and exploration of space. The "Manned Maneuvering Unit" invites visitors into a gravity-free chamber to conduct a few simple tasks. The "Moon Voyager" simulates flight in a space craft for would-be space travelers. *Choose Health* investigates the issues of nutrition, fitness and the relationship between them; substance abuse is graphically shown and one's "impaired" reaction time is tested. *No Place Like Home* takes a look at how home appliances and plumbing fixtures operate, the environmental effects of common household products and why conservation efforts are necessary. *Kidscience* invites children from ages three to five to explore their environment in the Waterworks, Musical Staircase, and Whisper Tubes (sound waves) exhibits. The *Traveling Exhibition Hall* invites the best scientific exhibits from around the country. Featured exhibitions have ranged from "Greenhouse Earth," an exploration of global warming to "Super Heroes," the world of comic and movie wonders.

The museum's blockbuster IMAX Theater is one of only a few such theaters in Florida. The IMAX at Cape Canaveral is associated with the Space Center. IMAX, an acronym for "image maximum," employs a new technology in film production and projection screening. Visual images are projected onto a screen which is 60 feet high and 80 feet wide. The size of the screen and image creates a powerful impact. Complementing the visual technology, there is an overwhelming clarity of sound from the six-channel, 42-speaker sound system. IMAX screenings have included *To the Limits*, an exploration of the limits of physical endurance on the human body; *Blue Planet*, a view of the earth from space; *Antarctica*, an exploration into the icy region of Antarctica; and *Rolling Stones at the MAX*, a concert tour. Call for schedules. *Ph. 463-IMAX.*

MODS offers summer camp programs, field trips, Saturday activities for children, special membership events, volunteer activities and *MODulations*, a quarterly magazine for members featuring interesting articles, film viewings, museum programs and special events. *401 SW Second Street. Ph. 467-6637.*

Events and Attractions

Riverwalk

Riverwalk is a mile-and-a-half brick pathway that runs along the New River in the heart of downtown Ft. Lauderdale. The eastern boundary of Riverwalk is just west of Las Olas Boulevard at Stranahan House. The Arts/Science District and Cooley's Landing (a new, modern marina) is located at the western end of Riverwalk. It is a linear park which follows the natural landscape of the waterfront with pathways linking it to government, cultural and downtown office centers.

Riverwalk was designed with an emphasis on creating an animated yet peaceful park setting. Civic planners envisioned a gathering place and a dynamic center for cultural programs, entertainment, leisure activities, and dining along the New River waterfront. Riverwalk's tropical landscape, benches facing the river, and boats cruising the waters create a serene atmosphere. It is a delightful area to stroll on the weekend and a lovely setting for a brown bag lunch during the week. Many of the bricks inset into Riverwalk's pathway were purchased by individuals who have inscribed personalized messages for posterity.

Riverwalk Blues Fest

This blues festival, held during the first weekend in November, begins on Friday evening and continues through Sunday. Popular and nationally recognized blues musicians and vocalists perform on the main stage; a second stage showcases local talent playing the blues; and a third stage, Blues Alley Cafe is used for non-acoustical music, usually a vocal and instrumental ensemble. The festival's restaurateurs set up booths and serve New Orleans Cajun-style food. *Bubier Park: Andrews Ave. & Las Olas Blvd. Ph. 761-5813.*

Las Olas Arts Festival

A high quality juried exhibition, this is sponsored by the Museum of Art during the first weekend in March. Celebrating its 25th season, it features fine art in all media from around the country. Approximately 260 artists are invited to participate in this two-day premier art event. *Bubier Park: Andrews Ave. & E. Las Olas Blvd. Ph. 525-5500.*

Sun Sentinel Jazz Festival

An annual three-day event in April, this celebrates the tradition and spirit of jazz. Nationally-known artists bring their unique sounds to the Broward Center for the Performing Arts. During the day, the sound of jazz can be heard along the New River as regional musicians and vocalists perform on the four outdoor stages. Street entertainers add to the festivities and participating restaurants provide a food feast. Special programs for children are designed to create a basic understanding of the musical structure of jazz and introduce some of the instruments. *400 SW 2nd Street. Ph. 761-5703.*

Starlight Musicals

A summer series of 10 outdoor concerts are offered on Friday evenings, beginning the third week in June. Each concert features a particular style of music, such as country and western, jazz, reggae, big band, and 50's oldies. Bring a blanket and spread out on the grass or dance to the music under the stars. Many people bring picnic dinners, but hotdogs and beverages are available at the refreshment stand. *Holiday Park: Federal Hwy. & Sunrise Blvd. Ph. 761-5362.*

The Fort Lauderdale International Film Festival

Taking place in November, this is presented by the Broward County Film Society and hosted by AMC theaters. During the two and a half weeks of the festival, more than 100 films from around the world are screened, including full length features, documentaries, experimental works, animation and short subjects. A series of seminars are presented through the sponsorship of Eastman Kodak. Parties, dinners and award ceremonies highlight the social events. *Ph. 563-0500.*

Winterfest Boat Parade

In celebration of the winter holidays, a parade of lavishly lit, decorated boats cruise the Intracoastal waterways from Port Everglades to Lake Santa Barbara (two miles north of Commercial Blvd.). People line the Intracoastal bridges from end to end to view this festive and colorful parade on the water. If possible, reserve a waterside table at one of the many Intracoastal restaurants for a spectacular view. *Ph. 767-0686.*

International Swimming Hall of Fame

The ISHOF is a focal point for aquatics, international and national competitions, and a training site for Olympic teams. Its museum showcases legendary swimming stars and aquatic history. An Olympic-size pool and facilities are available to community residents for lap swimming and aerobics. *One Hall of Fame Drive. Ph. 462-6536.*

Bonnet House

The Bonnet House was the 35-acre oceanfront estate of artists, Frederick and Evelyn Bartlett. Designed and constructed by Frederick Bartlett in 1920, it reflects the essence of early Florida. The grounds are naturally landscaped with mangroves, native trees, and exotic plantings. Approaching the house, the lush courtyard has a fine collection of carousel animals. The estate was deeded to the Florida Trust for Historic Preservation and is on the National Register of Historic Places. Tours are available from May through the end of November. *900 N. Birch Road. Ph. 563-5393.*

Water Taxi Historical Tour of the New River

Sponsored by the Fort Lauderdale Historical Museum, the water taxi offers a lively history lesson on the New River. A two-hour narrated tour presents the legends, anecdotes and history of Ft. Lauderdale's growth, which began along the New River. The *Stranahan House*, the oldest residence of Ft. Lauderdale (circa 1901), is one of the featured sights. Reservations are required. *Ph. 463-4431.*

Everglades Holiday Park

The Everglades Holiday Park offers a one-hour narrated tour aboard an airboat which glides through the marshy waters of the Everglades. The captain stops along the way to identify alligators and animals, exotic birds and varieties of plant life which habitate this tropical wilderness. A visit to the Seminole Indian village and alligator wrestling are highlights featured in the tour. *21940 Griffin Road. Ph. 431-8111.*

Five Star Rodeo

Professional rodeo competition is held once a month on Friday and Saturday evenings in a covered indoor/outdoor arena. Seven events are scheduled each night: saddle bronco riding, bare back, calf roping, team steer roping, barrel racing and bull riding. Concession stands, vendors, and country and western performers round out the evening fun. *6591 SW 45th Street, Davie. Ph. 437-8800.*

Don't Miss

Hailing a Water Taxi. The water taxi is a colorful part of the Ft. Lauderdale living experience. You can hail one from the docks along the waterway or call for a pick-up. This unique fleet of nautical cabs cruises seven miles of Intracoastal waterways with drop-offs at favorite spots, such as waterfront restaurants, marinas, Las Olas shops, New River attractions, and museums. All-day passes permit unlimited taxi hopping. *Ph. 565-5507.*

Shopping Las Olas. Las Olas Boulevard is a charming, upscale shopping district in the heart of downtown Ft. Lauderdale. Stroll the tree-lined streets illuminated with gas lamps and browse through the fashionable boutiques, one-of-a-kind shops, and art galleries. Many of the courtyard restaurants, patio cafes, and bistros along Las Olas have a European ambience.

A Giant Flea Market. The Ft. Lauderdale Swap Shop is the largest indoor/outdoor flea market in the South. It combines an international bazaar, country fair, farmer's market, and garage sale in one marketplace. There are vendors galore with something for everyone, from ruby red tomatoes to fine gold jewelry. The indoor air conditioned center features a circus arena, concert stage and food court. *Sunrise Blvd. between I-95 and the Florida Turnpike. Ph. 791-7927.*

A Little Gambling. Seminole bingo, held on tribal grounds seven days a week, is a large scale bingo game with high jackpots. If you enjoy a little gambling and some local flavor, plan an evening at the bingo parlor. *Ph. 961-4519.*

Going Western Style. Davie, a tropical southern city geographically, has a western theme and architectural design in its downtown center. Davie has become known for its stables of horses, miles of trails, ranches, western-style fashion and entertainment. *Do Da's American Country*, which borders Davie in Plantation, is a local saloon and dance hall for Florida's own cowboys and cowgirls. *Ph. 792-6200.*

Recreation

Spectator Sports

Ft. Lauderdale's Yankee Stadium is the winter home of the New York Yankees; they play 20 exhibition games from early March through mid-April. *Ph. 776-1921.*

Joe Robbie Stadium is home to the Miami Dolphins, *Ph. 620-2578,* and the Florida Marlins. *Ph. 779-7070.*

The Ft. Lauderdale Strikers play professional soccer from May through September at Lockhart Stadium. *Ph. 928-1584.*

The Carquest Bowl, played at Joe Robbie Stadium on New Year's Day, invites major college teams which represent their respective conferences. *Ph. 564-5000.*

The Federal Express Orange Bowl invites one of the Big Eight Conference teams and an independent team to play at Miami's Orange Bowl on New Year's Day. *Ph. 371-4600.*

Golf

There are more than 50 golf courses in Broward County. Many have driving ranges.

American Golfers Club
5101 W. Commercial Blvd.,
Tamarac.
18-hole course. *Ph. 731-2600*

Arrowhead Golf and Sports Club
8201 SW 24th St., Davie.
18-hole course. *Ph. 475-8200*

Bonaventure Country Club
200 Bonaventure Blvd.
Two 18-hole courses. *Ph. 369-2100*

Colony West Country Club
6800 NW 88th Ave., Tamarac.
Two 18-hole courses. *Ph. 726-8430*

Jacaranda Golf Club
9200 W. Broward Blvd.,
Plantation. Two 18-hole
courses. *Ph. 472-5855*

Pompano Beach Golf Course
1101 N. Federal Hwy.,
Pompano Bch. Two 18-hole
courses. *Ph. 781-0426*

Oak Ridge Country Club
3490 Griffin Rd., Ft. Lauderdale.
18-hole course. *Ph. 987-5552*

Sabal Palms Golf Course
5101 W. Commercial Blvd.,
Tamarac.
18-hole course. *Ph. 731-2600*

Note: Jacaranda Golf Club is home to Jimmy Ballard Golf Workshop.

Many hotels and resorts have golf facilities which are available to the public, especially during the summer months. The Greater Ft. Lauderdale Convention and Visitors Bureau has a complete listing of golf courses in Broward County. *Ph. 765-4466, ext. 711.*

◆ WATER SPORTS

Sailing, deep sea fishing, swimming, water skiing, snorkeling represent some of the water sports enjoyed along the many miles of scenic waterways.

Fishing

The Greater Ft. Lauderdale waterways abound with fish and fishermen engaged in four types of angling.

- Bottom or drift boat fishing along the reefs less than two miles offshore for snapper, grouper and smaller kingfish.
- Pier fishing along a boardwalk which juts out into the ocean at Fisherman's Wharf in Pompano or Angler's Fishing Pier in Lauderdale-by-the-Sea.
- Deep sea fishing for large sport fish, such as sailfish, dolphin, wahoo or blue marlin; charters are available at Bahia Mar Yachting Center, Cove Marina and Fish City Marina.
- Inland and backwater fishing for freshwater game fish, such as large mouth bass; boats and guides are available at Everglades Holiday Park.

Snorkeling

Greater Ft. Lauderdale has become a major destination for snorkelers in search of diving wrecks and artificial reefs. There are 80 dive sites along a 23-mile reef for snorkeling and scuba diving operations.

Beaches

Ft. Lauderdale Beach, 17th St. Causeway & A1A, *Ph. 468-1597*
Amenities: Metered parking and lots; newly designed promenade for strolling; playground, surfing area, Hobie Cat rentals, volleyball. Cafes and restaurants are located across the street from the beach.

The Ft. Lauderdale Beach underwent a cosmetic change during a recent revitalization project. The oceanfront streetscape has porticos and columns as entrance ways leading to the ocean. A wave design is the central theme. Wave crests and designs appear on the gateways, on the beach wall, and the walkways along the pedestrian promenade. Palm trees and beach plantings emphasize the tropical flavor while special street lighting creates a charming accent.

Directory of Services

9-1-1 Emergency Only   **POLICE • SHERIFF • FIRE • MEDICAL • RESCUE**

AGENCY	DESCRIPTION	BROWARD (305)
ALCOHOL & DRUG ABUSE	Intervention & Referral	800-252-6465 765-4589
CRISIS HOTLINE	24 Hour Help Line	467-6333
ABUSE CENTER: WOMEN IN DISTRESS	Provides Help and a Safe Place	761-1133
POISON CONTROL & INFORMATION CENTER		800-282-3171 355-4400
SENIOR SUPPORT FIRST CALL SENIORS	Telephone Reassurance & Support	522-5220
TEEN HOTLINE		467-8336
TELEPHONE SUPPORT FOR LATCHKEY CHILDREN		523-1222
TIME/TEMPERATURE		748-4444
WEATHER FORECAST		763-5353

County Services

AGENCY	DESCRIPTION	BROWARD (305)
GOVERNMENT CENTER	115 S. Andrews Avenue	876-7000
PUBLIC INFORMATION	Information & Referral	357-7585
ANIMAL CONTROL		359-1313
BOARD OF EDUCATION		765-6000
COUNTY COOPERATIVE EXT.		370-3725
COUNTY COURTHOUSE		765-4575
EMERGENCY MGMT	Disaster Readiness Training & Evacuation Information	765-5020 791-1090

FIRE PREVENTION		357-8248
FL. HIGHWAY PATROL	All Interstate Roads & Turnpikes	467-4550
GARBAGE COLLECTION		765-4202
LIBRARY		357-7444
LICENSES	Auto Tag	765-5050
	Parking Permit - Handicapped	765-5050
	Boating Registration	765-5050
	Fishing & Hunting	468-3474
MASS TRANSIT	Bus Route Information	831-8400
	Tri-Rail	800-874-7245
PARKS AND RECREATION		831-8100
PASSPORT INFORMATION		765-5173
PROPERTY APPRAISER		357-6830
SHERIFF		765-8900
TAX COLLECTOR		765-4600
TRAFFIC VIOLATION INFORMATION		765-4573
VOTER REGISTRATION		831-7050
WATER/SEWER	Emergency/After Hours	765-4710

Human Services

AGENCY	DESCRIPTION	BROWARD (305)
AMERICAN ASSOC. OF RETIRED PERSONS (AARP)	Florida State Headquarters Provides source for local contact	813-576-1155
AMERICAN RED CROSS	Hurricane Shelter Information Disaster Relief, Blood Banks, Educational Programs	763-9900
	After Hours	768-9906
CHILD CARE (Child Care Connection)	Information & Referrals on Licensed Child Care Centers & Registered Family Care Providers	486-3900
INFORMATION & REFERRAL SVCES, Community Service Council	Connects You with the Appropriate Person or Agency Who Can Answer Your Question or Assist You With A Particular Need	467-6333
HANDICAPPED/DISABLED SERVICES		831-6150

HEALTH DEPARTMENT		467-4700
I R S	Location & Hours of Local Offices Tax Information Tax Forms	800-829-1040 904-354-1760 800-829-3676
SENIOR CITIZEN SERVICES (Senior Connection)	Information/Assistance and Programs for Seniors	484-4357
SOCIAL SECURITY		800-772-1213
SOCIAL SERVICE TRANSPORTATION	Reduced Fares, Dial-A-Ride Transport for Seniors and Special Groups	357-6795
UNITED WAY	An Excellent Resource for Community Information	467-2756
VETERAN'S ASSISTANCE		356-7926
VOLUNTEER CENTER	A Clearinghouse for Community Volunteer Positions	522-6761
RETIRED SENIOR VOLUNTEER PROGRAM (RSVP)		563-8991

City Numbers

GOVERNMENT CENTER Information Desk	Ft. Lauderdale City Hall 100 N. Andrews Avenue	761-5000
CITY CLERK		761-5002
POLICE (Non Emergency)		761-5700
FIRE (Non Emergency)		831-8200
DRIVER'S LICENSE		467-4488
ELECTRICAL SERVICE	FL Power & Light	797-5000
GARBAGE COLLECTION		761-5046
LIBRARY		357-7444
PARKS & RECREATION		761-5346
TELEPHONE COMPANY	Southern Bell	780-2355
VOTER'S REGISTRATION		357-7050
WATER AND SEWER Emergency/After Hours		771-0880 776-5151

Civic Organizations

Greater Ft. Lauderdale Chamber of Commerce	462-6000
Public Information Office	761-5931
Broward Economic Development Council	524-3113
Greater Ft. Lauderdale Convention & Visitors Bureau	765-4466

Miami

The city's origins date back to 1826 when slaves were brought to work on the Miami River. The actual settlement did not take root until 1842 when William English named the village Miami, a derivation of "Mayaime," the Tequesta Indian word for "Indian Lake." At that time, property sold for $1 per lot. After the Civil War, new settlers arrived and began to build an agricultural community and trading economy. Growth was slow until Julia Tuttle, considered the true patron of Miami, urged Henry Flagler to bring the railroad southward to Miami. Helped by the Great Freeze of 1895, which wiped out most of Florida's citrus crop except for that of Miami, her dream was realized in 1896. Development quickly followed and, within 15 years, 5,000 people had settled in Miami. The 1920's saw more growth in both residents and tourists and by the mid 1930's Coral Gables, Hialeah and Miami Springs were populated. The art deco trend reached Miami Beach and the city began its sprawling rise.

Its multi-national focus began in the 1950's when thousands of Cubans fled the government of Fidel Castro. Miami became a center of trade to the Americas, with significant ties to the Caribbean, Latin America and South America in the areas of banking and commerce. Just as Flagler's railroad opened the doors to the north, the Port of Miami became the passageway to the south.

Today the City of Miami presents a triplex of images. Its downtown hub is a center of government, business, cultural arts, and health care. Its reflecting glass towers and colorful buildings form an elegant and "funky" skyscape. As a business center, it has become a Mecca for international trade as well as tourism. Miami is the second largest international financial district in the United States and is home to more than 100 multi-national corporate headquarters. The Port of Miami is the largest cruise passenger port in the country.

Surrounding the downtown area is a Miami of many colorful and ethnic neighborhoods, each reflecting the cultural heritage of its residents. Caribbean and Latin Street festivals, cultural events, entertainment and ethnic cuisine add a valuable dimension. The contributions are many , but so are some of the problems. Today the ethnic mix is nearly half Hispanic, one fifth black and a little more than one third white. Many of the ethnic communities remain self-focused, continuing to struggle with survival issues and receiving their slice of the economic pie. Some neighborhoods have become hotbeds of crime. Although Coconut Grove is not crime-free, it does represent an integrated mixture of people from different ethnic groups, including professionals, artists and business people.

A third image of Miami is its tropical island ambiance, coastal waterways and beautiful sandy beaches. Deep sea fishing, sailing, wind surfing, water skiing, and swimming in the blue-green ocean waters provide year-round vacation and relaxation. Long walks along the beach and the peaceful sound of ocean waves are some of Miami's pleasures for those who enjoy the water in a more passive way.

Miami continues to attract thousands of people who enjoy its many virtues and distinct personality. Rand McNally ranked it 20th among the most desirable places to live in their *Places Rated Almanac*. In addition to the City of Miami, each of the surrounding municipalities has its own unique and interesting profile.

Demographics

◆ Size

The Greater Miami Area refers to Miami and its surrounding municipalities within Dade County. Eleven of the 27 cities in Dade County are less than a square mile in size. The City of Miami is by far the largest municipality in the county, covering an area of 35.6 square miles. Dade County spans a total area of 1944.5 square miles, with its unincorporated areas accounting for 1813.9 square miles.

◆ Population

Dade County has a population of 1,937,094 residents. The 27 municipalities in the county total 909,023 people; unincorporated areas total 1,028,071 or more than 50% of the population.

City	Location	Population	City	Location	Population
Bal Harbour	NE	3,045	Miami	Center	358,548
Bay Harbor Islds	NE	4,703	Miami Beach	NE	92,639
Biscayne Park	NE	3,068	Miami Shores Village	NE	10,084
Coral Gables	SW	40,091	Miami Springs	NW	13,268

El Portal	NE	2,457	N. Bay Village	NE	5,383
Florida City	SW	5,806	North Miami	NE	49,998
Golden Beach	NE	774	N. Miami Bch	NE	35,359
Hialeah	NW	188,004	Opa-locka	NW	15,283
Hialeah Gardens	NW	7,713	South Miami	SE	10,404
Homestead	SW	26,866	Surfside	NE	4,108
Indian Creek Village	NE	44	Sweetwater	SW	13,909
Islandia	SE	13	Virginia Gdns	NW	2,212
Key Biscayne	SE	8,854	West Miami	SW	5,727
Medley	NW	663			

Island Cities: Bal Harbour, Bay Harbor Islands, Golden Beach, Indian Creek Village, Key Biscayne, Miami Beach, North Bay Village, Surfside

Source: U.S. Bureau of the Census, 1990. University of Florida, Bureau of Business and Economic Research

◆ Age Demographics of Dade County

0-14	20.2 %
15-24	14.0 %
25-44	31.5 %
45-64	20.4 %
65 and over	13.9 %

The median age in Dade County is 34.2. The largest percentage of people who are 65 years and older reside in Bal Harbour (59%) and Bay Harbor Islands (44%). The largest percentage of people under 18 years of age live in Florida City (37%) and Opa-locka (36%).

◆ Climate

Elevation: 15 feet
Annual Rainfall: 57.77 inches
Average Summer Temperature: 82 degrees
Average Winter Temperature: 68 degrees

Taxes

◆ Property Taxes

The unincorporated areas of Dade County have a millage rate of 24.3900 per $1,000 of assessed property value. The City of Miami levies a millage rate of 32.1023 and 31.6023 respectively, depending upon the property location and its relationship to the downtown area. The city of Opa-locka has the lowest millage rate, 21.665. The highest millage rate, 36.016, is appropriated by Indian Creek, an exclusive island community. In most of the municipalities throughout Dade County, millage rates range from 24.0 to 30.0.

◆ Sales and Use Tax

Dade County collects a 6 1/2% sales and use tax. Six percent is levied by the state and the additional 1/2% is a county tax.

Voting and Elections

To facilitate voter registration, Dade County offers more than 500 voter registration sites throughout the area. The County has deputized various banks, real estate firms and businesses in easily accessible locations to accommodate residents. *Ph. 375-4600; 375-3150.*

Dade County

There are 13 county commissioners elected from single-member districts for a four-year term of office. A chairperson and a vice-chairperson are elected by fellow commissioners. Every two years, either six or seven of the district seats are up for election.

Miami

The City of Miami is governed by four city commissioners and a mayor who are elected at-large by the entire elecorate for four years. Every two years, residents elect two commissioners. The next election for mayor will take place in 1997. All municipal elections are held in odd years, only. Primaries are scheduled for the first Tuesday, after the first Monday in November. The general election is held on the Tuesday following the primaries. *Ph. 375-5553.*

Supervisor of Elections, Government Center, 111 NW 1st Street, Miami, FL 33101.

Pet Registration

Dogs must be innoculated for rabies at four months of age. Pet owners must show proof of vaccination each year in order to register their dogs and obtain a county license tag. Although cats must also be innoculated for rabies, they do not have to be licensed. Leash laws, which are in effect, do not permit dogs to wander by themselves. Dogs must tolerate those uncomfortable dog days of summer, for they are not allowed on the county beaches. According to some residents, they seem to be more welcome along the strip past the Rickenbacker tollgate leading to Key Biscayne.

The Humane Society of Greater Miami is a private, non-profit organization which shelters unwanted pets and provides adoption services for orphaned animals. Its health care clinic innoculates, spays and neuters animals brought to the clinic or prior to adoption. The society's pet cemetery offers burial sites for deceased pets. A plot may be purchased with annual maintenance or perpetual care. On a lighter note, the Humane Society brings puppies and kittens to nursing homes to cheer up recovering patients. The program is called *Pet Therapy. Ph. 696-0800.*

Transportation

Air Travel

MIAMI INTERNATIONAL AIRPORT
NW 21st Street & 42nd Avenue (Le Jeune Rd.)
Miami, FL 33159
Main Number: *Ph. 876-7000*
Administration: *Ph. 876-7300*

Miami International Airport has the highest concentration of airlines in the world at its gates. There are 52 foreign and 17 domestic scheduled passenger airlines. Its extensive air system covers 190 cities in four continents – North America, South America, Europe and Africa – as well as Central America and the Caribbean. It has service to more cities in the Caribbean and Latin America than any other airport in the country. American, United and Iberia airlines have hubs at Miami International. Miami International Airport is approximately 15 miles from downtown Miami.

Amenities. Moving walkways are located on the third floor of the terminal building and provide easy access throughout the terminal and between the terminal and parking garages. From the parking garage, take the elevator to the fourth level and follow the signs to "Moving Walkways." The fourth level of the garage is equivalent to the third level of the terminal.

A full-service bank is located on the fourth floor of concourse B. On the second floor between concourses B & C, a limited branch office is available for transactions. ATMs are at both banking locations. Foreign currency exchange booths are situated in each concourse; a 24-hour exchange is located on the second level at concourse E. Two Passenger Service Centers are also on the second level, between concourses B & C and concourses G & H. At these centers, there are telephones, courtesy paging phones, telephones for the hearing impaired, stamp machines and mail boxes, ATM banking, and airport & airline information assistance. A full-service post office is located on the fourth level of the terminal at concourse B.

Pharmaceuticals: There are two 24-hour pharmacies located in the terminal lobby – one near concourse D and one near F. Prescription drugs are available at the concourse F location. Have your physician call the airport pharmacist. *Ph. 876-0556.*

Relaxation: If you need a quiet place to relax away from the hustle and bustle of the airport, there are several gardens with benches located on the second level deck. If you arrive at the airport too early or your flight is delayed, for a nominal fee you can use the health club on the eighth floor of the airport hotel. It has a heated swimmming pool, track, racquetball, steam bath, sauna, whirlpool and Nautilus equipment. If you are not the athletic type, the Top of the Port Lounge, also on the eighth floor, offers cocktails and an expansive view of the skyline and airfield.

Ground Transportation. Airport Limousine *(Ph. 423-5566)* and Transtar *(Ph. 856-7777)* provide a full range of transportation services, including stretch limos, luxury sedans, shuttle vans and buses. Ashtin Leasing, Town & Country and Yellow Cab provide taxi service.

Public Transit. Metro-Dade Transit has four bus routes which service the airport. Buses depart regularly from the airport en route to Downtown Miami; Coconut Grove and Coral Gables; Miami Beach; and Hialeah. For exact routing and scheduling, call Metro-Dade Transit Agency.

Chalk's International Airlines provides daily seaplane service to Key West, Bimini and Paradise Island from Watson Island Terminal (opposite the Port of Miami). *1100 Lee Wagener Blvd. Ph. 359-0414.*

Local Transportation
The Metro-Dade Transit Agency

- **Metrorail** is an electrically powered, elevated rapid transit system with standard size trains which are conductor-operated. It spans 21 miles, servicing areas which include downtown Miami, Coconut Grove, and Coral Gables along a route which begins in Kendall and terminates in Hialeah. There are 21 stops, approximately one every mile. The first train leaves Kendall at 5:15 am and arrives in Hialeah at 6:06 am; the last train departs from Kendall at midnight. Metrorail connects with Metromover, Metrobus and Tri-Rail. *Ph. 638-6700.*

- **Metromover** is a fully automated people mover which is computer operated. The individual trams loop around downtown Miami on an elevated track every 90 seconds. There are nine stops servicing major downtown locations with 12 more under construction. *Ph. 638-6700.*

- **Tri-Rail** is a commuter train linking Dade, Broward and Palm Beach Counties. Trains operate during peak commuter hours and midday during the week, Saturday, and most holidays. There is free parking at most Tri-Rail stations. Tri-Rail connects with Metrorail at the "Metrorail Station" near Hialeah.

- **The Metrobus** system covers 63 Dade County routes with approximately 565 buses. More than 19 routes service Downtown Miami and the Beaches daily. Metrobuses operate Monday through Friday, from 4:30 am until 2:00 am. Schedules change on the weekend and holidays. Buses connect to Metrorail, Metromover, and Tri-Rail providing a bus-to-rail network. Handicapped residents, seniors and students in the 12th grade or under using the system during school hours are entitled to half fares and transportation passes. *Ph. 638-6700.*

- **The Breeze Connection** offers frequent shuttle service from downtown Miami to South Beach on Friday and Saturday, 7 pm - 4 am and Sunday noon - 6 pm. Call Metro-Dade Transit for more detailed information.

The Metro-Dade Transit Agency is located on the ninth floor of the Government Building, *111 NW First Street. Ph. 638-6700.* Contact them for special transportation needs and services. *Ph. 263-5400.*

Postal Service

The postal system of Dade county is unique due to its ever changing boundaries. A Main Post Office services the Greater Miami Area with zip code designations of 331 and 332. At this main facility, all mail is distributed to branches and stations located within the various municipalities and unincorporated areas which have these postal designations. Zip codes are defined by geographic boundaries, not municipality guidelines. A given zip code encompassing a given geographic area may cross two cities. Opa-Locka, Homestead, and Hialeah are the only municipalities in Dade County not serviced by the Miami Main Post Office. There are associate main offices with branch networks in each of the three cities which provide full postal service.

For information on the postal branches and stations closest to you, call the Main Office in your designed area. They will also provide a listing of the postal contract stations in your community.

Post Offices & Zip Codes

Miami Main Office 33100-33299	2200 NW 72nd Street	470-0642
Opa-Locka Main Office 33054-33056	550 Fisherman Street	681-7489
Homestead Main Office 33030-33035	739 Washington Avenue	247-2641
Hialeah Main Office 33010-33017	325 E. First Avenue	888-6491

Newspapers and Magazines

THE MIAMI HERALD is a daily newspaper with international, national and local coverage. Its primary circulation areas are in Dade, Broward and Monroe Counties. It serves the local communities on Thursdays and Sundays with a zoned insert called *Neighbors*, a section dedicated to news and happenings in specific communities in the Greater Miami area. *Tropic*, the Sunday magazine, features stories about people, places and events in South Florida. Special interest sections devoted to arts and culture, business, home and design, home buying, and travel are published on various days during the week. *Weekend,* an entertainment guide, appears on Fridays. *Ph. 376-2909.*

EL NUEVO HERALD, published daily by The Miami Herald, is the country's largest Spanish-language daily. Although it is the sister newspaper to the Herald, it has an independent format and coverage appealing to the Hispanic community. During the week, El Nuevo prints international, local, and sports news along with a special features section which focuses on a different topic every day. *Viernes,* the weekend supplement, provides coverage on area entertainment: movie reviews, restaurant reviews and local events and attractions. It is circulated in Dade, Broward and Palm Beach counties. *Ph. 376-3535.*

DIARIO LAS AMERICAS is published six days a week; there is no Monday edition. It is a Hispanic newspaper dedicated to local and international news as well as an emphasis on sports, health and social items. *Ph. 633-3341.*

◆ Other Ethnic Publications
(Newspapers) MIAMI JEWISH TRIBUNE; EXITO; (Magazines) CAMACOL MAGAZINE, MIAMI MENSUAL.

MIAMI DAILY BUSINESS REVIEW, published five days a week, features real estate, business and law. Columnists analyze the real estate markets with a focus on residential resales, condominiums, and commercial properties; listings (and prices) of homes that sold, foreclosures, mortgages and deeds; features on finance, including a financial analysis of local companies and investment news, as well as business relocations and stories on local entrepreneurs. *Ph. 347-6644.*

◆ Other Business Publications
MIAMI TODAY, INTERNATIONAL BUSINESS CHRONICLE, SOUTH FLORIDA BUSINESS JOURNAL. For information, refer to Ft. Lauderdale's Newspapers and Magazines.

NEW TIMES is a local newspaper which publishes area news and entertainment including theater reviews, musical reviews, restaurant reviews and listings of area nightclubs. The classified section has a unique musical billboard for musicians.

SOUTH FLORIDA MAGAZINE is a regional magazine circulated throughout Dade, Broward, Palm Beach and Monroe counties. It features South Florida lifestyles, new trends, current issues in the community, spotlights on people, culture, health, fashion, sports, travel, restaurants, and dining reviews. Special editions include: *Travel* (June); *Best and Worst of South Florida* (August); *Fashion* (September); *Restaurants and Dining, Profiles on Chefs and New Trends in Cuisine* (November/April). *Ph. 445-4500.*

Library System

Main Library
101 West Flagler Street
Ph. 375-5016

The Miami-Dade Library System includes the Main Library, 25 neighborhood branches, and four regional libraries. The county library system services residents within the Dade County Library Taxing District. Residents of Bal Harbour, Bay Harbour, Hialeah, Miami Shores, North Miami, North Miami Beach, Opa-locka and Surfside are serviced by their own municipal libraries; they must pay an annual fee to obtain a Miami-Dade library card.

The Main Library is located in the Metro-Dade Cultural Center. In the center of the complex, an open courtyard plaza with tables and chairs invites visitors to sit, eat or read at their leisure. The Miami-Dade Library System is committed to creating as many bridges as possible to connect people with the many services the library offers.

The *Porta Kiosk*, a modular structure located on the platform of the monorail station, is a library designed to serve commuters. Patrons can borrow the latest selections directly at the kiosk or use the computer to access publications at other branches. *Biblio Beat*, a televised program, broadcasts the special programs and services offered by the library system. A special segment of the program presents upcoming events and entertaining interviews with special guests. If you want to know what's happening at the library, tune in to Cable 34. *Dial-Up On-Line Catalog Service* is a 24-hour library service. Residents with a personal computer and modem can access the library files and search for publications by author, title, subject or key words.

The Imagination Factory presents "Storytelling To Go," an outreach program which takes storytelling on the road to schools, daycare centers and youth facilities. The repertoire includes a variety of American and international tales designed to stimulate young imaginations. *Miami Kidfest*, held at various library locations, acquaints children with the library and provides a line-up of entertainment while community sponsors supply free ice cream. Many of the performers engage the children in the 'art of the story' through storytelling, mime, folk songs or puppet shows.

Project L.E.A.D. (Literacy for Every Adult in Dade) has received recognition for its one-on-one tutoring in basic reading skills and family literacy workshops. With the large number of immigrants residing in Dade County, this program has significantly benefitted the community. *Multicultural Awareness Programs* provide a perspective of the cultural and ethnic heritage of different peoples around the world through visual media and performing arts. The library hosts exhibits in ethnic photography, paintings and folk art as well as performances in music, dance and folklore of the featured country and/or ethnic population.

A strong focus on special events and weekly programs have made the Miami-Dade Library System a hub of diverse and exciting cultural events and activities as well as a learning center. Its programs include lectures, discussions, and workshops which cater to many special interests; vocal and instrumental concerts; dance performances; art/design workshops; book reviews; art films; fine art exhibits; etc. The *Quarterly Schedule of Programs* describes upcoming events at the various libraries throughout the system. *Library Happenings*, a newsletter published by the Friends of the Miami-Dade Libraries, Inc., highlights the events and happenings at different branches.

Health Care

There are 37 hospitals serving the Greater Miami Area. Several are affiliated with Miami's renowned medical schools as well as a variety of hospitals which provide special services. A small sampling of hospitals are listed below.

Cedars Medical Center
1400 NW 12th Avenue
Ph. 325-5803

Founded in 1961, Cedars Medical Center merged with Victoria Hospital in 1993 under the aegis of Columbia Hospital Corporation. It is presently the largest private medical center in South Florida. As a teaching hospital, it is affiliated with the University of Miami School of Medicine and the Barry University School of Pediatric Medicine.

Cedars Medical Center has 500 private rooms and a 585 licensed bed capacity. All nurses are trained in specialties to provide quality care. Cedars has received recognition for many of its special programs, which include:

- The Cancer Center has been designated a Comprehensive Community Hospital Cancer Center by the American College of Surgeons Commission on Cancer.
- Cardiac Services offers a 62-bed dedicated unit for the care of cardiac patients and performs open heart surgery.
- The Breast Care Center provides mammography units which are accredited by the American College of Radiology.
- The Geriatric Center runs a program of primary health care (and free transportation) for seniors.
- The Microsurgery Unit offers specialized procedures for hand trauma and limb reattachment.
- The Headache Treatment Center provides biofeedback, stress reduction and physical therapy.
- The Sleep Disorder Center diagnoses and treats sleep disorders with a focus on apnea.

The Cedars Inn is located within the hospital to accommodate family and friends of patients.

Jackson Memorial Hospital

1611 NW 12th Avenue
Ph. 325-7429

Jackson Memorial Hospital is a direct descendent of the Miami City Hospital which dates back to the early 1900s. A not-for-profit institution, it is the second largest hospital in the United States. It is an accredited major teaching institution for the University of Miami School of Medicine and together they share a 67-acre site in downtown Miami. The University of Miami/Jackson Memorial Medical Center was cited in *The Best in Medicine* as one of the top 25 medical centers in the nation. Jackson Memorial Hospital was also honored as one of the nation's top hospitals in *The Best Hospitals in America*.

Dedicated to patient care, it has a 1,448-bed capacity and a staff 1,150 physicians (approximately 600 University of Miami School of Medicine faculty members and 550 house staff physicians and residents). Although a full-service comprehensive facility, about one third of its beds are dedicated to special care. The Medical Center is a regional resource for trauma, burn, cancer, newborn special care, neurological and spinal cord injury, rehabilitation, psychiatric, and organ transplant. Jackson Memorial has also contributed to the South Florida Aids Network by providing care and counseling to patients in need.

Jackson North Maternity Center is a satellite facility in North Dade.

Mount Sinai Medical Center Of Greater Miami
4300 Alton Road
Miami Beach
Ph. 674-2121

Mount Sinai is a private, not-for-profit teaching facility with 600 physicians who have medical privileges on staff. Its specialties include:

- Cardiac care and open heart surgery.
- Women's medical services including a comprehensive breast center.

Every woman taking a mammogram is seen by a physician. If indicated, physicians are equipped to perform a breast biopsy, thereby avoiding unnecessary delays.

- Infertility programs and in-vitro fertilization.
- Orthopedic specialties and rehabilitation.
- Alzheimer's Memory and Disorder Center.

Miami Children's Hospital
6125 SW 31st Street
Ph. 666-6511

Miami Children's Hospital, founded in 1950 as a Variety Children's Hospital, is affiliated with the State University of New York.

It offers over 40 medical specialties to youngsters from birth to 21 years of age. While serving the Dade community as a pediatric medical center, it also is a regional referral center for children in need of specialized medical care throughout South Florida and the Southeast. As a trauma network affiliate, its trauma response team provides immediate care to children in critical emergencies who are transported by helicopter.

In 1986, Miami Children's Hospital opened a new facility with 208 beds. The hospital is renowned for providing optimal care for children with medical problems ranging from the most common to the rarest childhood diseases. With the new expansion project, the hospital can accommodate more children with its 60 additional beds; other projects, which will provide increased space for medical services, are currently on the drawing boards.

As a leader in research and education.....

- It is the only dedicated *Pediatric Teaching Hospital* in the Southeast.
- Its *Research Institute,* which began operation in 1991, is currently studying genetic diseases at the molecular level. Such research plays a vital role in understanding disease and developing genetic therapy.
- Its annual *Pediatric Post-Graduate Course,* offering updates, courses and seminars, is the largest continuing education program for pediatric physicians in the United States.
- Its *Scientific Newsletters* present current medical research, information and new strategies for health care to pediatricians throughout the world.
- Its *Pediatric Advanced Life Support Course* televises medical information to foreign physicians in Latin America through satellite telecommunications; its other telecommunications programs reach over 50 countries on five continents.

North Shore Medical Center

1100 NW 95th Street
Ph. 835-6000

North Shore Hospital, a not-for-profit full service medical center, opened its doors in 1953 with 110 beds for patient care. Since then, it has become a mainstay in the health community and presently accommodates 357 beds. Its nationally recognized programs and special services include the *Miami Women's Health Center,* the *Neo-*

natal Intensive Care Unit, the *Griffith Cancer Center* and the *Advanced Imaging Facility.*

The Miami Women's Care Center, created in 1985, was a 'first' in the area and has since served as a model for subsequent programs in South Florida. It was based on the fact that women have specific and unique health needs and recognized that women's health issues needed a forum to be addressed adequately. Miami Women's Care Center has received national acclaim for its commitment to communicating honest and accurate medical information and providing opportunities for women to understand and participate in their own care. The Women's Center offers health talks, discussion panels, and support groups. 'Special Saturdays' features a series of famous women who have challenged traditional role boundaries as well as men who have insights into women's issues. The Women's Resource Library contains a wealth of articles, books, videos and cassettes. Registered nurses specializing in women's health and wellness are trained to answer questions over the telephone and/or will provide a packet of current information related to specific health concerns.

The C. Gordon Griffith Cancer Center and the American Cancer Society offer free cancer screenings for early detection of cervical, breast, uterine, skin, oral, colon-rectal, prostate and testicular cancers. Screenings are held monthly, on a first-call, first-served basis. *Ph. 634-7518.*

A Men's Wellness Program was initiated to promote awareness of men's health problems and recognize the necessity of physical examinations and early screenings. The Men's Wellness Series include health education classes; health screenings and support groups are also part of the program.

Pritikin Longevity Center
5875 Collins Avenue
Miami Beach
Ph. 866-2237

The Pritiken Longevity Center opened in 1976 offering a unique program for healthier living through better nutritional habits and exercise. Although a residential program is offered, many Florida residents select *Pritiken PM,* a four-week session with classes three evenings per week. The program is based on diet, exercise and education. It begins with a fitness evaluation which includes a blood chemistry panel and physical exam. After an exercise stress test, a physiologist provides a personalized exercise prescription. During the program, health care professionals present a comprehensive view of nutrition; new eating habits and cooking styles; alternative ways to manage stress; and related health issues. Exercise classes are conducted by the Center's physiologists who monitor participants' progress. At the end of the four weeks, exercise prescriptions are provided for continuing the program at home.

Bascom Palmer Eye Institute
900 NW 17th Street
Ph. 326-6000

The Bascom Palmer Eye Institute is the largest such facility in the southeastern United States and one of the leading eye institutes in the world. An integral part of the University of Miami School of Medicine, it opened as a separate institute in 1962 with a strong commitment to patient care, research and education. The Anne Bates Leach Eye Hospital and the William L. McKnight Vision Research Center are its two main facilities. The Eye Hospital has state-of-the-art operating room facilities and technologies. It treats more than 10,000 surgical patients each year. The Research Center has produced many major scientific advances in ophthalmology. Serving the School of Medicine, the Institute trains medical students, residents and fellows annually. It also offers seminars, conferences and continuing education programs to an international body of ophthalmologists and physicians.

Education

DADE COUNTY PUBLIC SCHOOLS
Department of Information Services
1450 NE. Second Avenue
Miami, FL 33132
Ph. 995-2388

In the Dade County Public School System, there are 192 elementary schools, 49 middle schools, 28 senior high schools, 14 special schools and centers, and 11 vocational/adult education centers (not located at other secondary schools).

Dade County has the largest school district in the state and the 4th largest in the United States. As a result of its sprawling size and large student population, the county is divided into six administrative educational regions. Each region has a superintendent who reports to a central administrator, the Deputy of Education. Within each region, there are four "feeder patterns" or neighborhood educational units. Similar to a pyramid, local area elementary schools feed into middle schools which feed into a central high school at the top.

In addition to the traditional neighborhood school, Dade County also supports several Magnet Schools and 54 Magnet Programs. Complementing a disciplined academic program, they offer concentrated study in various fields of student interest. There are three free-standing dedicated magnet high schools which are available to students from any geographical area in the county; the two magnet middle schools and one magnet elementary school have restricted geographical requirements. The magnet programs within neighborhood schools attract students from an extended geographic area of 20 miles.

◆ Magnet High Schools

Marine and Science Technology High School, MAST Academy, is located on Virginia Key, adjacent to Key Biscayne. Students interested in marine science and technology are offered an enriched program in marine biology, oceanography and related subjects as well as hands-on laboratory experiences. Graduates are qualified to continue their education, enter the military or apply their skills in various careers. *Ph. 365-6278.*

Design and Architecture Senior High (DASH) is located in the heart of the Miami Design District. The program offers concentrated study in one of four areas of design: architecture, landscape architecture, interior design and fashion design. Students develop a portfolio in a selected area in preparation for post-secondary design schools and universities. College level courses in the various design disciplines are offered through the dual enrollment program. *Ph. 573-7135.*

New World School for the Arts, located in downtown Miami, provides students with the opportunity for a continuous education, beginning in the 10th grade and continuing through four years of college. Students receive a rigorous academic program as well as artistic training in their particular area of interest. There are four divisions in the arts program: dance, music, theater and visual arts. Students may earn dual enrollment college credit for a portion of their arts credits. After receiving a high school degree, they may choose to follow a career path; continue on for a two year associate degree or a four year bachelors degree at the New World School; or apply to another post-secondary school. *Ph. 237-3135.*

Magnet Programs which have been integrated into the academic curriculum offer students enriched programs within a particular area of interest.

Elementary & Middle School Magnet Programs: Montessori programs; Writing and Literature; Science and Mathematics; Zoo Science/Math; Aerospace Science/Math; Computer Technology; International Studies; Visual and Performing Arts.

High School Magnet Programs: International Baccalaureate; Visual and Performing Arts; Media Arts; Medical Arts and Allied Health Professions; Tourism and Travel; Aviation Science; Business and Finance; Engineering Science; Teaching; Professional Education; Legal and Public Affairs; Professional Leadership.

◆ Gifted Programs

Dade County also offers nine full time programs to motivate gifted students who need a more rigorous and stimulating academic program.

◆ Special Programs

Fannie Mae Academy offers inner city minority students and at-risk students an opportunity to prepare for careers in finance, business and mortgage banking while enrolled in a high school curriculum. The program is supported by the Federal National Mortgage Association. Students who receive high grades may qualify for free college scholarships.

Conflict Resolution Programs are scheduled to be integrated into the learning curriculum at all levels of the educational system. Students in grades K-12 learn how to deal with conflicts constructively by identifying and understanding the cause of conflicts and effective techniques for resolving them.

Multimedia-Assisted Large Group Instruction introduces large-screen videos into the classroom. For a generation raised on videos and visual images, American History and World History are presented through instructional films three times a week. A master teacher reviews the significant themes and answers questions.

Pre-Kindergarten Programs are considered a necessity for all children enrolled in the county's 188 elementary schools. Young children gain self confidence as they develop abilities to express themselves and learn how to socialize with other children. Exceptional and at-risk students have benefited from pre-school programs for many years.

English as a Second Language is not a specific program, but encompasses several educational programs and special services which are available to students (and their families) who do not speak English fluently. Contact the Board of Education for more information.

UNIVERSITIES AND COLLEGES

The University of Miami opened its doors to the first class of students in October, 1926. Approximately 14,155 students are presently enrolled, with more than 12,000 full-time students.

The University System is comprised of two Colleges (Arts & Sciences, Engineering) and 11 Schools (Architecture, Business, Communication, Continuing Studies, Education, International Studies, Law, Marine and Atmospheric Science, Medicine, Music, Nursing, and Special Joint Programs). It has approximately 105 undergraduate programs, 98 graduate programs, and eight professional areas. *Ph. 284-2211.*

The Coral Gables Campus houses both colleges and nine schools. It has a "residential college" on campus which provides housing for faculty members and their families. This concept, borrowed from the British, permits faculty members to be more visible and accessible as they interact with students, participate in student activities, and host informal student gatherings.

The Rosenstiel School of Marine and Atmospheric Science, located on Virginia Key in Biscayne Bay, is in an area well suited to experiential learning. The Schools of Nursing and Medicine are located in downtown Miami, the hub of one of the busiest medical complexes.

Florida International University is a part of the State University system. It opened in 1972 with an enrollment of only upper division and graduate students, but by 1981, freshmen and sophomores were added to the student body. A few years later, FIU received authorization to offer doctoral programs. With an enrollment of 24,000 students and over 950 full time faculty members, it is presently the largest public university in South Florida and the fourth largest in the State. For the past five years, FIU has been listed as one of the best universities in the country by the *US News and World Report* survey of "America's Best Colleges."

There are 11 colleges and schools which offer Baccalaureate, Masters and Doctoral degrees. They include the following colleges and schools: Arts & Sciences; Business Administration; Education; Engineering & Design; Health; Accounting; Computer Science; Hospitality Management; Journalism and Mass Communication; Nursing; and Public Affairs and Services. In addition to the academic departments, FIU supports interdisciplinary centers and conducts research projects which address important social and economic concerns.

FIU has two campus locations: the Main Campus at University Park in Miami and the North Miami campus. Apartment-style housing is available on both campuses.

St. Thomas University was founded in 1961 as a four-year liberal arts institution. Its main campus, which has on-site residences, is located in a lovely, secluded area of North Dade. Its two satellite schools in Hialeah and Southwest Dade attract commuter and evening students. In addition to a full spectrum of liberal arts courses, the undergraduate school features a curriculum in tourism and hospitality, sports administration, business, and education. A Master's degree is also offered in many of these programs as well as a degree in the pastoral ministries. St. Thomas University also houses the School of Law, which attracts students from diverse ethnic backgrounds.

The University, which is sponsored by the Catholic Archdiocese of Miami, is a nonsectarian institution which has been recognized for its varied population of international and multicultural students. Its small student body of 2,570 permits a low student/faculty ratio. *Ph. 628-6546; outside of Florida, 1-800-367-9010.*

Barry University was founded in 1940 as a small Catholic women's college. Since then, it has grown considerably and educates 7,000 students annually as a coeducational institution. Sponsored by the Dominican Sisters, the university offers a selection of 85 undergraduate and graduate programs. Barry University houses the

School of Podiatry, the only one in the Southeast and one of seven in the country. *Ph. 899-3000.*

Miami-Dade Community College, established in 1960, presently incorporates five campuses throughout Dade County and provides an education to 54,000 students. It has received national recognition for its innovative programs and its high number of student graduates. In addition to general studies, there are featured programs which are the signatures of each campus. *Ph. 237-3000.*

- The North Campus, located in northwest Dade, provides programs in the protection services and specialized training for paramedics, police officers, and fire fighters. It also offers programs of study in funeral services and operations; graphic arts technology; electronic engineering and American sign language.
- The Kendall Campus, formerly the South Campus, has a strong liberal arts curriculum leading to an AA degree. Its child care program qualifies students for HRS licensing. A new community outreach center focuses on business skills and careers, with many courses available for credit.
- The Wolfson Campus, in downtown Miami, is the most visible. It plays host to various cultural groups and organizations in the City. The New World School of the Arts, located on the campus, is a Dade County Magnet High School in partnership with Miami Dade Community College. Wolfson Campus also offers a strong curriculum in interior design and technology; hospitality; international commerce; and paralegal accreditation.
- The Medical Center Campus, located in the heart of the Civic Center (one of the busiest medical hubs in the country), specializes in allied health technologies and nursing. Surrounded by four medical facilities, students are afforded enriched practical study experiences.
- The Homestead Campus is a nucleus for business support in the Homestead community. Its program relates to business needs and activities.

The Cultural Scene

Gusman Center for the Performing Arts

As the old, worn out Olympia Theater was about to breathe its last breath, philanthropist Maurice Gusman purchased the building and donated a large sum of money for restoration. The movie palace, which dates back to 1925, was built by Paramount Enterprises at a cost of $1.5 million. It was designed as an "atmospheric theater" at a time when the movie house itself was both part of the entertainment and the fantasy. The lavish interior was built to resemble the walled garden of a Mediterranean palace with rococo statues and columns enhancing the grandeur. A simulated sky with drifting clouds and stars creates the illusion of an ampitheather under a moonlit sky. When vaudeville arrived at the theaters, patrons were entertained for hours by live performers, films or newsreels, and the fabulous Wurlizer organ.

In 1975, the Gusman Center was deeded to the City of Miami. In 1984, it was listed in the National Register of Historic Places. With a seating capacity of 1,700, it is host to the prestigious Florida Philharmonic Orchestra, the New World Symphony, and the Miami Film Festival. *174 E. Flagler Street, Ph. 374-2444.*

Greater Miami Opera

The Greater Miami Opera, which was founded in 1941, is the seventh oldest opera company in the United States. During its many performing seasons, the company has attracted internationally acclaimed artists, including Luciano Pavorotti, who made his US debut with the Greater Miami Opera in 1965. During the last decade, it has dedicated itself to performing a repertoire of popular traditional operas as well as introducing new innovative works. Projected English translations above the stage as well as a scene-by-scene synopsis in the program makes the opera more accessible. The company performs four operas every season, beginning in January and continuing through April. Opera Previews, which are held the Sunday prior to a new performance, provide informative and entertaining commentaries about the composers and the historic context of the upcoming opera. Maestro James Judd serves as both the Musical Director of the Greater Miami Opera and the Musical Director for the Florida Philharmonic. Mr. Judd, a highly acclaimed symphonic and operatic conductor, has performed as a guest conductor for both the Berlin and Israel Philharmonic Orchestras as well as performing in the major concert halls of Europe. *2901 W. Flagler Street. Ph. 854-1643.*

Center for the Fine Arts

The Center for the Fine Arts is located in the Metro-Dade Cultural Center, a Mediterranean-style complex. As a major art institution in South Florida, it is dedicated to displaying major art exhibitions on loan from museums and private collections around the world. Although it only opened its doors in 1984, its reputation has attracted more than 100 exhibitions, including works by Picasso, Toulouse Lautrec and Frank Lloyd Wright. Although similar to a museum, the Center for the Fine Arts does not own or collect any art. Exhibitions represent different eras, genres and styles. The two large gallery areas permit two (and sometimes three) exhibitions, which change every two months. The open patio courtyard, with its tiled floor and wrought iron doors, is a delightful setting for sculpture workshops, concerts and parties. Sunday at the center is family day. Special programs, including guided tours and workshops, are planned around the exhibition. Thursday evenings are set aside for gallery tours, lectures and performances related to the exhibition. The membership is invited to participate in local visits to many of South Florida's museums and galleries. Museum trips and viewings of private collections are also scheduled to places such as Washington, DC, La Jolla, CA, and New York City. *101 W. Flagler Street. Ph. 375-3000.*

South Florida Art Center

The South Florida Art Center provides affordable studio space for visual artists working in different media. Artists, whether they are emerging or established, must submit a portfolio of work to a committee prior to acceptance. Presently, more than 85 artists have studio space in the arts district of Lincoln Road. SFAC supports three exhibition spaces. The Ground Level is a major exhibition and performing space; #922 is a smaller space located above the Ground Level; ClaySpace is dedicated exhibition space for a cooperative of clay artists. The Ground Level hosts a curated exhibition every month, beginning with a reception on the third Friday of the month. Many of the exhibits integrate the visual and the performing arts. It is not unusual to experience a musical program, poetry reading, or interpretive dance being performed at the reception.

Studio classes for beginning and advanced students in different media are conducted by artists. Individual tutorials are held in studio space while group classes are held in larger workshop areas. Lectures and forums are also hosted by SFAC. In addition to expanding its community education programs, it is also providing more offerings to artists. An editing facility for film and video artists and a screening room for film viewings are new additions to the center.

The Administrative offices, open Monday through Friday, offer maps and addresses of the artist's studios. *924 Lincoln Road, Miami Beach. Ph. 674-8278.*

Florida Philharmonic Orchestra

This is a regional orchestra which performs as a resident company for the cities of Miami, Ft. Lauderdale, Boca Raton and Palm Beach. *836 Biscayne Blvd. Ph. 945-5180.*

For more detailed information on the Florida Philharmonic Orchestra, refer to "The Cultural Scene In Ft. Lauderdale."

Coconut Grove Playhouse

Coconut Grove Playhouse is Florida's largest regional professional theater. Originally built in 1926 as a movie palace, it was converted to an Air Force training school during WW II. It reopened as a theater in 1956 and during the next 21 years attracted an impressive list of actors. In 1979, it was acquired by the State of Florida. With the appointment of Jose Ferrer as Artistic Advisor in the early 1980's, the Coconut Grove Playhouse became nationally known. In 1985, Arnold Mittelman succeeded Jose Ferrer and guided it towards further growth.

The Playhouse presents international, national and Southeast premiers of the highest caliber, often by renowned playwrights. The Mainstage has a seating capacity of 1,130. There are six shows produced during the season with four-week engagements scheduled for each one. The Encore Room is a much smaller, more intimate theater with a capacity of 135. Two plays are produced, with 10-week engagements scheduled for each one. The Playhouse was highly praised for its Encore Room production of *The Lady From Havana*. Both English and Spanish versions of the play were performed by the same cast.

The Playhouse sponsors the *Young Actor's Performance Program*, a six-week rehearsal and performance workshop for young people from 14-17 years of age. *Acting Classes*, which are offered to the entire community, introduces people with an interest in acting to the theater; the *Professional Apprenticeship Program* is a rigorous program for individuals with formal training. *3500 Main Hwy. Ph. 442-4000.*

Vizcaya Museum and Gardens

Vizcaya, a majestic villa overlooking Biscayne Bay, was built between 1913 and 1916 as the winter retreat of industrialist James Deering. Enamored with European art and architecture, Deering fashioned the 76-room villa after an Italian Renaissance country home. The 34 decorated rooms, designed around a central courtyard, showcase Deering's exquisite collection of 15th-19th century European furniture, tapestries and decorative arts. Guides are available to present anecdotal stories and describe the furnishings. The 10 acres of surrounding gardens are adorned with statuary, fountains and pools. A boat tour presents a view of the house and gardens from the bay.

A visit to Vizcaya's Museum Gift Shop is a must! It has high quality replicas of European decorative arts and unique gift items.

Vizcaya offers a membership to museum patrons. Throughout the year, special events such as balls, parties and concerts are held in the courtyard or on the verandah. *3251 S. Miami Avenue. Ph. 579-2708.*

Events and Attractions

Coconut Grove Arts Festival

The Coconut Grove Arts Festival began as a promotion for Irma La Douce, a 1963 production of the Coconut Grove Playhouse. As an artist's colony, Coconut Grove was the perfect place to publicize the French musical by staging a "Left Bank Affair" art show. Today, the Coconut Grove Arts Festival has evolved into an outdoor arts festival of major scale and significance. It is traditionally held during President's Day Weekend in February, beginning on Friday. The Grove is converted into a pedestrian mall with booths of colorful art work from all different media lining the streets. More than 2,000 artists throughout the US and abroad apply for exhibition space; only 300 are accepted by a juried panel of experts. The high quality of art selected for exhibition has been widely acclaimed. Festival bands and well-known musicians perform in scenic Peacock Park which overlooks Biscayne Bay. An outstanding variety of ethnic foods and culinary treats are prepared by food vendors who are also juried into the show; acceptance is based on taste and presentation. *Ph. 447-0401.*

Note: Because of its reputation, the Coconut Grove Arts Festival is host to approximately 750,000 visitors. If possible, get there early to avoid the crowds and the strong afternoon sun.

Miami Film Festival

Held on the first Friday in February, the festival is produced by the Film Society of Miami. Movie aficionados look forward to this 10-day event which premiers international films of artistic value. During the festival, 28-30 films from countries around the world are previewed, with a question and answer session after each one. Producers, directors, actors, screen writers, and critics are invited as special guests to present seminars and participate in panel discussions.

During the year, the Film Society presents premier screenings; retrospectives of films from a particular country, director or genre; and various social events and gatherings. *Gusman Center for the Performing Arts. Ph. 377-3456.*

Miami Book Fair International

Every year, the Miami Book Fair attracts over 500,000 visitors during its eight-day fair in November. More than 200 authors, publishers, booksellers, and guests converge for this literary extravaganza which celebrates the art of great writing and the enjoyment of reading. More than 300 national and international exhibitors display selections of books. In addition to the fun of wandering through the various book stalls, special programs highlight the event. *Miami-Dade Community College. Ph. 237-3258.*

- On Monday through Friday, "Evenings With..." presents readings and informal discussions with a different author each night. A number of authors from different literary genres participate in readings, panel discussions and autograph sessions during the final three days of the fair.
- Young children are introduced to childrens' literature through personal encounters with authors and illustrators, discussing and autographing their books at Children's Alley. The "art of the story" is also presented through children's theater, storytelling and puppet shows.
- Celebrity authors from Latin America and Spain present their literary perspectives in Spanish to audiences of Hispanic origin as part of the International Program.

- Renowned chefs/authors discuss their cookbooks and give tasty demonstrations of their particular culinary art in *Epicure Row*.
- Collectors of rare editions may find a special book or two in the *Antiquarian Annex*.

The Lipton Tennis Championships

These are held during the middle of March every year. This 10-day event is the fifth largest tennis tournament in the world, hosting both male and female players in singles and doubles competition. During the first eight days, there are day and evening qualifying rounds among the top seeded players. The championship matches are played during the second weekend; the women's finals are held on Saturday and the men's finals on Sunday. The Lipton Championships are televised in 60 countries. As you wander through the crowd, you will observe a very international flavor. In 1992, spectators came from 28 different countries and 32 states.

A new stadium, with Florida motifs and palm trees, was recently constructed to seat 14,000 fans. Seating is arranged in an octagonal design which permits greater seating and viewing capacity at the lower and middle levels; there are no bleachers! Chairs are provided for spectator comfort. In addition to the main stadium, there are 10 other courts used during the eight days of competition prior to the finals. Throughout the park, there is an atmosphere which is very relaxed, yet festive and exciting. There are many concession stands offering a variety of high quality catered menus as well as snacks. *7300 Crandon Blvd. Ph. 446-2200.*

Miami International Boat Show and Sailboat Show

This features a display of virtually every type of marine craft, electronics and accessories available in the national and international markets. It had its premiere show in 1941 and is presently the largest boat show in the world. During the five-day event, scheduled over President's Day weekend, boating experts present informative seminars and answer on-the-spot questions. There are three locations to preview a variety of exhibitions and attractions. The *Miami Beach Convention Center*, which is the hub of the show, is also the main stage for showcasing power boats ranging from personal water craft to high performance boats and luxury yachts. Fashion shows display the latest in nautical designs; radio controlled boat races and contests provide family fun; and the Ski Lake attraction features ski shows and clinics. On the water, boating exhibits are located at the *Biscayne Bay Marriott Marina*, 1633 N. Bayshore Drive in downtown Miami. Visitors may view a spectacular variety of powerboats in water as they stroll the docks. The **Miami International Sailboat Show** is held at the *Miami Beach Marina*, 300 Alton Road. Exhibitors showcase everything from large luxury yachts to small sailboats and accessories. Showgoers are invited to board the yachts and speak with the captains. The American Sailing Association offers free mini-sailing lessons and sailing excursions on the bay. *Miami Beach Convention Center, 1901 Convention Center Drive. Ph. 673-7311.*

Continuous shuttle service provides easy access to the three locations. For more information, call Bruce Rubin Associates. *Ph. 448-7450.*

Fairchild Tropical Garden

Named after the famous plant explorer, Dr. David Fairchild, this lush tropical garden opened in 1938. Covering 83 acres with 5,000 varieties of plants, it is the largest tropical botanical garden in the continental United States.

The landscape design sets the stage with its winding paths, lakes and vistas. Botanical highlights are the Tropical Rain Forest, the Sunken Garden, the Flowering Vine Pergola, the Cycad Circle, the Hibiscus Garden, and the Rare Plant House. Plants are grouped in designated areas and labeled for easy identification. One of the Fairchild's objectives is to help perpetuate rare and endangered plants of Florida, the Caribbean and the tropics. Fairchild Tropical Garden is also committed to community education. There is a guided tram tour which provides information on the different plant communities; walking tours look into areas not reached by the tram. Courses in horticulture and botany are available throughout the year as well as lectures, plant shows, and special events. *10901 Old Cutler Road, Ph. 667-1651.*

Fruit and Spice Park

The Fruit and Spice Park is the only botanical garden of its kind in the United States. This tropical Eden, which is situated in a 20-acre park, showcases over 500 varieties of exotic fruit, vegetables, herbs, spices and nuts from around the world. As you explore the grounds, you are invited to sample any of the fallen fruits. Expert advice is available on how to plant and care for different fruits, vegetables and spices, as well as canning and freezing tips. During the year, park professionals conduct classes and workshops on sweet and spicy topics, such as Cooking with Tropical Fruits and

Vegetables; Tropical Fruit Wine Making; and Herbs and Spices for South Florida. Florida Fruit Safaris travel to South and Central America to collect indigenous fruits and plants. For those who have the interest, but not the time to be away from home, farm tours of South Florida are also offered. The Fruit and Spice Park also hosts different events and festivals throughout the year. Tours of the gardens and grounds are conducted on Saturday and Sunday afternoons. *24801 SW 187th Avenue, Homestead. Ph. 247-5727.*

Miami Metrozoo

An afternoon at Miami's Metrozoo will delight children and adults alike. In addition to its fascinating residents, Metrozoo itself has received much praise for its tropical beauty. Situated on 290 acres, there are more than 300 species of exotic and rare animals living in natural habitats. Embarking on an international safari, you will pass through Asia, Europe and Africa, recreated by detailed landscaping and the free roaming animals. In addition to its many natural habitats, Metrozoo offers a full 'immersion' exhibit – a new trend in zoo design. Asian otters may not yet realize that they are living in captivity! Their habitat is an authentic environment complete with fog, jungle sounds, tropical foliage and even fragments of an ancient temple.

Metrozoo also offers membership as well as a variety of special programs.

- A *Behind the Scenes* guided tram tour presents a special look as animals are being washed, fed and quarantined for delivering their babies.
- *Zoo Camp* is an eight-week program which provides an in-depth approach to animal handling, care and training.
- Special *Children's Programs* are scheduled during the year with popular stars such as the Sesame Street Gang, the Flintstones and other favorite cartoon characters. Kids get to 'meet and greet' these friends after the show.
- *Feast with the Beast, Black Tie Dinner Gala* is held at the zoo. Tables are arranged for evening dining on the grounds of the zoo with selected restaurants on site catering different foods and delicacies. Music can be heard throughout the park as the partying continues into the morning hours with the nocturnal beasts. *12400 SW 152nd St., South Miami. Ph. 251-0400.*

The Nature Connection

The Nature Connection offers a look at Greater Miami's natural environment – its coastal areas, plant, bird and marine life – through unique guided tours and trips. Offerings include Fossil Rock Reef Walks; Naturalist-Led Bike Trips; Beach Walks; Hikes and Canoe Trips; Hands-On Marine Exploration; and Interpretive Talks on Local History. *Ph. 556-7320.*

Holocaust Memorial

The Holocaust Memorial is a passionate reminder and tribute to the six million Jews who died in the Nazi concentration camps during World War II. At the center of the Memorial is a 42-foot bronze arm arising from the earth, the final act of a dying person. A concentration camp number is burned into the forearm. Figures of tortured human victims, clinging to the taut skin and trying to escape, depict the horror of the Holocaust. Around the monument are images of the death camps; a photographic mural which is etched into black granite; and a Memorial Wall with an inscription of the names of loved ones who perished. The Holocaust Memorial, which opened in February, 1990, was designed by Miami-based architect and sculptor Kenneth Treister. *1933-1945 Meridian Avenue, Miami Beach. Ph. 538-1663.*

Art Deco District of South Beach

The Art Deco District, which lies at the southern end of Miami Beach, includes one square mile of buildings constructed between 1923 and 1943. Although architectural styles vary and include Streamline Moderne, Spanish Mediterranean as well as Art Deco, the buildings are scaled to similar size. Trendy art deco hotels, restaurants and street cafes line the picturesque Ocean Drive at South Beach. Many people are actively engaged in a favorite pastime – people watching. People on foot, on bicycles, or on roller blades offer a spectacular array of costumes – from outrageously colorful to casually elegant. On a sunny day, thousands of people line the beach to enjoy the sun, play, swim or just relax under a tree and read. The district comes alive at night with an animated, vibrant ambiance, restaurants offering new world cuisine, chic clubs, and nightspots.

The Art Deco District was listed on the National Register of Historic Places in 1979. On Saturday morning, The Art Deco Welcome Center gives walking tours describing the architecture of this designated historic district. Bike tours are available on Sunday morning. *5th to 23rd Street, Miami Beach. Ph. 672-2014.*

Ethnic Festivals

During the year, many colorful festivals are held to celebrate the culture and ethnic background of Miami's diverse populations. *Carnaval Miami/Calle Ocho*, the largest Hispanic celebration in the United States, honors the proud roots of Miami's Latin residents. The nine days of festivities during March attract more than one million people to the world's largest block party.

The *Goombay Festival* celebrates the Bahamian blacks who settled in Coconut Grove and were some of Miami's earliest immigrants. Their merchant ships and wrecker/salvagers contributed to Miami's merchant business community. Every June, the Goombay Festival honors the Bahamian black pioneers and their place in the history and growth of Miami. It is the largest black heritage festival in the country.

Don't Miss

Old Town Trolley. The Old Town Trolley is a very pleasant way to see downtown Miami, visit neighboring communities, and learn about the history of the area. A 90-minute narrated tour takes you to attractions in Miami, Coconut Grove, Coral Gables and Miami Beach.

Mayfair Mall. As you pass through the portals of the Mayfair Plaza in Coconut Grove, you will see a shopping arcade of unparalleled beauty. The open air interior courtyard is designed with tropical foliage, hanging greenery, trellises, ponds and waterfalls. The ornamental use of glazed ceramic tile, carved stone, copper sculpture, wrought iron, mahogany and glass creates a stunning visual effect of contrasting elements.

Cocowalk. Cocowalk, which is also located in the Grove, is a charming multilevel complex with a European village ambiance. It invites leisurely strolling and window shopping around the square while street entertainers perform in the central plaza and artisans attract attention with their crafted wares. Many people enjoy sitting in one of the colorful outdoor cafes with a cool drink in hand, engaged in the favorite pastime of people watching.

Stone Crabs. Once you have been introduced to stone crabs, you may be able to get by in the months when stone crabs are not available, but you will not be happy about it. The sweet and succulent taste of this seafood delight is unbeatable!

A Bicycle Ride across the Rickenbacker Causeway into Key Biscayne. With magnificent waterways on both sides of Key Biscayne, this route is not for serious bikers. Blue skies, vibrant blue green waters with splashes of color from wind surfers, water skiers and boaters combine to create a panorama that is visually breathtaking and soothing to the soul.

Recreation

Football
The Miami Dolphins highlight the football season from September through December. They play home games at Joe Robbie Stadium. *2269 NW 199th Street (Greater Miami North). Ph. 620-5000.*

Baseball
The Florida Marlins, a national league baseball team, played their first season in 1993. Joe Robbie Stadium is home to the Marlins from April through October. *Ph. 628-7417.*

Basketball
The Miami Heat, a young NBA franchise, debuted in 1988. The Miami Arena is home to this exciting team. Its season begins in October and continues through April. *721 NW 1st Avenue (Downtown Miami). Ph. 577-HEAT.*

Special Sporting Events
The Miami Classic, an International Soccer Tournament, hosts the best soccer teams from South and Central America, the Caribbean, Europe and North America. *Ph. 669-0101.*

Metropolitan South Florida Fishing Tournament is the largest fishing competition, attracting thousands each year. *Ph. 376-3698.*

Federal Express Orange Bowl Football Classic is an annual New Year's day event featuring two nationally ranked college football teams. *Ph. 371-3351.*

Golf

Although there are many public golf courses in Greater Miami, it is advisable to make reservations. Most of the courses feature a lighted driving range, putting green, clubhouse, restaurant or snack bar, pro shop, instruction and equipment rental. Call Tee Time Services 24-hour reservation line: *Ph. 669-9500.*

Bayshore Golf Course
6401 Kendale Lakes Dr., Kendall
Three 9-hole courses.
Ph. 382-3930

Bayshore Par Three Golf Course
2795 Prairie Avenue, Miami Beach
9-hole course.
Ph. 674-0305

Biltmore Golf
1210 Anastasia Ave., Coral Gables
18-hole course.
Ph. 460-5364

Briar Bay Golf Course
9373 SW 134th Street. Kendall
9-hole course.
Ph. 235-6667

Fontainebleau Golf Club
9603 Fontainebleau Blvd.
(West of Airport)
Two 18-hole courses.
Ph. 221-5181

Golf Club Of Miami
6801 Miami Gardens Dr.,
N. Miami Beach
Three 18-hole courses. *Ph. 829-4700*

Granada Golf Course
2001 Granada Blvd., Coral Gables
9-hole course.
Ph. 460-5367

Greynolds Park
17530 W. Dixie Hwy.
N. Miami Beach
9-hole course. *Ph. 949-1741*

Kendale Lakes Golf &
Country Club
2301 Alton Road, Miami Beach
18-hole course. *Ph. 532-3350*

The Links at Key Biscayne:
6700 Crandon Blvd.
Championship 18-hole course.
Ph. 361-9129

Melreese Golf Course
1802 NW 37th Ave.
(Airport Area)
18-hole course. *Ph. 635-6770*

Miami Shores Country Club
1000 Biscayne Blvd.,
Miami Shores.
18-hole course. *Ph. 795-2366*

Miami Springs Country Club
650 Curtiss Pkwy.,
Miami Springs.
18-hole course
Ph. 888-2377

Normandy Shores Golf Course
2401 Biarritz Dr., Miami Beach
18-hole course.
Ph. 868-6502

Palmetto Golf Course
9300 SW 152nd Street, Miami
18-hole course.
Ph. 238-2922

Presidential Country Club
19650 NE 18th Avenue
N. Miami Beach
18-hole course. *Ph. 933-5266*

Haulover Park
10800 Collins Ave., Miami Beach
9-hole course.
Ph. 940-6719

Redland Golf & Country Club
24451 SW 177th Avenue,
Homestead
18-hole course. *Ph. 247-8503*

Beaches

The residents of Miami and neighboring inland cities head to the shores of Miami Beach and Key Biscayne to feel the sand and ocean waters at their feet. Ten miles of beach with graceful palms and oceanfront hotels line the A1A coastal highway, from South Miami Beach at 1st Street to Sunny Isles Beach at 192nd Street.

The Rickenbacker Causeway leads to five miles of beach along the shores of Key Biscayne: Hobie Beach, Virginia Beach, Crandon Park, and Bill Baggs Beach (Cape Florida State Recreational Area).

South Pointe, 1Washington Ave., Miami Beach, *Ph. 673-7730*
Amenities: Barbecue grills, shelters, playground.

Lummus Park, South Beach, Ocean Drive: 5th-15th Sts., Miami Beach, *Ph. 673-7730*
Amenities: In the heart of the Art Deco District; volleyball, waverunners, roller skating, playground, chairs & umbrellas.

Bill Baggs Park, Cape Florida State Recreation Area, 1200 S. Crandon Blvd., Key Biscayne, *Ph. 361-5811*
Amenities: Family oriented; swimming, picnicking, fishing, chairs & umbrellas.

Crandon Park, 4000 Crandon Blvd., Key Biscayne, *Ph. 361-5421*
Although hurricane Andrew destroyed some of the amenities in the park, people continue to enjoy the three-mile beachfront.

In addition to visiting the beaches, residents have a wealth of water sports available to them. Deep sea fishing excursions are popular, as well as scuba diving, snorkeling, sailing, power boating and jet skiing.

Directory of Services

9-1-1 Emergency Only	POLICE • SHERIFF • FIRE • MEDICAL • RESCUE	
AGENCY	**DESCRIPTION**	**DADE (305)**
ALCOHOL & DRUG ABUSE	Intervention & Referral	800-821-4357 358-4357
CRISIS HOTLINE	24 Hour Help Line	358-4357
ABUSE CENTER	Women in Distress North Dade South Dade	758-2546 247-4249
POISON CONTROL & INFORMATION CENTER		800-282-3171
SENIOR SUPPORT	Contact the Alliance for Aging	670-6500
TIME		324-8811
WEATHER/SURF INFORMATION		661-5065
HURRICANE HOTLINE		596-8735

County Services

AGENCY	DESCRIPTION	DADE (305)
GOVERNMENT CENTER	140 W. Flagler	375-5656
PUBLIC INFORMATION	Citizen Information	375-5656
ANIMAL CONTROL		884-1101
BOARD OF EDUCATION		995-1000
COUNTY COOPERATIVE EXTENSION		248-3311
COUNTY COURTHOUSE		375-5775
EMERGENCY MGMT	Disaster Readiness Training & Evacuation Information	596-8700
FIRE PREVENTION		470-3760
FL. HIGHWAY PATROL	All Interstate Roads & Turnpikes	470-2510
GARBAGE COLLECTION		594-1500
LIBRARY		375-2665

LICENSES	Auto Tag	375-3591
	Parking Permit - Handicapped	375-5226
	Fishing & Hunting	375-5820
MASS TRANSIT	Bus Route Information	638-6700
PARKS & RECREATION		857-3350
	Claude Pepper Federal Bldg.	536-5359
PASSPORT INFORMATION	51 SW 1st Avenue	536-4448
		536-4681
PROPERTY APPRAISER		375-4020
SHERIFF		595-6263
TAX COLLECTOR		375-5455
TRAFFIC VIOLATION INFORMATION		324-5151
VOTER REGISTRATION		375-4600
WATER/SEWER		665-7471
Emergency/After Hours		274-9272

Human Services

AGENCY	DESCRIPTION	DADE (305)
AMERICAN ASSOC. OF RETIRED PERSONS (AARP)	Florida State Headquarters Provides source for local contact	813-576-1155
AMERICAN RED CROSS	Hurricane Shelter Information, Disaster Relief, Blood Banks, Educational Programs	326-8888
CHILD CARE	Community Coordinated Day Care Referrals	375-4670
INFORMATION & REFERRAL SERVICES	Connects You with the Appropriate Person or Agency Who Can Answer Your Question or Assist You With A Particular Need	358-1640
HANDICAPPED/DISABLED SERVICES		375-3566
HEALTH DEPARTMENT		325-2500
IRS	Location & Hours of Local Offices	800-829-1040
	Tax Information	904-354-1760
	Tax Forms	800-829-3676
MEDICARE		800-333-7586

NEWCOMERS CONTACTS:	Cuban American National Foundation	592-7768
	Haitian Catholic Center	751-6289
	Greater Miami Black Resource Guide	571-9505
SENIOR CITIZEN SERVICES	Information/Assistance and Programs for Seniors	358-6060
SOCIAL SECURITY		800-234-5772
SOCIAL SERVICE TRANSPORTATION	Reduced Fares, Dial-A-Ride Transport for Seniors & Special Groups	638-6448
UNITED WAY	Community Information	579-2200
VETERAN'S ASSISTANCE		795-1511
VOLUNTEER CENTER	A Clearinghouse for Volunteer Positions	579-2300
RETIRED SENIOR VOLUNTEER PROGRAM (RSVP)		375-5335

City Numbers

GOVERNMENT CENTER *Information Desk*	Miami City Hall 3500 Pan American Drive	250-5300
CITIZEN RESPONSE CTR	Information on City Agencies	579-2457
CITY CLERK		250-5360
POLICE (Non Emergency)		579-6111
FIRE (Non Emergency)		579-6300
DRIVERS LICENSE		751-9212
ELECTRICAL SERVICE	FL Power & Light	442-8770
GARBAGE COLLECTION		575-5130
LIBRARY		375-2665
PARKING GARAGES	Location & Rates	373-6789
PARKS & RECREATION		575-5240
TELEPHONE COMPANY	Southern Bell	780-2355
VOTER'S REGISTRATION		375-4600
WATER AND SEWER		575-5261
Emergency/After Hours		665-7471

Civic Organizations

Greater Miami Chamber of Commerce	350-7700
Greater South Dade/South Miami Chamber of Commerce	661-1621
Italian-American Chamber of Commerce	577-9868
Coconut Grove Chamber of Commerce	444-7270
Little Havana Development Authority	324-8127
Latin Chamber of Commerce of the USA	642-3870
Miami-Dade Chamber of Commerce	751-8648
Women's Chamber of Commerce of Dade County	446-6660
Miami Convention and Visitors Bureau	539-3063

Naples

The coastal city of Naples is famous for its white sandy beaches, upscale shopping and ecological splendors. Naples is a sophisticated area with just the right blend of old, new, elegant and simple. Its natural environment is a treasure, with its many parks, sanctuaries, islands, bays and beaches offering a respite from city life. Many residents use boats and water taxis to get around. It has long been a favorite residence of affluent CEO's and retirees, but is now expanding its vision to become a greater business base and year-round community. It hugs the Gulf in Collier County's southwestern corner. Ft. Myers, a growing metropolitan city, lies to its north, while Everglades City, the gateway to Everglades National Park, is its southern neighbor.

Naples is known as the Golf Capital of the World, boasting more golf holes per capita than any other place. But her past was not always sand, fairways and greens. After the Civil War, pioneers used the area as a base for fishing camps. Mullet was caught, salted and sold to traders – and as late as 1885, only two families actually lived within the city limits. Others were thwarted by the razor-like grass, dense palmetto scrub, and the ever-present mosquitoes. It was not really 'discovered' until 1923 with the creation of Collier County, named for New York City millionaire, Baron Collier. At one time Collier owned over a million acres of Florida land. Four years later, the railroad arrived – and with it, a boom in population. In 1946, the city benefited from the vision of Henry Watkins. He and two partners hired a land planner to develop the Naples Plan, the current framework of this jewel of the southwest. Today a new highway connection to Ft. Lauderdale and Miami and a major airport expansion offer increased opportunities for business development, cultural happenings and international tourism.

Demographics

◆ **Size**

Collier County includes the City of Naples and Everglades City. Defined geographic areas or communities, which are unincorporated, comprise the remaining areas of the county. There are 12 such communities: North Naples, Central Naples, Golden Gate, East Naples, South Naples, Marco Island, Royal Faka-Palm Creek,

Urban Estates, Rural Estates, Corkscrew, Immokalee and Big Cypress.

Collier County is the largest in Florida, encompassing nearly 2000 square miles, 99.4% of which is unincorporated. The City of Naples, which is the hub, is 10.7 square miles; Everglades City is .9 square miles.

◆ Population
As of the 1990 census, Collier County's population was 152,099. Permanent residents in the City of Naples totaled 19,505; Everglades City had a population of 321.

◆ Age Demographics in Collier County

Age	Percentage
Under 18	20%
18-24	8%
25-44	27%
45-59	15%
60-74	21%
75 plus	8%

Collier County has a median age of 40.7; in the City of Naples the median age is 60.6; the median age in Everglades City is 35.4.

◆ Climate
Elevation: 4 feet
Annual Rainfall: 51.40 inches
Average Summer Temperature: 82.4
Average Winter Temperature: 67.8

Taxes

◆ Property Taxes
The millage rate in unincorporated Collier County is 14.3331 mills per $1000 of assessed property value. The City of Naples has a millage rate of 13.7379; Everglades City has a millage rate of 20.5359.

◆ Sales and Use Tax
Collier County collects a 6% tax levied by the State of Florida.

Voting and Elections

Elections Office: Building F, Collier County Government Center, 3301 Tamiami Trail East, Naples, FL 33962. *Ph. 774-8450.*

Collier County is governed by a board of commissioners who serve for a four-year term of office. The County is divided into five districts; each district elects a commissioner who resides there. Every two years, either two or three of the district seats are up for election.

The City of Naples is governed by a mayor and six council members who are elected at-large. The mayor may serve only one four-year term of office. The council members, also elected for four years, may serve two consecutive terms. The city manager is appointed by the council. Every two years, three of the council seats become available. Elections are held during the first Tuesday in February. *Ph. 434-4717.*

In Everglades City, five council members are elected to serve a four-year term of office; the mayor is elected for a two-year term. The city clerk is appointed by the council to manage the daily business and affairs of the city. *Ph. 695-3781.*

There are approximately 300 outreach locations in Collier County to register new voters or process changes. Call the Supervisor of Elections for a listing of the various banks, public schools, libraries and real estate offices which have deputized officials to process voter registration.

Pet Registration

Dogs and cats, six months of age, must be inoculated and licensed. If neutered, there is a saving in licensing fees. County ordinances require dogs to be on a leash. Although there are pooper-scooper regulations for the county, peer pressure from neighbors often generates the most effective adherence to the law. There are no pets allowed on the beaches.

The Humane Society of Collier County receives pets from owners who can no longer take care of them. If you are thinking of purchasing a pet, consider adopting one from the Humane Society.

Their newsletter, *Humane Society of Collier County*, is published four times a year. *Ph. 643-1555.*

Transportation

Air Travel

NAPLES AIRPORT AUTHORITY
160 Aviation Drive N., Naples, FL 33942

The Information Center is open from 8 am until 5 pm. *Ph. 643-073.* The Naples Airport Authority is a small, tropical regional airport with the flavor of a Caribbean terminal. There is no fee for airport parking. The airport is approximately three miles east of downtown Naples.

Commuter Airlines include:
US Air (service to Tampa and Orlando)
American/Eagle (service to Miami)
Delta/Comair (service to Orlando)

Ground Transportation. There is ground transportation from the airport. Taxi and limousine service are available at the terminal. If you prefer a rental car, Avis, Hertz, National and Budget are on the airport grounds.

SOUTHWEST FLORIDA INTERNATIONAL AIRPORT
16000 Chamberlain Pkwy.
Fort Myers, FL 33913
Communications Center – *24 Hr. Ph. 768-1000*
Paging Service: *Ph. 768-1000*
Parking Information: *Ph. 768-1818*

Southwest Florida International Airport (coded RSW) is a bright, airy, modern two-level terminal which is easy to access. From the first level, escalators (and elevators) lead to security clearance and the boarding gates. RSW is a regional airport serving a five-county area. It provides gateways for more than a dozen major airlines with non-stop and direct service to cities within Florida, the United States and Canada. Certified for operation in 1983, it has grown remarkably. A US Customs facility is available to process international charter flights from Canada. RSW is presently applying for gateways to provide regular scheduled carrier service to and from

Canada. Future plans include international service to European cities. The airport is 30-35 miles from downtown Naples.

Amenities. If you are flying home for a visit with family and friends, you can purchase some gift items which are unique to Florida at the Florida Pantry. If you are without money, the automatic teller machine can assist you. Amenities also include a postal center to mail letters and purchase stamps. For parents traveling with infants, there is a nursery/changing room.

Ground Transportation. Naples Taxi Company provides door-to-door passenger shuttle service between Naples/Marco Island and the airport. *Ph. 643-2148.* For other forms of transportation, contact the Ground Service at the airport. *Ph. 768-4457.*

Major Airlines include:
American
American Trans Air
Continental
Delta
Northwest
TWA
United

Commuter Service includes:
US Express (service to Tampa & Orlando)
American Eagle (service to Miami)

Local Transportation

There isn't any! If you do not have a car, boat, bicycle or roller skates, you will have to rely on taxis or the good nature of friends.

Postal Service

The City of Naples has one Main Post Office and one branch office.

Main Office	1200 Goodlette Road, N. Monday-Friday: 8:30-5:00 pm Saturday: 8:30-noon	262-5411
Downtown Station	856 3rd Avenue, S. Monday-Friday: 8:30-5:00 pm Closed Saturday	262-1355

148 Naples

| Express Mail Inquiries | If needed, on-demand home pick up is available for an extra fee. | 800-962-2250 800-872-6211 |

Contract Stations

Contract stations perform all postal services. Call for specific hours of operation.

North Naples Pharmacy North Naples Contract Station	9331 Tamiami Trail, N.	597-8129
Lely Card Shop East Naples Contract Station	4939 Rattlesnake Hammock Rd.	774-1991
Glass-Ma-Taz Ridgeport Contract Station	5425 Airport Road, N.	566-8080
Postal Station Berkshire Commons	7231 Radio Road	353-5988
Shipping and Mailing Sta. Neapolitan Contract Station	838 Neapolitan Way	267-4933
Beacon Shipping Northgate Contract Station	1845D Isle of Capri Blvd.	455-8447
Party World Central Contract Station	2069 Tamiami Trail, N.	263-7771
Quick RTO Gulfgate Contract Station	1650 Airport Road, S.	774-4471

Stamp Vending Machines

Park Shore	4200 Tamiami Trail, N.
Courthouse	3301 Tamiami Trail, E
East Naples Carrier Annex	3573 Progress Avenue
North Naples Pharmacy	9331 Tamiami Trail, N.
Main Office	1200 Goodlette Road, N.
Downtown Station	856 3rd Avenue, S.

Newspapers and Magazines

NAPLES DAILY NEWS is a daily publication. Each day of the week is devoted to a different theme dealing with Naples lifestyle and happenings. Sunday's People Section lists meetings of clubs and organizations scheduled for the upcoming week. Friday's *Applause* is a weekend guide featuring theater, film, arts, and entertainment. The first day of each month, the Daily News publishes a calendar of scheduled events for that month. *Ph. 262-3161.*

◆ **Special Editions**

A *Newcomer's Guide* is published twice a year, at the beginning of December and again in February. A *Visitor's Guide* is published the first Thursday in March. It is a six-part guide to Collier County with coverage ranging from the environment to the arts.

MATURE LIFESTYLES is a monthly publication with a news magazine format, focusing on the positive side of living for its 50-plus readership. Special features offer suggestions for effective living. In addition to its travel, health, finance/business segments, a local section profiles community personalities, entertainment, recreation and local happenings. It is distributed throughout the four counties of Lee, Collier, Charlotte and Pinellas. *Ph. 482-7969.*

GULF SHORE LIFE, a magazine with distribution along the Gulf from Naples to Sarasota, publishes 10 issues during the year. It features area lifestyles and profiles active people in the community. There are special highlights on local happenings, book reviews, and a calendar of events. *Ph. 643-3933.*

Library System

Headquarters Library

650 Central Avenue
Naples. *Ph. 262-4130*

Headquarters Library is the main library of the Collier County Library System. There are five branch libraries within the county. All offer video cassettes on loan. Most of the county libraries have IBM compatible or Macintosh computers for public use as well as public domain software. A new meeting room at Headquarters, which can accommodate 100 people, is also available on "loan" to community groups. It has a satellite TV receiver and a projection TV screen. Talking books for the blind and programs for children and young adults are special offerings at Headquarters. Call for locations and numbers of the branch libraries.

Health Care

Naples Community Hospital

350 Seventh Street, N.
Naples. *Ph. 262-3131*

Naples Community Hospital is a not-for-profit, 376-bed, acute care facility providing comprehensive medical/surgical services, with the exception of open heart surgery.

Some of its special services include a Cardiac Rehabilitation Program, offering the patient educational and psychological support, behavior modification, and a monitored, supervised progressive exercise program. An emphasis on health enhancement is the foundation of its Wellness Center. Some of the activities include cardiovascular and Nautilus conditioning; classes in aerobics, aquacise and yoga; race walking classes; and a better back program. A professional staff directs and monitors the exercises, following the guidelines of the American College of Sports Medicine.

North Collier Hospital

1501 Immokalee Road,
Naples. *Ph. 597-1417*

North Collier Hospital, a subsidiary of Naples Community Hospital, is a 50-bed facility with 24-hour emergency care. Its new birthing center has private rooms with accommodations for the new father, if he wishes to remain overnight.

◆ Emergency Care Centers

There are several emergency care centers which are affiliates of Naples Community Hospital. They provide minor emergency and routine medical care.

East Naples Urgent Care Center

5432 Rattlesnake Hammock Road
Ph. 775-2220

Golden Gate Urgent Care Center

5038 Coronado Pkwy.
Ph. 455-6300

North Collier Health Center
1501 Immokalee Rd.
Ph. 591-7760

Marco Island Urgent Care Center
40 Heathwood Drive S.
Marco Island
Ph. 394-8234
Open 24 hours a day, seven days a week.

Naples Day Surgery offers an alternative to hospitalization. They perform elective outpatient surgery, endoscopic diagnostic procedures, and medical procedures to alleviate chronic pain. They have two locations:

South Location
Naples Day Surgery
790 Fourth Avenue North
Ph. 263-3863

North Location
Naples Day Surgery North
11161 Health Park Blvd.
Ph. 598-3111

Southwest Florida Regional Medical Center
3785 Evans Avenue
Fort Myers.
Ph. 939-1147

The Southwest Florida Regional Medical Center is a private, 400-bed, acute care medical/surgical facility which is under the umbrella of Columbia Healthcare Corporation. It has become well known for its Florida Heart Institute which has the third largest open heart surgery program in Florida and one of the highest success rates in the country. The Medical Center also houses the Eye Institute and Neurological Institute. Patients arrive from different countries for its highly acclaimed surgical services, which also include kidney transplants. Other specialties include a Wound Care Center, Rehabilitation Center (with a second location in Naples), and Hyperbaric Medicine, which uses pure oxygen to treat conditions such as diver's bends, gas gangrene, hard to heal wounds, smoke inhalation and the toxin from the brown recluse spider.

◆ Community Health Programs

Community Home Services, Inc. is a not-for-profit agency affiliated with Naples Community Hospital. It provides professional home care assistance and rehabilitative services seven days a week. In recognition of its fine service, the Joint Commission on Accreditation of Healthcare Organizations has awarded it accreditation with commendation. *Ph. 263-7113.*

The **Briggs Health Resource Center**, under the auspices of Naples Community Hospital, is an information referral center. It has a directory of physicians who specialize in certain types of medical problems; a library with health and medical publications providing information on specific medical conditions; and health related videos. Its touch screen computer is programmed to display the names of physicians and their specialty, medical services, access to more medical information. A directory of other life services and resources in the community can also be accessed by computer or printed materials. Its informal living room creates an inviting and relaxing setting to browse through the available literature on health issues. The Health Resource Center has expanded its services to include a variety of newcomer information, job services and free tax assistance. *Ph. 262-4221.*

The **Alzheimer's Day Care Center** is under the auspices of the local chapter of the Alzheimer's Association. Family members who are care givers can gain some relief and time to themselves while patients are engaged in supervised activities at the center. *Ph. 775-2233.*

Education

COLLIER COUNTY BOARD OF EDUCATION

Administration Center
3710 Estey Avenue
Naples, FL 33942
Ph. 643-2700

◆ Collier County Public Schools

The Collier County Board of Education provides a public school education through 16 elementary schools, five middle schools, and four high schools. Collier's public schools are fully accredited by the Southern Association of Colleges and Schools (SACS). Collier County was the first in the state to receive accreditation for its elementary schools, ensuring that educational standards are met at the lower grade levels, as well as the middle and high school levels.

School Notes. All elementary schools have full-day kindergarten programs.

Collier County was among the first in Florida to introduce classroom computers and a computer literacy program.

The dual enrollment program offers qualifying high school students enhanced educational opportunities. Students can take courses at Edison Community College in Naples for college credit while fulfilling high school curriculum obligations.

Highlights. Teachers are encouraged to develop innovative programs for the classroom; the best programs are awarded mini-grants.

Collier County and the Conservancy co-sponsor an enriched environmental educational program beginning with students in the elementary grade levels.

The Collier School System hosts the annual *Young Authors' Conference,* a special event for students in grades K-8. Students receive an invitation only if they have authored a book; they are encouraged to share their work with other students and attend special presentations and workshops for young writers. Students and their parents have the opportunity to mingle with recognized authors who are invited as guest speakers.

◆ Programs for Special Needs

The Infant Toddler Program provides activities for children who are moderately or severely handicapped, from birth to three years of age. Parents may choose to have homebound or center-based services. The Pre-Kindergarten Program mainstreams 3-5 year old handicapped children with others who are non-handicapped at a traditional elementary school.

The Vocational Training Program for moderately or mildly handicapped students offers vocational study and a supportive job site program within the school, leading to independent employment in the community. This step-by-step guided program has received much praise.

Collier County has a full-time *Gifted Program* at the middle-school level throughout the district. Students are enrolled in an advanced program which focuses on the four basics – language arts, science, social studies and mathematics – five days a week. There is also a pilot program for gifted children at the elementary school level.

COLLEGES AND UNIVERSITIES

Edison Community College, a satellite of Ft. Myers, has a new 50-acre campus in Naples. Edison Community offers two different degree programs. Students who major in accounting, business, computers, health technologies or nursing receive an Associate of Science degree. Students who enroll in a liberal arts program may transfer to a four-year college or university with an Associate of Arts degree. *Ph. 732-3700.*

International College of Naples is primarily a business college with four-year bachelor degree programs in accounting, computer management, business management and business administration. It also offers associate degree programs in medical records, paralegal studies and two-year business programs. International College is nationally accredited by the Accrediting Commission of Independent Schools and Colleges. *Ph. 774-4700.*

Barry University, which is based in Miami, has extension facilities in Lee and Collier Counties. It offers a special program for adult students who did not complete their education. Students may earn a four-year bachelor's degree by enrolling in evening classes. The Bachelor of Liberal Studies degree builds upon previous courses and life experiences which are evaluated for equivalency in credits. The Bachelor of Professional Studies degree builds upon the student's current career and offers credits for career experience. Areas of study include human resources management, public administration, business administration and health care management. Barry University is accredited by the Southern Association of Schools and Colleges. *Ph. FL. 800-388-2279; 278-3041.*

Walden University offers a Ph.D. in administration/management, health services, human services and education as well as an Ed.D.

This self-directed program requires completing a series of papers on different modules. Walden's non-traditional educational program is accredited by the North Central Association of Colleges and Schools. *Ph. 261-7277.*

Florida Gulf University, a new Florida State University, has scheduled plans to open for the 1997-98 school year. It will be located in Lee County, on a site near Ft. Myers. Students will be able to complete undergraduate and graduate studies close to home. A strong program in environmental studies will be part of the FGU curriculum.

The Cultural Scene

Philharmonic Center for the Arts

Combining the visual and the performing arts in one facility, the Philharmonic's unique and pleasing architectural design incorporates both form and function. Hayes Hall, the main performing arts and concert hall, seats 1,221, while the Daniel's Pavilion, a smaller informal theater, can seat 200 patrons. The four art galleries and two sculpture gardens are integrated into the design. The "Phil" (as it is called) is the permanent home to the Naples Philharmonic and the Gulf Coast home to the Miami City Ballet. Its concert hall presents theater, music, dance and special performances; the smaller theater, which does not have permanent seating, may be used for chamber music, cabaret, dance or magic carpet concerts for children. The season begins in November and continues through April with special holiday concerts during spring and summer. The art galleries at the Phil house a permanent art collection; exhibit works on loan from museums; and showcase local artists, whose work is for sale. Prior to a performance or during intermission, you can visit the galleries or walk through the beautiful sculpture gardens. Guided tours through the complex and galleries are available. *5833 Pelican Bay Boulevard. Ph. 597-1900.*

Adult Education at the Phil
- Exhibition Lecture Series: Usually, at the beginning of a new exhibition, a gallery lecture is presented to enhance the visual experience. Whenever possible, the exhibiting artist is invited to present the lecture and discuss the work.
- Art Lecture Series: A series of four lectures are given from different art disciplines during the season.

- Conductor Preludes: The Musical Director of the Philharmonic, Christopher Seaman, delivers an informal lecture on the evening's selection of classical music, one hour before the scheduled performance.
- Music Lectures: "What to Listen For in Music" is an adult education series of lectures presented by a Naples Philharmonic musician.
- Dance Preview: The Artistic Director of the Miami City Ballet, Edward Viliella, discusses the dance program, background of the production and choreography prior to the performance.

The Naples Philharmonic

The Naples Philharmonic was founded in 1983. Since its inception, it has grown in the number of resident musicians, diversity of concerts, and acclaim for the quality of its performances. Today the orchestra has expanded to 42 resident musicians which forms the core of its 84-piece symphony. Its musical director, Christopher Seaman, is well known in his homeland of Great Britain where he conducted the BBC Scottish Symphony. He has guest conducted orchestras on most continents and continues as the conductor-in-residence of the Baltimore Symphony. The Philharmonic Pops principal conductor, Erich Kunzel, is often referred to as the "Prince of Pops." He shares his time as the music director of the Cincinnati Pops Orchestra and makes guest appearances to conduct pops concerts throughout the country.

The **Classical and Pops Concerts** are the main events of the musical season. The Naples Philharmonic offers a six-performance series of classical selections on weekends from November through April. Those who enjoy the sound of "pops" can hear the orchestra play a lighter fare of timeless favorites during the three concert series beginning in January. During the season, the 82-voice Philharmonic Center Chorale accompanies the orchestra for two concerts.

Special Seasonal Concerts selected for the holidays feature the musical sound of the Pops as they celebrate Halloween, Christmas, New Years, and pay tribute to Memorial Day. The **Casual Classics** presents a series of three concerts which are lighter and not as formal as the classical series. Some of the serenades and melodies are likely to be familiar to audiences.

Members of the resident orchestra comprise the small **Chamber Musical Ensembles**. The **Candlelight Music Series** of three concerts is performed in the fall and again in the spring. These chamber evening programs take place in the intimate setting of the Daniels Pavilion. Other programs include chamber quintet, quartet, and trio ensembles. The Chorale is also featured in a special performance with a chamber ensemble.

The Miami City Ballet

A resident company of the Naples Philharmonic Center for the Arts, the Miami City Ballet shares its time between the two coasts of Florida. It presented its premier performance in October, 1986. The 39 dancers were selected from major dance companies around the world. Edward Villella, a principal dancer with the New York City Ballet for more than 30 years, has served as its artistic director, sharing the neo-classical vision and style of his mentor, George Balanchine. The company presents a series of four different programs. Three to four ballets, some of which are world premieres, are performed during each program. The season begins in October and extends to April. The Nutcracker Suite is traditionally performed before the Christmas holidays. For more detailed information, refer to Miami's Cultural Scene. Philharmonic Center for the Arts. *Ph. 532-4880 (Miami Office).*

Naples Players

In existence for 40 years, the Naples Playhouse is a community theater of amateur, but experienced actors presenting professional quality performances. Theater productions include a rich variety of musicals, comedies and drama. There are eight shows scheduled each year; five during the winter season and three during the summer. Throughout the year, Naples theatergoers are also treated to some special productions which are performed at the playhouse. *Naples Playhouse, 339 Goodlettte Road, S. Ph. 263-7990.*

Jazz on the Green

During the summer season (from May through September), the Naples Beach Hotel and Golf Club hosts Jazz on the Green. During May, June, August and September, the concerts take place on the third Saturday night of the month. In July, the concert is scheduled for the fourth Saturday evening. If it rains, there's always Sunday. To fully relax under the stars, bring your own chairs or blankets; although no coolers are allowed, food and beverages are for sale on the premises. *Naples Beach Hotel and Golf Club, 851 Gulf Shore Blvd., North. Ph. 261-2222.*

Naples Art Association

The Naples Art Association, a nonprofit organization founded by local artists, offers classes and "famous artist" workshops. The gallery features members' juried works each month. If you are not a hands-on artist but love the arts, you may wish to attend some of the informal lectures, demonstrations or the lecture series on a particular area of art history. Every year, the Naples Art Association raises scholarship money to benefit high school graduates continuing their art education. *970 5th. Avenue North. Ph. 262-6517.*

Music In the Park

The City of Naples sponsors concerts in Cambier Park on Sunday afternoons, November through April. Relax to the sound of old favorites, classical selections, well-known marches, and big band music presented by local musicians. *Ph. 434-4690.*

Note: Local community theater groups also perform at Cambier Park in the Norris Auditorium. Contact Parks and Recreation, Community Services Dept. for a listing of cultural events.

Naples Depot Cultural Center

The Naples Depot, a restored railroad station dating back to 1927, is presently the homesite for civic and cultural activities. It hosts several civic groups and provides space for art exhibits, lectures and workshops. The *Council On World Affairs* meets at the Depot weekly and invites guest speakers to address subjects of universal concern in the interest of promoting a greater understanding of the events and issues affecting Americans today. The Council also sponsors a Great Decisions program which uses an assigned text and covers eight topics of current global concern. *1051 Fifth Avenue South. Ph. 262-1776.*

The United Arts Council of Collier County

This is a state designated local arts agency, a resource center and liaison between the community and the various arts organizations. They financially support the public school system with cultural enrichment programs. A favorite for adults is the 'Arts Alive at Five,' a cultural bimonthly social at the Naples Depot. Local artists showcase their work in a party setting with live music. *Ph. 263-8242.*

Events and Attractions

Tropicool Fest

Tropicool Fest has become a tradition in Naples. It is the major event of the year, with constant partying during the first two weeks in May. Although it began as an end-of-season celebration, it has, in fact, extended the Naples season. The Great Dock Canoe Race and Taste of Collier are two of the highlights.

The *Great Dock Canoe Race* takes place at the Great City Dock on the second Saturday in May. Each year there is a different theme for the Canoe Race. Participants are encouraged to dress in costume and decorate their canoes in accordance with their interpretation of the theme. A canoe outfitted as "Polyester Princess" was the winning entry of *Nerds In Paradise,* a theme used a few years ago. Spectators, or those without canoes, are also encouraged to dress in costume. There are three heats during the day with a total of 150 canoes participating. The proceeds support local charities.

A *Taste of Collier* is sponsored by the Collier County Chapter of the Florida Restaurant Association. Everybody looks forward to this gourmet feast which is held on the first Sunday in May. Thirty area restaurants participate, offering their most delectable delights. The proceeds benefit mental health.

Tropicool also hosts Bay Day, a cleanup of the bay followed by a four- or eight-mile educational bicycle tour around the bay, Sand Castle Contests, Art Shows, Sporting Events, Musical Performances, and more. There are a total of 45 events during the two weeks, concluding with the Tropicool Music Fest in Cambier Park. *Ph. 591-1754.*

Swamp Buggy Races

Swamp Buggy Races began in 1949 with a group of hunters. Special vehicles were necessary to get through the swamp lands for the hunting season in the Everglades. After somewhat boastful conversations about the quality and performance of their respective vehicles, the group of hunters decided to put their buggies to the test and the races began.

Today, the Swamp Buggy Race is a high-speed sport through mud and water on a half-mile oval track. It has been designed with mud holes which can be as deep as 5 1/2 feet. At certain places along the track, buggies disappear, with only the driver's head emerging above the mud. There are eight different classes of buggies, ranging from small jeeps to custom-built, racing vehicles. In total, there are about 80 buggies competing in the different categories.

The Swamp Buggy Races take place three times during the year. The Winter Classic is at the beginning of March; the Memorial Championship is during the Memorial Day weekend; and the Fall Championship is at the end of October. Each event is two days. During the first day, the qualifying races take place. The second day features the finals and championship races. At the close of the day, the champion escorts the swamp buggy queen to the mud bath. She dives into the mud, crown and all, for the ceremonial closing event. All money raised during the events is donated to local charities. *Ph. 774-2701.*

Corkscrew Swamp Sanctuary

This is a peaceful haven for nature lovers and for the wildlife inhabiting the area. Your visit is hosted by the National Audubon Society who maintains and operates the Sanctuary. Meandering along a two-mile boardwalk, which winds through a forest of towering 500-year-old bald cypress trees, you gain a sense of nature's grandeur. The Sanctuary is also home to nesting wood storks (seven and eight pound birds with 66-inch wing spans), a variety of wading birds, and many species of small birds, turtles, alligators, foliage and wildflowers. There is an illustrated self-guided tour book of the Boardwalk. *Off Rte 846, Immokolee Road. Ph. 657-3771.*

Everglades National Park Boat Tours

The Everglades National Park is the third largest national park as well as the largest subtropical wilderness in the United States. Slow moving fresh waters move across thousands of acres of sawgrass. Its mangrove islands, swamps and jungle provide a habitat for a great variety of wildlife, fish and plants. Park naturalists guide and narrate the boat tours through the Everglades. *One half-mile past Everglades City State Road 29. Ph. 695-2591 or 800-445-7724.*

The Naples Nature Center and the Briggs Nature Center

These two facilities are operated by the Conservancy, an environmental organization which arose in response to estuarine concerns about a proposed roadway over Rookery Bay linking Naples and Marco Island. This was in 1964. Today, Rookery Bay is a national estuarine sanctuary. The role of the Naples Conservancy has expanded to ensure the appreciation and preservation of its beaches, waterways, islands, fisheries and wildlife.

The Naples Nature Center. Situated on 13.5 acres, the Center has several nature trails and a tidal lagoon.

- The *Wild Animal Rehabilitation Clinic* cares for sick or injured wildlife and nurses them back to health.
- The *Natural Science Museum* features a sea turtle aquarium with sea turtles and other salt water fish; a "mini-ocean" display with live shells, crabs and sea horses; Southwest Florida native birds and wildlife; a serpentine exhibit with 14 native snakes; and a live bees' nest and honeycomb ensconced in a tree with protective glass surrounding it.
- The *Nature Trails* present three different ecosystems for the visitor to explore on foot. Walk the mangrove swamp trail, hardwood hammock trail or subtropical hammock trail; if you want to relax, take a 45-minute complementary boat ride along the lagoon which travels through the mangrove forest.
- A series of five lectures are presented by noted environmental guest speakers, beginning in January.
- Every Wednesday, October through May, the Conservancy hosts a *Newcomer's Social* to introduce new residents to Florida's subtropical environment as well as the special programs and activities offered by the Conservancy. *1450 Merrihue Drive. Ph. 262-0304.*

Briggs Nature Center. The Briggs Nature Center encourages interpretative educational experiences, exploring the environment as a means of learning about it.

- They offer guided canoe trips through Rookery Bay to explore the mud flats, oyster beds, and birds as well as sunset canoe trips through the ABC islands to identify the birds in the mangroves. Both are preceded by a slide presentation and lecture. This is a "hands-on" experience. The Nature Center also has pontoon boat trips through the waterways, including one to a shelling area.
- The *Wilderness Adventures* offer canoeing and combination hiking and boating excursions on Saturdays.
- As part of their adult education program, a series of four *Learn Hands-On Nature Workshops* are presented during the first quarter of the new year. Previous workshops have included subjects

such as "beginning bird watching," "home aquaria" and "all about shells."
- A stroll along the half-mile boardwalk demonstrates the changes in the ecosystem as you proceed from the swamp mangroves which inhabit the wetlands to the scrub oaks and slash pines in the drier areas. *Shell Island Road. Ph. 775-8569.*

The Edison House

And last but not least, a wonderful treat awaits you at the Edison Ford Winter Estates – on your way to Sanibel Island. A guided tour takes you back to the life and times of Thomas Edison and Henry Ford.

In the spring of 1885, Thomas Alva Edison traveled to St. Augustine, seeking the warmth of the South. But an unusual cold and dreary Spring brought him to Ft. Myers and its tropical climate, which was more inviting. The estate which he built along the banks of the Caloosahatchee River covers 14 acres. His home, with its large breezeway and porches, as well as the lush botanical gardens, was designed to reflect tropical living. Edison thrived in his new surroundings and in 1916 his dear friend Henry Ford purchased a home next door.

The tour includes the Edison and Ford homes, the tropical gardens, Edison's laboratory and museum. Edison built a research laboratory on his estate to explore native sources of rubber after many discussions with his friends, Ford and Firestone. All of the laboratory equipment remains as it was during his experiments. After discovering that goldenrod was the best source of rubber, he produced a hybrid that could grow to 14 feet in height. Examples of rubber products produced from goldenrod are displayed in the museum. Edison's inventions, which include the phonograph, batteries, the ticker tape machine, movie projectors and an assortment of light bulbs, are featured exhibits at the museum. During his lifetime, Edison held 1,093 patents for his inventions. Visitors will be delighted by some of his inventions which they may not know about. *2350 McGregor Blvd. Ft. Myers. Ph. 334-7419.*

Don't Miss

Sunset at Naples Pier. It has been said that the dynamic cloud formations are Florida's mountains, giving it depth and perspective. A view of the ever-changing colors as the sun fades below the horizon is spectacular at the Naples Pier. At sunset, the sky may appear as a beautiful abstract landscape painting of muted pastels or may cast a more dramatic effect with its vibrant saturated glowing colors. If the atmospheric conditions are right, you may also see a green flash, a phenomenon which appears the moment the sun crosses over the horizon.

Christmas Walks. Naples welcomes the Christmas holiday at the end of November with the Festival of Lights, sponsored by the Third Street Shops and a Christmas Walk arranged by the Fifth Avenue Business District. The warmth and spirit of the holiday season is sparked off with the tree lighting festivities, choirs and Christmas carols, refreshments and eggnog.

Village on Venetian Bay. Elegant and unique boutiques, galleries and restaurants are surrounded by water in this Mediterranean-style village. It is a delightful way to shop, enjoy a cup of cappuccino overlooking the bay, or relax on one of the benches in this charming setting. *4200 Gulf Shore Blvd. North. Ph. 261-0030.*

Naples Water Taxi. The water taxi provides transportation to various restaurants and nightspots overlooking the bay. It will pick you up at home (if home is on the water) or at the city dock. They also offer a choice of different excursions, including a sunset cruise to view the "million dollar" homes along the bay and canals. *Ph. 774-7277.*

Sanibel & Captiva. For a quick getaway, head towards Ft. Myers and explore the beaches along Sanibel and Captiva Islands. Sanibel Island is well known as the shelling capital of the world. Strolling along the beach, you'll be surrounded by the many interesting shells that wash ashore. Bicycle along the island arteries and side roads to feel the flavor of the tropics with its lush vegetation.

Recreation

The Grapefruit League

Neapolitans have a choice of teams to follow in the Grapefruit League. The Minnesota Twins hold their spring training at the Lee County Sports Complex in Fort Myers. *Ph. 800-28-TWINS.* But, if you're a baseball fan from Boston, you'll want to get tickets to a Red Sox game in the City of Palms Park, located in downtown Ft. Myers. *Ph. 334-4700.*

Public Golf Courses

With more than 35 golf courses, Naples is a golfer's dream. There are more golf holes per person than any other statistically measured area. It is best to make reservations during the season.

Hibiscus Golf Club
175 Doral Circle
An 18-hole, 6242-yard course with par 72. Facilities include a driving range, putting green and practice green with sand trap. Club rentals are available. *Ph. 774-0088.*

Ironwood Golf Club
205 Charity Court
A short 18-hole challenging course. Arthur Hill designed this 2,500-yard course with par 54. Facilities include a putting green, club rentals, lessons, pro shop and restaurant. *Ph. 775-2584.*

Lely Flamingo Island Club
8004 Lely Resort Blvd.
An 18-hole, 7,171-yard course with par 72, designed by Robert Trent. Facilities include a driving range, putting green, club rentals, lessons, pro shop and restaurant. *Ph. 793-2223.*

Marco Shores Golf and Country Club
State Rd. 951
An 18-hole, 6,370-yard course with par 72, designed with nine water holes. Amenities include driving range, putting green, club rentals, lessons, pro shop and restaurant. *Ph. 394-2581.*

Pelican's Nest Golf Club
4450 Bay Creek Drive SW
Bonita Springs
An 18-hole, 6,908-yard course with par 72, designed by Tom Fazio. Facilities include a driving range, putting green, club rentals, lessons, pro shop and restaurant. *Ph. 947-4600.*

Riviera Golf Club
52 Marseille Dr.
An 18-hole, 4,090-yard executive course with par 62. Facilities include a putting green and club rentals. *Ph. 774-1081.*

Beaches

Naples has 10 miles of public beachfront. There is public access to the beach from every avenue which ends at the Gulf. You can walk past million dollar beach homes without trespassing, as long as you remain on the beach. Don't expect to see any life guards; there aren't any!

To make your beach experience more pleasant, the City of Naples will issue a beach permit for your car – at no cost. The permit entitles residents to park at a metered space on a public street adjacent to the beach – free of charge. Parking is permitted from 5 am until 11 pm. In order to qualify for a permit, you must provide proof of residency.

Naples, Seagate Drive (North), Gordon Pass (South)
Amenities: Fishing pier, bait.

Clam Pass Park, Seagate Drive
Free trams over boardwalk which is surrounded by mangroves and a tidal bay.
Amenities: Water equipment rentals.

Bonita Beach, Hickory Blvd. & Bonita, Beach Rd.; southern end of Bonita Beach

Lowdermilk Park, Gulf Shore Blvd. at Banyan Blvd.
Amenities: Children's play area.

Tigertail Beach, Hernando Dr., Marco Island
Amenities: Sailboat rentals, playground, and snack bar.

Vanderbilt Beach & Park, North Naples, Delnor Wiggins Pass State Pk.(North), Vanderbilt Drive (South)
Amenities: Wheelchair access, boat ramp, fishing, and observation tower.

Directory of Services

9-1-1 Emergency Only   **POLICE • SHERIFF• FIRE• MEDICAL• RESCUE**

AGENCY	DESCRIPTION	COLLIER(813)
ALCOHOL & DRUG ABUSE	Intervention & Referral AA: 24 Hr.	800-821-4357 262-6535
CRISIS HOTLINE	24 Hour Help Line: PROJECT HELP	262-7227
ABUSE CENTER	Shelter for Abused Women	775-1101

166 Naples

POISON CONTOL & INFORMATION		800-282-3171 263-5700
SENIOR SUPPORT	Telephone Reassurance & Support Responds to People Living Alone	263-7777
TIME/TEMPERATURE		263-5050

County Services

AGENCY	DESCRIPTION	COLLIER (813)
GOVERNMENT CENTER	3301 Tamiami Trail E.	774-8999
ANIMAL CONTROL		597-4880
BOARD OF EDUCATION		643-2700
COUNTY COOPERATIVE EXTENSION		353-4244
COUNTY COURTHOUSE		774-8800
EMERGENCY MANAGEMENT	Disaster Readiness Training and Evacuation Information	774-8444
FIRE PREVENTION		394-2575
FL. HIGHWAY PATROL	All Interstate Roads & Turnpikes	455-3133
GARBAGE COLLECTION		597-6088
LIBRARY		262-4130
LICENSES	Auto Tag Parking Permit - Handicapped Boating Registration Fishing & Hunting	774-8177 774-8177 774-8176 774-8176
MOSQUITO CONTROL		436-1000
PARKS AND RECREATION		353-0404
PASSPORT INFORMATION		774-8314
PROPERTY APPRAISER		774-8141
SHERIFF		774-4434
TAX COLLECTOR		774-8171
TRANSPORTATION SERVICES		774-8191
TRAFFIC VIOLATION INFORMATION		774-8105

Directory of Services 167

VOTER REGISTRATION		774-8450
WATER/SEWER		434-5050
	Emergency/After Hours	649-2823

Human Services

AGENCY	DESCRIPTION	COLLIER (813)
AMERICAN ASSOCIATION OF RETIRED PERSONS (AARP)	Florida State Headquarters Provides Source for Local Contact	813-576-1155
AMERICAN RED CROSS	Hurricane Shelter Information Disaster Relief, Blood Banks, Educational Programs	261-8903
CHILD CARE OF SOUTHWEST FLORIDA	Information & Referrals on Licensed Child Care Centers & Registered Family Care Providers	643-3908
INFORMATION & REFERRAL SERVICES	Connects You with the Appropriate Person or Agency Who Can Answer Your Question or Assist You With A Particular Need	649-1404
HANDICAPPED/DISABLED SERVICES		643-5900
HEALTH DEPARTMENT		774-8200
INTERNAL REVENUE SERVICE	Location & Hours of Local Offices Tax Information Tax Forms	800-829-1040 904-354-1760 800-829-3676
MENTAL HEALTH INFORMATION		261-5405
NEWCOMERS CLUBS	Contact the Chamber of Commerce	394-8704
SENIOR CITIZEN SERVICES *SENIOR AID LINE*	Information/Assistance Programs for Seniors	774-8443
SOCIAL SECURITY		800-772-1213
UNITED WAY	An Excellent Resource for Community Information	261-7112
VETERAN'S ASSISTANCE		774-8448
VOLUNTEER CENTER	A Clearinghouse for Volunteer Positions	649-4747
RETIRED SENIOR VOLUNTEER PROGRAM (RSVP)		263-3671

City Numbers

GOVERNMENT CENTER *Information Desk*	Naples City Hall 735 Eighth Street, South	434-4601
CITY CLERK		434-4701
POLICE (Non Emergency)		434-4844
FIRE (Non Emergency)		434-4730
DRIVERS LICENSE		434-5004
ELECTRICAL SERVICE	FL Power & Light	262-1322
GARBAGE COLLECTION		434-4747
LIBRARY		262-4130
PARKS & RECREATION		434-4683
PARKING PERMITS: BEACH		434-4600
TELEPHONE COMPANY	United Telephone	262-8666
VOTER'S REGISTRATION		774-8450
WATER AND SEWER	Emergency/After Hours	434-4745

Civic Organizations

Naples Area Chamber of Commerce	262-6141
Marco Island Chamber of Commerce	394-7549
Economic Development Council of Collier County	263-8989

Melbourne

The sister cities of Melbourne and Palm Bay represent the two largest population centers in Brevard County. While Palm Bay has a large residential population, Melbourne is the metropolitan center of the area. Situated in the southern part of the county, Melbourne and its neighbors are home to many of the space coast industries such as aerospace, high-tech oriented companies and electronics firms. Many young people are employed in these industries, creating an active and family-oriented population. Brevard County is the east coast home of the US space program, resulting in an influx of diverse and upwardly mobile, new residents. Patrick Air Force Base, the headquarters for missile testing and development, has an annual impact of $500 million. During the past 10 years, the county has experienced a 63% growth in the labor force, bringing a new vitality to the area. Today, there are 10 Fortune 500 companies located in South Brevard county alone.

The history of Melbourne dates back to the Civil War when it served as a military base. After the war, liberated slaves came to Melbourne and were the first to establish a city in the late 1860's. The first white family did not arrive until 1877. Soldiers, who had discovered the beauty of Melbourne and its beaches during the war, returned to the area, spurred on by the availability of inexpensive homesites along the Indian River. The city was not officially named until 1879, in honor of its first postmaster, a native of Melbourne, Australia. The Florida East Coast Railroad brought more settlers and tourists to Melbourne as well as facilitating the transport of citrus, vegetables and fish to other areas. Growth continued, but the mainland was not connected to the beaches until the 1920's when a bridge was built across the Intracoastal Waterway and the beachfront community of Indialantic was developed.

Since then, South Brevard has seen the growth of many waterfront municipalities. Presently, Viera which is situated at the northern end of South Brevard, is being developed as a "model city." With the County Government Operations Center and the School Board Services Facility located in Viera, it has become an administrative center for the county. Its 38,000 acres will be the site of many different styles of residential communities; recreational facilities including new parks and golf courses; cultural activities and attractions; commercial and business operations; and service industries.

Although Melbourne may not be as widely known as some of the other cities in Florida, its economic growth, youthful population and 33 miles of natural beach area are attracting a large number of new residents. Melbourne is a blend of both the old and the new. It possesses the special charm of old world Florida, but is also a modern-day city with an emphasis on development and new facilities. It is well situated midway between Miami and Jacksonville and is only a hop, skip and a jump to Orlando's playground.

Demographics

◆ Size

Brevard County, one of the longest in Florida, is 72 miles long and 18 miles wide. Due to its elongated shape, three main areas have evolved: North Brevard, Central Brevard and South Brevard. In 1990, Brevard had a population of 398,978 people. North Brevard has a population of approximately 80,500. Its major population center is in Titusville, which is the county seat; it is directly across the river from the Kennedy Space Center.

◆ Population

Central Brevard's population is 110,000. Its major communities include Cocoa Beach, Cocoa, Rockledge, Cape Canaveral, and Merritt Island. Port Canaveral is also situated here, making it a center for cruising, shipping, and fishing. South Brevard includes Melbourne, Palm Bay and eight other municipalities which comprise over 50% of the county's population. More than 207,000 residents now call this area home. By the year 2000, the population is projected to reach 263,217.

Palm Bay, the largest city in South Brevard, has 62,632 people living within 65 square miles. Melbourne is the second largest city with 59,646 people in a 30-square-mile area.

Neighboring Municipalities In South Brevard

Indian Harbour Beach	6,933
Indialantic	2,844
Malabar	1,977
Melbourne Beach	3,021

Melbourne Village	591
West Melbourne	8,399
Palm Shores	210
Satellite Beach	9,889

The population within the incorporated areas totals 154,142. The unincorporated areas have a population of 53,293 people.

◆ Age Demographics in South Brevard County

Under 18	22.0%
18-24	8.8%
25-49	36.0%
49-59	9.6%
60-64	5.9%
65-plus	18.5%

The average age in South Brevard county is 39 years. Median ages in Melbourne and Palm Bay are 35.1 and 31.7 respectively.

◆ Climate
Elevation: 6-26 feet
Annual Rainfall: 47 inches
Average Summer Temperature: 82 degrees
Average Winter Temperature: 63 degrees

Taxes

◆ Property Taxes
The following are the millage rates per $1,000 of assessed value: Melbourne – 19.6648; Palm Bay – 20.6013; Unincorporated areas surrounding Melbourne range from 18.6894 to 18.7950.

Neighboring Municipalities: Indialantic – 20.1052; Indian Harbour Beach – 18.4794 or 18.5819; Malabar – 16.7197; Melbourne Beach – 18.8552; Melbourne Village – 20.2133; Palm Shores – 17.3862; Satellite Beach – 20.1922; West Melbourne – 17.3862.

These rates include tax liabilities for the general fund, library, fire protection, law enforcement and school taxes.

◆ Sales and Use Tax
Brevard County collects a 6% sales tax levied by the State of Florida.

Voting and Elections

Brevard County

Brevard County is governed by a board of commissioners from five districts. The five commissioners are elected by single-member districts for a four-year term. A chairperson is appointed from among fellow commissioners. Every two years, either two (or three) of the district seats are up for election.

All new voters must register with the county. They are then automatically eligible to vote in federal and city elections as well.

SUPERVISOR OF ELECTIONS, Government Center, 2725 St. Johns Street, Melbourne, FL 32940

County Registration

- Titusville Courthouse, *Ph. 264-6740*
- Merritt Island Service Complex, *Ph. 455-1400*
- Brevard Service Complex, 1515 Sarno Road, Melbourne, *Ph. 255-4455*
- Government Center - Viera, 2725 St. Johns Street, Melbourne, *Ph. 633-2124*
- First Federal of Osceola, 6000 S. Babcock Street, Palm Bay, *Ph. 768-2811*

MELBOURNE. Melbourne is governed by a city council consisting of seven members, including the mayor, who are elected at-large. The mayor may reside in any part of the city, but the other six members must live in the district which they represent. Council members serve a four-year term of office. Elections are held on even numbered years, during the first Tuesday, following the first Monday, in November. Half of the district council seats become available every two years. *Ph. 727-2900.*

PALM BAY. Palm Bay is governed by a city council consisting of four members and a mayor, all of whom are elected at-large to serve a three-year term of office. Municipal elections are conducted the first Tuesday after the first Monday in November. *Ph. 952-3414.*

Pet Registration

All dogs and cats must be inoculated for rabies when they reach four months of age and be licensed by the county. Cats, as well as dogs, must wear a tag indicating the date of vaccination. Renewals are annual.

Dogs must be on a leash when not on the owner's property, unless under strict voice command (with no ifs or buts for not responding). Although the county does not have any pooper-scooper laws in effect, many communities do have regulations prohibiting defecation on public property. Pets are not permitted on any of the beaches or within most of the county parks, especially where there are picnic areas and playgrounds. They are invited, however, to a few of the county parks which have camp sites. Contact the Department of Parks and Recreation to find out which ones welcome pets.

The Humane Society of Brevard is an active organization which has several volunteer programs to assist in the care of sheltered animals. The society has a *Foster Care* program for animals who are sick or injured, as well as an *Adoption Center*. *Pet Therapy* has been a successful program which so often brings a smile to people under the weather. Dogs are brought to residents of nursing homes for weekly visits. The Humane Society publishes a newsletter which features programs, events and pet news.

Transportation

Air Travel

MELBOURNE INTERNATIONAL AIRPORT
One Air Terminal Parkway
Melbourne, FL 32901
Main Number: *Ph. 723-6227*
Security: *24 Hr. Ph. 951-3361*
Paging: *Ph. 723-2214*
Parking: *Ph. 727-7866*

The airport serves Brevard, Indian River, and St. Lucie counties. It recently underwent a $23 million expansion and renovation program. A 60-foot atrium, with tropical plants and palm trees, greets passengers in the main terminal. New concourses with sloped ramps lead to loading bridges which shelter travelers from the heat or rain. Increased ticketing and parking facilities were also part of the expansion project. Over 750,000 passengers use the airport each year. Due to the accessibility of services and the manageable size, it is a very user-friendly airport.

Beginning as a small regional facility, it achieved a new status as an international airport in 1993; it was designated as a US custom's port of entry to process international cargo. By 1995, plans include pre-cleared charter and scheduled passenger service from Canada and the Bahamas. Additional overseas routes are also on the drawing board along with plans for a federal inspection station.

Note: The Melbourne International Airport is approximately three miles from downtown Melbourne and five miles from Palm Bay.

Amenities. Amenities include services for handicapped travelers, a tourist information center, travel agency, restaurant and lounge, and a game room.

Ground Transportation. There are five car rental agencies on the airport grounds. The airport is also served by Melbourne Shuttle and Taxi, which provides door-to-door service to destinations en route to Titusville in the northern part of the county and Port St. Lucie to the south. Shuttles leave twenty minutes after each arriving flight. Reservations are only necessary for transportation to the airport. Shuttles charge a flat fare; taxi service is based on mileage. *Ph. 724-1600.*

Major Airlines include:
Continental
Delta
US Air

Commuter Carriers to destinations within Florida:
American Eagle
Comair
US Air Express
United Express

Call the airline directly for flight and passenger information.

Sea Travel

Port Canaveral is a major deep-water port of entry, providing both cargo and passenger accommodations. Premier and Carnival cruise lines offer three- and four-night trips to the Bahamas. Premier also visits the secluded Abaco Islands in the northern part of the Bahamas. SeaEscape offers a number of six-hour cruises for those interested in briefer excursions. *Ph. 783-7831.*

Local Transportation

The **Space Coast Area Transit (SCAT)** provides public transportation for Brevard county residents. The bus fleet consists of 29 wheelchair-lift-equipped vehicles and travels 20 different routes throughout the county, seven of which are within South Brevard. They run from 6 am to 6:45 pm with stops at hospitals, shopping centers, cultural institutions and senior living centers.

If you are a commuter however, do not rely on SCAT for public transportation. From 6 am to 9 am and from 3:30 pm to 6:30 pm, most of the SCAT buses are contracted to agencies, with three exceptions. SCAT provides three buses for early morning passengers. One bus departs from Palm Bay, one from Coco Beach and one from Titusville – all converge at the hub in Viera at 8 am. Similarly, the same three buses depart from Viera shortly after 5 pm en route to Palm Bay, to Coco Beach and to Titusville. For bus routing and scheduling information: *Ph. 633-1878.*

Beach shuttle service from Melbourne and Palm Bay is available to Satellite Beach on a regular basis. Call for schedule.

Special Services

- *Space Coast Commuter Assistance Program:* Provides carpool matching, ridesharing, and other driving alternatives for the single commuter. *Ph. 633-1878.*
- *Vanpool Program:* Surveys area residents for their transportation needs and matches people who are interested in carpooling, walking or bicycling with others to similar destinations. *Ph. 952-4563.*
- *Transportation Disadvantaged Program:* Serves residents who are mentally and physically handicapped or those who are transportation disadvantaged and do not have access to an automobile. Call as early as possible to make reservations. *Ph. 633-1878.*

- *Special Fares:* Senior citizens, students and handicapped individuals are entitled to use the system at half fare.

Postal Service

There are eight full service post offices in the Melbourne/Palm Bay area. All accept mail and parcels, sell stamps, and offer postal boxes. Zip code information is available through any branch. The postal system does not process U.S. passports.

Post Offices

Eau Gallie	681 St. Claire St. Monday - Friday: 8:30 am - 5:00 pm Saturday: 8:30 am - 2:00 pm	254-3433
Palm Bay	4660 Lipscomb St. Monday - Friday: 8:00 am - 5:00 pm Saturday: 8:00 am - noon	723-8838
Melbourne	640 East New Haven Monday - Friday: 8:00 am - 5:30 pm Saturday: 8:00 am - 2:00 pm	723-5135
Indialantic	200 N. Palm Ave. Monday - Friday: 8:30 am - 5:00 pm Saturday: 8:30 am - noon	723-1162
Melbourne Beach	504 Ocean Ave. Monday - Friday: 8:30 am - 5:00 pm Saturday: 9:00-noon	723-4255
Satellite Beach	210 Jackson Ave. Monday-Friday: 8:30 am - 5 pm Saturday: 8:00 am - noon	773-8306
Interchange Square	1155 Malabar Rd. Monday-Friday: 9:00 am - 4:30 pm Saturday: 10:00 am - 2:00 pm	No Phone
Sun Tree	6105 N. Wickham Rd. Monday-Friday: 7:30 am - 5:00 pm Saturday: 8:30 am - 2:00 pm	255-3406

Contract Stations

Call for services provided and hours of operation.

Ace Hardware	3221 W. New Haven	724-6510
Belk-Lindsey	Melbourne Square Mall	726-6455
Trailer Haven	1102 Salem Ave.	723-6030
Bealls Dept. Store	285 E. Eau Gallie Blvd.	773-0477

Bealls Dept. Store	5270 Babcock St. NE	951-7616
Rac's Cards & Gifts	160 Malabar Rd. #115	984-7561
Shady Oaks	6050 Babcock St. SE	952-0656

Newspapers and Magazines

FLORIDA TODAY, which had its beginnings in 1966, provides international, national and local coverage for Brevard County residents. A daily upbeat newspaper with a Sunday edition, the format is patterned after its parent Gannett newspaper, *USA Today*. Special sections include *Money Monday*, a financial and business weekly; *Lifelines*, a monthly issue with features on medical issues, healthy living and nutrition; and weekly community sections with extensive local coverage. The *Times*, which focuses on Melbourne and the *Bay Bulletin*, with its focus on Palm Bay, are published every Wednesday. They present personality profiles, community news, local happenings, classes, club/organizational meetings and upcoming events in South Brevard. The *Star Advocate* and the *Tribune* highlight community news in Titusville and Coco. *Florida Today* also publishes a variety of yearly special editions, which include *Back to School; Pools and Patios;* and the *Space Coast Fact Book*, a great resource for newcomers. Ph. 242-3500.

THE ORLANDO SENTINEL is the leading newspaper in the Orlando area. It offers extensive and comprehensive coverage of state, national, and international news and entertainment seven days a week. It does not have a bureau in Melbourne but uses assigned reporters to write about events and happenings in the local section of the Brevard edition. The *Calendar* magazine, published on Friday, reports on the movie, entertainment, and cultural events of the coming week. Ph. 639-1605.

Library System

Melbourne Library
540 E. Fee Avenue
Ph. 952-4514

The Brevard County Library System has 14 libraries, with more than 730,000 volumes in its collection. South Brevard has eight of the libraries in its domain, which includes Melbourne's main branch and its two community libraries. All are connected by an on-line computer cataloging system.

The Brevard library in Coco, situated in the central part of the county, is the largest one in the system. It has a Newsbank to locate articles from major newspapers around the country and an index of magazines articles.

The library houses an extensive genealogy collection. Volunteers from the Geneaology Society are available to assist others who are interested in learning how to trace family origins.

Through funding programs for the Humanities, the library invites authors to give readings from their own books followed by a group discussion. Another popular program is the five-week *Poetry Series:* five contemporary poets are studied through readings and commentaries presented by invited scholars. An innovative library offering for seniors, the *Older American's Discussion Group*, is an eight-week session which utilizes a reading list for discussing issues common to older Americans.

The *Summer Library Reading Program* for school age children uses a theme to encourage children to read as well as a reward incentive system. *Read the Zoo* is a five-week program. Each week, *Florida Today* publishes an article about a different zoo animal with a suggested library reading list. Students who complete the readings about the various animals are honored at a special party with invited guests, along with the residents at the zoo.

The County Reserves Program mails books to the homebound or will send a catalogue to help in the decision-making process.

The *Brevard Literacy Coalition*, sponsored by the Library System, is an advocate of adult literacy. It provides tutors for adults who either are unable to read or speak English as a second language. Volunteer teachers are trained and provided with materials for tutoring, but they are asked to stay with the program for at least one year. Ph. 633-1809.

The Melbourne Library sponsors historical programs related to Melbourne's history; films which include classic westerns as well as foreign films; poetry readings; and presentations by local authors. Children's programs include story hours and readings which make use of the library's vast collection of puppets.

The library offers meeting rooms to various community groups and clubs. Monthly newsletters alert residents to upcoming lectures, programs, and events.

Health Care

Holmes Regional Healthcare System

1350 S. Hickory Street
Melbourne
Ph. 727-7000

A not-for-profit medical/surgical complex in Melbourne, Holmes Regional Medical Center has 528 beds situated in an eight-story building. A smaller community facility is located in Palm Bay. Over 300 physicians covering 80 specialties are affiliated with the hospital. The Heart Center at Holmes provides cardiac catherization, balloon angioplasty and open heart surgery. Other medical specialties include an approved cancer care program, renal dialysis, gastroenterology, pulmonary medicine, and maternity care. Comprehensive diagnostic capabilities include full-body CAT scanning, magnetic resonance imaging, electrodiagnostic procedures and a computerized clinical laboratory. At a moment's notice, a critical transport helicopter and trained flight team are prepared to respond to referring hospitals and emergencies. To assist with day-to-day health care and exercise prescriptions, Holmes Regional has a Pro-Health & Fitness Center, monitored by a professional staff.

Resulting from a strong community commitment and educational focus, Holmes offers an ongoing lecture series covering a variety of medical topics; a *Heart-to-Heart* series with cardiologists; and a monthly newsletter, *Heartbeat*, featuring updates on medical news, health care, and community programs. In association with the South Brevard Women's Center, it coordinates and offers a program which focuses on health care and lifestyle issues for women and about women. Held twice monthly, the seminars are led by different professionals, covering a variety of topics.

Palm Bay Community Hospital

1425 Malabar Road NE, Palm Bay
Ph. 722-8000

The Palm Bay Community Hospital is an affiliate of the Holmes Regional Medical Center. As a 60-bed facility, it offers medical and surgical services with an intensive care unit. It has a full-service emergency department and also provides outpatient diagnostic services. A professional medical building with eleven physicians in eight specialties has recently opened. Being part of the Holmes medical network, the Palm Bay Community Hospital is involved in a variety of community outreach programs.

Melbourne Neurologic

1317 Oak Street
Ph. 725-5300

This is the largest neurological referral center along the eastern coast of Central Florida. Its staff of physicians specialize in the diagnosis and management of disorders affecting the spine, brain, nerves and muscles. Patients are cared for at Holmes Regional Medical Center.

Devereux Hospital & Children's Center of Florida

8000 Devereaux Drive
Ph. 242-9100

The Devereux Hospital, part of the Devereux Foundation, opened in 1988 on 50 acres in Melbourne. It is licensed as a psychiatric hospital and intensive residential treatment facility for autistic, emotionally disturbed, and multi-handicapped children and adolescents.

Community Psychiatric Center Palm Bay Hospital

4400 Dixie Highway NE, Palm Bay
Ph. 729-0500

CPC is a 35,000 square foot, 60-bed facility designed exclusively to meet the needs of adolescents who have psychiatric or chemical dependency problems. It houses a gymnasium and swimming pool for patient therapy. CPC Palm Bay offers free testing to adolescents with potential psychiatric or chemical dependency concerns.

Sea Pines Rehabilitation Hospital

101 E. Florida Avenue
Ph. 984-4600

Sea Pines is an 80-bed medical inpatient/outpatient treatment facility. Its comprehensive programs and services assist patients recovering from cancer, stroke, head injury, spinal cord injury, as well as those who are afflicted with chronic pain, neuromuscular diseases, arthritis, and other disabling conditions. Through specialized medical and therapeutic modalities, patients are helped in reaching their highest level of independent functioning.

The Easter Seal Center
3661 S. Babcock Street
Ph. 723-7280

Ventures in Living is a day-care center for physically disabled adults or those beset by early stages of Alzheimer's disease. The days are structured with activities which are therapeutic and entertaining. If medically permitted, clients may use the swimming pool facilities. The Center is staffed with a full-time nurse. There is also a special unit for individuals with more advanced cases of Alzheimer's. The fee includes door-to-door transportation and a hot lunch. The hours are from 7:30 am until 5:15 pm. Hourly rates are also available, if you need a few hours respite.

Education

BREVARD COUNTY SCHOOL BOARD
2700 St. Johns Street
Melbourne, FL 32940
Ph. 631-1911

The Brevard County School System has a population of more than 7,000 students. There are 13 elementary, six middle/junior, and four high schools in the Melbourne/Palm Bay area. Brevard County School District ranks as the 56th largest among the nation's 16,000 school systems.

◆ School Highlights
Student participation in the annual *State Science Fair* over the past several years has resulted in more than 575 awards. Language arts and mathematics are stressed in the curriculum. The 1993 National Teacher of the Year, Tracey Bailey, teaches at Satellite High School.

The school district is dedicated to computer literacy. More than 2,750 microcomputers are available to students in all grades, resulting in a ratio of one PC for every 12 students. Summer enrichment computer camps are also offered.

Elementary age children are encouraged to increase cultural awareness. An annual concert is performed by the Brevard Symphony Orchestra for all fifth grade students. The Symphony has a joint program with the Brevard School District to provide string music instruction. The Brevard Arts Council also presents concerts throughout the school district. Art exhibits at each elementary school are sponsored through Project Team, a joint effort of the school system and the Melbourne Junior League. During the summer, senior high students can enroll in the musical theater program.

To enhance an understanding of the governmental system at work, selected students from the county's high schools are invited to participate in a model student senate. One hundred students are given the opportunity to assume the role of a U.S. senator. Others serve as pages, clerks and secretaries. Research on issues, interviews with senators, and committee assignments give a large number of participants the chance to simulate the U.S. Senate in action.

The Brevard School District is responding to the critical need to build self esteem at an early age and to educate students on the effects of substance abuse. Class time has been allocated to explore these issues, beginning in kindergarten and continuing through high school.

The Brevard School Foundation raises funds to supplement tax revenues in its efforts to maintain a high standard of education. The additional financial support is applied towards creative classroom projects, student scholarships, and teacher recognition.

The school system has special programs for the learning disabled. There are also two private schools which specialize in learning disabilities, dyslexia, academic problems, and lack of motivation. Contact the Brevard Learning Clinic *(Ph. 676-3024)* and the Sylvan Learning Center *(Ph. 255-0662)* for more specific information.

UNIVERSITIES AND COLLEGES

Florida Institute of Technology is the only independent university of technology in the southeast United States. The student population of 2,800 undergraduates and 3,200 graduate students originate from 50 states and 90 countries. The educational emphasis is on the preparation for careers in engineering, science, business, psychology, aviation, communication, the humanities and pre-law.

Over 85% of the faculty hold a Ph.D. in their respective fields. Classes are small, averaging 32 students. The 175-acre campus is located in Melbourne. Student activities include fraternities and sororities, academic societies, sports participation in NCAA Division II, and a diverse number of cultural organizations representing students of Black, Chinese, Japanese, Indian, Muslim, and Caribbean origins.

Research and computer facilities include 24-hour dial-up access, 40 work stations, with MAC and IBM compatible software and PCs.

The graduate school offers doctoral degrees in 17 disciplines. The Florida Tech School of Aeronautics is one of the largest aviation operations in the world. It has its own fleet of 50 aircraft and a flight center at the Melbourne airport. *Ph.768-8000.*

The **University of Central Florida** has a Brevard Campus. State-supported, it serves the students of Brevard County who are entering their junior or senior years or enrolling in graduate programs. The program is available to students who have attained an Associate degree from Brevard Community College or wish to transfer after two years from other approved colleges and universities. The curriculum focuses on business administration, public administration, criminal justice, education, and nursing. *Ph. 632-4127.*

Brevard Community College is a two-year junior college attended by more than 15,000 students, of which almost 6,000 are enrolled at the Melbourne Campus. 'Open' campuses consisting of 13 adult educational centers are also part of their extensive outreach to more than 50,000 people each year. Their offerings include: a *University Program*, for those who want to continue their education towards the attainment of a B.A. or B.S. degree at another institution; *Technical Education,* for students who wish to earn an associate of science degree in computer programming, electronic technology, medical laboratory technology, nursing, or criminal justice; and *Vocational Education,* a series of one-year programs, such as automotive mechanics, cosmetology, horticulture, industrial electronics, welding, or practical nursing. *Ph. 254-0305.*

Rollins College has branch campuses in Rockledge and at Patrick AFB. It offers courses in the evenings and on weekends. Major fields of study include accounting, business administration, computer science, the humanities, and the social sciences. Students can earn an associate degree, a bachelor of arts degree, or a bachelor of science degree while working. *Ph. 632-9575.*

Barry University, based in Miami, has a Brevard County branch campus. It offers programs for working adults in both business and the liberal arts. Credits are awarded for work experience. *Ph. 453-6253.*

Phillips Junior College, in Melbourne, offers a two-year associate degree and six non-degree programs such as accounting, secretarial skills, and tourism. *Ph. 254-6459.*

The Cultural Scene

Maxwell C. King Center for the Performing Arts

Brevard's Performing Arts Center has a 2,000-seat theater which can be converted into either a 1,200-seat or an 800-seat theater for smaller events. A dynamic season of entertainment includes touring Broadway musicals and comedy, classical and pops concerts, opera, dance companies, vocalists, and popular artists. Theatergoers can mix and match to create their own subscription series of any four performances. The Black Box Experimental Theater, with 250 seats, showcases new plays and aspiring writers to the community.

Prior to a performance in the main theater, the Black Box Theater offers a pre-theater dinner buffet with live music and a cash bar.

The Center for the Performing Arts is also used as a facility to teach music, dance, theater and art. Available for community use, it has two dance studios, rehearsal halls, classrooms, and workshops for art and ceramics. 3865 N. Wickham Rd. Melbourne. *Ph. 242-2219.*

The Hennegar Center

The Hennegar Center, the oldest public building in the county, was constructed in 1919 as a school for third-sixth grade students. Through restoration and refurbishing, it has been renewed with a 1920's motif. Noted Broadway stage designer, Peter Feller remodeled the old school auditorium, which can seat 500 guests. During the year, the Melbourne Civic Theater, a resident theater, performs a series of six professionally directed plays. Touring companies are also invited to stage off-Broadway productions and other forms of entertainment in the Hennegar Theater.

In celebration of Black History month, a program of Negro spirituals and choral music are presented for a week in February. Black artists from Brevard and neighboring counties are invited to showcase their work in the Center's exhibition gallery. During the year, the Hennegar Center invites artists from the Artist's Forum to exhibit their works, which are also for sale. The exhibition changes every six weeks.

The Children's Theater Program, designed for students in elementary school, presents curriculum-based theater performances. This has proven to be an effective and innovative learning strategy. The Hennegar Center also sponsors a summer circus camp for children in sixth and seventh grades. Professionally trained staff teach unicyling, juggling, face painting, and clowning during the one week program.

The Hennegar Center actively promotes Brevard's community arts and civic organizations, providing space for classes, meetings and seminars of community interest. *625 E. New Haven. Ph. 407-723-8698.*

Melbourne Civic Theater

The Melbourne Civic Theater (formerly the Indian River Players) has been in the community since 1952. The actors who audition for each show are from the local area. During the theater season, six productions selected from well-known musicals, mysteries or comedies are staged at the Hennegar Center. Seven performances of each show are presented during two consecutive weekends. In addition to the main theater series, a special Christmas show is performed in celebration of the holiday; a special summer production extends the season and two extra seasonal shows keep theater patrons busy throughout the year.

A small, upstairs Black Box Theater permits more intimate and avant guard plays. Each year, the Civic Theater hosts a playwright competition which is juried by a panel of judges from the theater arts. The winning play is casted and performed by the Melbourne Civic Theater. *Hennegar Center, 625 E. New Haven. Ph. 723-1668.*

Phoenix Production Company

The Phoenix Production Company is a small, non-equity community theater group. A variety of seven contemporary plays, each scheduled for six weeks, are performed. Its repertoire includes dramas, musicals, comedies, and mysteries. The small and intimate 93-seat theater creates a sense of involvement between the actors and the audience. *817 E. Strawbridge Ave. Ph. 952-5717.*

Brevard Symphony Orchestra

The Symphony, which began in 1954, has been a mainstay of the Brevard community, presenting concerts in the north, central and south parts of the county. It performs a five-concert series in Melbourne's Maxwell C. King Center for the Performing Arts each season. Four of the concerts are classical and the fifth, a pops performance. Nationally recognized guest performers often appear with the Symphony. Before each concert, the conductor or associate conductor presents a lecture on the musical selections which will be played during the program. The musical director and principal conductor, Kypros Markou, has been with the Symphony since 1986. During his career, he has appeared as a guest conductor for symphonies, opera companies and dance ensembles throughout the United States. *1500 Highland Ave. Ph. 242-2024; 242-2219.*

The Symphony Guild has a very active membership and hosts many social events to support the symphony.

Melbourne Municipal Band

A gathering of volunteer musicians from diverse professions perform for residents free-of-charge, year-round. Formed in 1965 with only 16 members, the Melbourne Band presently has approximately 80 musicians. It has performed hundreds of concerts over the years with performances in Brussels, Belgium and Amsterdam. It enjoys a full and active season, averaging 33 concerts annually. During the summer, a Concert in the Park series is presented on Sunday afternoons. The band also offers music classes to all age groups. *Ph. 724-0555.*

Brevard Art Center and Museum

BACAM is a visual arts and cultural center with six exhibition galleries. The Museum exhibits art from all media, all styles, and all periods. It has more than 4,000 pieces in its permanent holdings with an impressive antiquities collection of Asian and Egyptian decorative arts. It also has the largest body of work by Ernst Oppler, a turn-of-the-century German printmaker.

During the year, it hosts 8-12 exhibitions, including contemporary works by well-known artists on loan from other museums around the country. Curated shows and traveling exhibitions are featured in the main galleries. BACAM actively supports the local and regional art community through museum exhibitions, sponsorship of juried shows, and the purchase of works by Florida artists.

In keeping with its mission to be a community-based museum, it offers several programs to develop or enhance an interest in art. Museum docents give tours of the different galleries on a daily basis. A *Brown Bag Lecture Series*, which is held once a month, invites artists affiliated with the current exhibition to discuss the the works from historical, artistic and personal perspectives. The *Art History Series* presents monthly lectures on Sundays. *Museum Mondays*, sponsored by the Museum Guild, invites different speakers to address the group on a variety of interesting subjects, ranging from assessing the value of your antiques to gourmet cooking.

BACAM's art school is in an adjacent building and houses four large studios for the study of art. A full painting studio, a ceramics studio, a photography studio with black/white and color darkrooms, and an all-purpose art studio provide space for the five-week programs offered during the day, evening and also weekend workshops. Children's programs include after-school classes and a summer art camp.

The Museum hosts many social activities for its members as well as monthly trips to different museums in Florida. Call for a calendar of events. *1463 North Highland Ave. Ph. 242-0737.*

The *Artists Forum of BACAM* is a cohesive group of artists working in all media under the umbrella of the Museum. They schedule various exhibitions during the year and play an active part in the community.

Space Coast Science Center

The SCSC has a touch and feel, user-friendly series of exhibits for young and old. The Nature Room is a rent-free domicile for live animals, such as baby sea turtles, frogs, tarantulas, and a variety of snakes in their natural habitat.

The Exhibit Room showcases four exhibitions each year which explore a facet of science. On permanent exhibit are hair-raising generators, computer games, and holograms which encourage discovery as well as observation. A radio station for ham operators becomes active during a space launch.

With a strong commitment to community outreach, SCSC offers many entertaining and educational programs for children. Favorite ones include *Electricity and How it Works*, featuring Dr. Zapp; *Air Amazing*, a discussion on gases and molecules; *Creepy Crawlies*, a puppet show with creepy insects; and *What's For Dinner*, an exercise which allows children to become part of the food chain. Call the Space Coast Science Center for a calendar of their exhibitions and monthly programs. *1510 Highland Ave. Ph. 259-5572.*

Brevard Cultural Alliance

The Cultural Alliance provides an array of services to artists, cultural organizations and the Brevard community. A monthly publication, Art-A-Fact, features a cultural calendar of events and spotlights various cultural groups and happenings in the area. The magazine is free with membership. *2725 St. Johns Street. Ph. 690-6817.*

Events and Attractions

Space Coast Art League Spring Festival

The Space Coast Art League Spring Festival is held the second weekend in February. This is an invitational and juried exhibit of more than 200 artists working in all artistic media and includes paintings; bronze, glass & wood sculptures and objects of art; jewelry; ceramics; and photography. *Atlantic Plaza, Satellite Beach.*

Melbourne Art Festival

The Melbourne Art Festival, held in April, is a two-day gala event which attracts over 60,000 people to historic downtown Melbourne. Approximately 250 artists participate in this juried show; prizes are awarded to the best works in each of eight categories. Entertainment is provided on a continuous basis, featuring different musical and dance groups. *KidsWorld*, an entertainment and activity center, features lively performances and craft projects for kids. A 5K *Flamingo Run* takes participants over the scenic Melbourne Causeway, returning in time to join in for a sampling of tasty delights from local restaurants. For those who dare 'to let it all hang out,' the *Flamingo Fling* is a Mardi Gras-style parade and costume contest for the uninhibited.

Brevard Porcelain Artists Exhibition

Brevard Porcelain Artists present their works at the Eau Gallie Civic Center in Melbourne during the last weekend in October. There are more than 30 member artists who participate. This is the largest porcelain show on Florida's east coast. Artisan pieces are all hand-signed and registered.

Botanical Gardens at Florida Institute of Technology

The gardens consist of 146 acres, featuring more than 300 species of ferns, palms, and other tropical foliage. Visitors walk along a one-mile paved trail as they explore Florida botany. The entrance to the garden is a one-room schoolhouse, the oldest in the county, which was built in 1883. The gardens may be enjoyed free of charge from dawn to dusk. *Florida Tech-Melbourne Campus. Babcock St. Entrance. Ph. 768-8000, ext. 6119.*

Brevard Zoo

The Brevard Zoo is a new and exciting face in the community. It has been designed as a geographical zoo with the animals arranged according to their home of origin rather than species. The Latin American Loop has an elevated walkway with animal enclosures along the shady tropical boardwalk. Jaguars, llamas, monkeys, giant ant eaters and exotic birds live in this Latin American community.

Paws On, an animal study zone, is an interactive learning center for both adults and children. There are five themes which focus on animal life: their homes, food, physiology, senses, and life styles. A multilevel ramp leads to different exhibits. Playgrounds for learning include a giant spider web which children can explore. At the top of the web is a kiosk with colorful graphs and information about spiders. Another exhibit features a play area which is a simulated bee's honeycomb. A kiosk at the top of the honeycomb presents information about bees. A re-creation of an eagle's nest has a telescope which allows you to see through the eyes of an eagle. Or, you may want to test your arm strength against that of an ape.

An *Animal Encounter Area* permits touching and petting of the zoo's miniature horses, goats, ferrets, and prairie dogs.

The mission of the Brevard zoo is to be an interactive playground and science center – to provide entertainment as it educates. Its expansion program calls for various stages of development. *Native Florida Exhibits* will be the next project, followed by an *Australian Aviary*. The last phase to be developed will be its habitat for African and Asian animals. *8225 N. Wickham Road. Exit 73 off I-95. Ph. 254-9453.*

Turtle Creek Sanctuary

Turtle Creek Sanctuary is a 60-acre property in the heart of Palm Bay. Visitors walk along an elevated boardwalk which passes through four different plant communities; view protected endangered species; and enjoy the tranquility of this "outdoor theater of environmental entertainment." A jogging trail and canoe dock are located within the Sanctuary. Guided tours can be arranged. *Ph. 952-3433.*

Wildlife Photography

If you enjoy 'shooting' wildlife, a visit to the Merritt Island National Wildlife Refuge is a must for photographers. Bird watching is another favorite activity, given the many different species which call it home. The refuge was created to protect endangered species and the wildlife of the area. There are both self-guided walking tours and driving tours into the park. Don't be surprised by the activity in the area; the Kennedy Space Center is its well-known neighbor. *Ph. 861-0667.*

NASA Kennedy Space Center: Spaceport USA

Spaceport USA at the NASA Kennedy Space Center showcases the history of our space program. In addition to the many models and displays at the Visitor's Center, such as samples of moon rock, Spaceport USA opened an exhibit which allows you to climb aboard a simulated space shuttle and visit the crew's living quarters. A two-hour guided bus tour visits different areas in the complex from the pads where the moon missions are launched to the sites where the astronauts train. Your space journey is not complete without experiencing the breathtaking IMAX viewing of *The Dream Is Alive* and *Blue Planet* on the IMAX 5 1/2-story panoramic screen. Through advanced cinematic technology, the viewer is swept into the action of the space flight. Plan to spend a total of six hours if you want to 'do it all' in one day. *Ph. 452-2121.*

U.S. Astronauts Hall of Fame

Nearby to Spaceport USA is the United States Astronaut Hall of Fame. Our first seven space heroes of the Mercury project are showcased in the museum. The exhibits reveal the story of their hopes, fears and accomplishments. The U.S. Space Camp for children is also housed in the same facility. Visitors can watch youngsters, who are participating in a five-day program, experiencing hands-on training as "future" astronauts. *Ph. 269-6100.*

Don't Miss

Turtle Watches. The largest sea turtle nesting area in the U.S. is located between Melbourne Beach and Sebastian Inlet. Annually between May and August, sea turtles come ashore during the evening hours to lay their eggs. This is an opportunity to see the giant leatherbacks, greens, and loggerheads, which are among the endangered species. Moonlight beach walks take on a new meaning in Melbourne.

Manatee Sightings. Crane Creek Promenade, located along part of Melbourne Avenue in the historic downtown area, is the popular spot for watching the much loved manatees. A 10-foot-wide boardwalk lined with oak trees, sabal palms, and decorative benches attract many nature lovers, especially at night with its uniquely lit setting.

Airboat Tour. Treat yourself to an airboat ride at Camp Holly on the St. Johns River in Melbourne. A 35-minute guided tour across seven miles of waterway presents a panorama of gators, wildlife, birds, and plants with interesting narrations about the area. *Three miles west of Interstate 95 and U.S. 192. Ph. 723-2179.*

Bargain Shopping. Bargain shopping at the Super Flea and Farmers Market begins on Friday and continues through Sunday from 9 am-4 pm. An open-air market with approximately 800 stalls, it sells everything from antiques and collectibles to farm ripe edibles. *The market is located on Eau Gallie Blvd., just west of Interstate 95. Ph. 242-9124.*

Leisure Saturdays & Sundays. Visiting the other towns in South Brevard County is a great way to spend a leisurely weekend day, year-round. Fifth Avenue in Indialantic is home to many specialty shops and a boardwalk stroll adds to the trip. Antiquing in downtown Eau Gallie on Highland Avenue is fun for those who enjoy wonderful relics. Others take pleasure in spending time along the 652-foot pier jutting into the Indian River at Melbourne Beach.

Recreation

Baseball

The Florida Marlins will train at Viera in a new complex, which includes a 7,500-seat stadium and five practice fields. February to April will take on new meaning for Melbourne sports fans as the Marlins and visiting teams 'play ball' during the spring training season.

Boating

Choose between the scenic Intracoastal or the rockier Atlantic. Public boating areas are found in Melbourne at Ballard Park, Eau Gallie Causeway, and Front Street Park; in Palm Bay, boating sites include Alex Goode Park, Fred Lee Park, and Pollark Park. Other public facilities are located in Grant, North Melbourne, and South Melbourne Beach. Contact the Greater South Brevard Chamber of Commerce for information on marina facilities. *Ph. 724-5400.*

Boaters should visit Pelican Island and Grange Islands, accessible only by boat, to see some interesting birds and wildlife. The endangered brown pelican nests on Pelican Island, but no foot access is permitted. Visiters are invited to explore the Grange Islands and to camp out there. Docking is available at no charge.

Sailboarding or windsurfing enthusiasts enjoy both the steady winds along the Indian River and the challenge of the Sebastian Outlet. Shops along the beaches rent equipment and also offer lessons.

Fishing

Deep sea fishing in the area can put dolphin, grouper, mackerel, snapper, and wahoo into your refrigerator – and marlin and sailfish on your trophy wall! Pier casters can look for flounder, snapper, trout, whiting, bluefish (spring and fall), and sea bass (late summer and early fall). Surf fishing usually puts channel bass, pompano, whiting and Spanish mackerel into the basket. During the spring and fall, bluefish, snook, and sea bass may be spotted.

Licenses are required for saltwater and freshwater fishing if you are between the ages of 15 and 65. *Melbourne: Ph. 242-6506; Palm Bay: 942-4540.*

Golf

There are many private and public courses in South Brevard County. Following is a list of the public courses.

Harbor City Municipal Course
2750 Lake Washington Road
Melbourne
An 18-hole, 7,025-yard championship course with par 72. Facilities include a driving range, club rentals, lessons, and pro shop. *Ph. 255-4606.*

Melbourne Municipal Golf Course
475 New Haven Avenue
An 18-hole, 6,026-yard course with par 71. Facilities include a driving range, club rentals, lessons, and pro shop. *Ph. 723-3565.*

Spessard Holland Golf Course
2374 Oak Street
Melbourne Beach
An 18-hole, 5,136-yard course with par 67, designed by Arnold Palmer. Facilities include a driving range, club rentals, lessons, pro shop and restaurant. *Ph. 952-4529.*

Habitat Golf Course
3591 Fairgreen Road
Valkaria (South of Palm Bay)
An 18-hole, 6,800-yard course with par 72. This championship course is situated on 200 acres. Facilities include a driving range, putting green, club rentals, lessons, and pro shop. *Ph. 952-6312.*

Surfing

Melbourne/Palm Bay is known by surfers as the "small wave capital of the U.S."

Surfers gather for the annual Easter and Labor Day surfing festivals held in Melbourne each year. Pro-surfers compete for prizes and challenges.

Tennis

Courts are available at the following locations. Call to find out if there is a fee for using the courts.

- Hoover Junior High School in Indialantic: *Ph. 952-4524*
- The Pines in Indian Harbor Beach: *Ph. 773-2000*
- Crane Field in Melbourne: *no phone*
- Fee Avenue Tennis Courts in Melbourne: *Ph. 727-2985*
- Melbourne High School: *Ph. 952-5880*
- Driskell Park Court in Palm Bay: *Ph. 952-3400*
- Roach Park Court in Palm Bay: *Ph. 952-3400*

Beaches

Along the 33 miles of South Brevard's coastline lie excellent areas, both busy and private, to sun, swim and surf.

Bicentennial Park, Indian Harbor Beach, U.S. A1A, *Ph. 773-0552*
Amenities: Free parking; boardwalk; volleyball; picnic facilities; snack bar.

Canova Beach Park, Eau Gallie Blvd. (east end), *Ph. 952-4580*
Amenities: Free parking; mobile concessions; dune crossover; covered pavilion with seating; picnic facilities.

James H. Nance Park, Indialantic, U.S. A1A, *Ph. 723-2242*
Amenities: Free parking; dune crossover; children's playground; volleyball; picnic facilities; snack bar.

Paradise Beach Park, Indialantic (North), U.S. A1A, *Ph. 952-4580*
Amenities: Free parking; volleyball.

Spessard Holland Park, Melbourne Beach, U.S. AIA, *Ph. 773-6458*
Spessard Holland Park has North and South Beach Areas.
Amenities: Free parking; dune crossover; mobile concessions; covered pavilions; picnic tables but no grills.

Directory of Services

9-1-1 Emergency Only	POLICE • SHERIFF • FIRE • MEDICAL • RESCUE	

AGENCY	DESCRIPTION	BREVARD (407)
ALCOHOL & DRUG ABUSE	Intervention & Referral Alco-hall Adult Children of Alcoholic & Dysfunctional Families	800-252-6465 632-5958 636-0880
CRISIS HOTLINE	24 Hour Help Line	631-8944
ABUSE CENTER:	Spouse Abuse & Domestic Assault Shelter for Abused Women	631-2764
POISON CONTROL & INFORMATION CENTER		800-282-3171
TEEN HOTLINE		631-4300
TIME/TEMPERATURE		725-4636

County Services

AGENCY	DESCRIPTION	BREVARD (407)
GOVERNMENT CENTER	2725 St. Johns Street Melbourne	633-2000
PUBLIC INFORMATION	Information & Referral	264-5200
ANIMAL CONTROL		633-1765
BOARD OF EDUCATION		631-1911
COUNTY COOPERATIVE EXTENSION		952-4536
COUNTY COURTHOUSE		952-4606
EMERGENCY MGMT	Disaster Readiness Training & Evacuation Information	633-1770
FIRE PREVENTION		633-2138
FL. HIGHWAY PATROL	All Interstate Roads & Turnpikes	690-3900
GARBAGE COLLECTION		633-2041
LIBRARY		633-1792

196   Melbourne

LICENSES	Auto Tag	255-4410
	Parking Permit - Handicapped	
	Boating Registration	
	Fishing & Hunting	
MASS TRANSIT	General Information	633-2019
	Bus Route Information	633-1878
PARKS AND RECREATION		633-2046
PASSPORT INFORMATION		264-5283
PROPERTY APPRAISER		255-4440
SHERIFF		632-2511
TAX COLLECTOR		255-4453
TRAFFIC VIOLATION INFORMATION	Contact Clerk of County Court	952-4604
VOTER REGISTRATION		255-4455
WATER/SEWER		633-2093
Emergency/After Hours		455-1338

Human Services

AGENCY	DESCRIPTION	BREVARD (407)
AMERICAN ASSOC. OF RETIRED PERSONS (AARP)	Florida State Headquarters Provides source for local contact	813-576-1155
AMERICAN RED CROSS	Hurricane Shelter Information Disaster Relief, Blood Banks, Educational Programs	723-7141
CHILD CARE ASSOC.	Information & Referrals on: Licensed Child Care Centers & Registered Family Care Providers	636-6613
	Before and After School Care	636-4948
INFORMATION & REFERRAL SVCE: UNITED WAY	Connects You with the Appropriate Person or Agency Who Can Answer Your Question or Assist You With A Particular Need	631-2740
HANDICAPPED/DISABLED SERVICES		633-6182
HEALTH DEPARTMENT		633-2015
I R S	Location & Hours of Local Offices	800-829-1040
	Tax Information	904-354-1760
	Tax Forms	800-829-3676

Directory of Services 197

MENTAL HEALTH INFORMATION		
CIRCLES OF CARE		723-3910
PARENTS STRESS LINE		631-8944
NEWCOMERS CLUBS		452-5583
SENIOR CITIZEN SVCS	Information / Assistance *Programs for Seniors*	631-2747
SOCIAL SECURITY		800-772-1213
SOCIAL SERVICE TRANSPORTATION	Reduced Fares, Dial-A-Ride Transport for Seniors & Special Groups	
SPACE COAST AREA TRANSIT		633-2019
HARBOR CITY VOLUNTEER AMBULANCE SQUAD		723-8480
UNITED WAY	An Excellent Resource for Community Information	631-2740
VETERAN'S ASSISTANCE		633-2012
VOLUNTEER CENTER	A Clearinghouse for Volunteer Positions	631-2740
RETIRED SENIOR VOLUNTEER PROGRAM (RSVP)		984-0479
WOMEN'S RESOURCE CENTER		727-2200

City Numbers

GOVERNMENT CENTER Information Desk	Melbourne City Hall 900 E. Strawbridge Avenue	727-2900
CITY CLERK		727-2901 Ext. 255
POLICE (Non Emergency)		259-1211
FIRE (Non Emergency)		255-4601
ELECTRICAL SERVICE	FL Power & Light	631-2000
GARBAGE COLLECTION		727-2901 Ext. 302
LIBRARY		952-4514
PARKS & RECREATION		952-4580
TELEPHONE COMPANY	Southern Bell	780-2355
VOTER'S REGISTRATION		255-4455
WATER & SEWER Emergency/After Hours		727-2900 255-4622

Civic Organizations

South Brevard Chamber of Commerce	724-5400
Brevard Economic Development Council	242-1800
Brevard Convention & Visitors Bureau	724-5400
Community Services Council	639-8770

Orlando

Behind the magic and glamour of Walt Disney World, entertainment parks, and vacation resorts, there is another Orlando which is more subdued and sophisticated. It is the Orlando where people live, work and raise their children. A high quality of life with affordable housing, cutting edge and innovative educational programs, and a dynamic and diversified economy are attracting families to the area. In addition to the continuing expansion of the tourism and entertainment industries, Metro Orlando has become one of the fastest growing high technology centers in the country. Manufacturing, warehouse/distribution, agribusiness, regional headquarters operations, and international business operations also provide a major contribution to the economy. Orlando's international business climate has attracted people from all over the world introducing many different cultures into the Orlando community.

Picturing Orlando today, it is difficult to imagine it 150 years ago when the city was little more than a soldier's campsite. Orlando's history dates back to the end of the Seminole War when Aaron Jernigan staked a claim on the land in 1842. According to legend, the community, which was called Jernigan, was later changed to Orlando's Grave in honor of Orlando Reeves. Reeves, a U.S. soldier on night guard, was killed by an Indian while protecting the campsite of his scouting party. In 1857, the name was again changed from Orlando's Grave to Orlando when it was deeded to the county. It was not until 1875 that it was given official status as an incorporated city with one square mile and 85 residents. In the late 1800's, the establishment of citrus groves and the arrival of the railroad brought growth to the area as it became a trade center. Although Orlando's citrus industry and land development had a major impact on its economy, it wasn't until the opening of Walt Disney World in 1971 that Orlando's growth skyrocketed.

Orlando's program for growth management may be a model for future cities in America. As Orlando continues to develop, the city will expand beyond its downtown infrastructure, with nodes or centers of population and business activity away from the hub. With careful planning of highway expansion, road construction, land development and housing, many of the surrounding areas will become centers of activity. City planners have a vision for growth extending into the 21st century.

Demographics

◆ Size
The Orlando Metropolitan Statistical Area includes Orange, Seminole, Osceola, and Lake Counties. Orange County encompasses 910 square miles; Seminole County is 298 square miles; Osceola County is 1,350 square miles; and Lake County is 1,163 square miles. The city of Orlando has an area of 43 square miles.

◆ Population
Orange County has a population of 701,292 residents. Its 13 municipalities contain approximately 55% of the total population.

City	Population
Apopka	14,283
Bay Lake	21
Belle Isle	5,543
Eatonville	2,208
Edgewood	1,055
Lake Buena Vista	24
Maitland	9,104
Oakland	707
Ocoee	14,220
Orlando	168,456
Windermere	1,631
Winter Garden	10,392
Winter Park	22,265

Bay Lake and Lake Buena Vista are two incorporated cities within the Disney domain. Although both have governing bodies, there are few actual residents. The incorporated areas of Orange County have a total population of 249,909; the unincorporated areas contain 451,383 people.

Neighboring Counties	
Seminole County	298,057
Lake County	157,061
Osceola County	114,411

Source: University of Florida, Bureau of Business and Economic Research Population Studies.

◆ Age Demographics of Orange County

0-14	20.7 %
15-24	15.9 %
25-44	34.8 %
45-64	17.8 %
65 and over	10.8 %

The median age in Orange County is 31.5. Within the four-county area, Lake County has the largest 65 and over population (27.7%).

Source: Florida Consensus Estimating Conference
Population & Demographic Forecasting, Spring 1992

◆ Climate
Elevation: 106 feet
Annual Rainfall: 52.35 inches
Average Summer Temperature: 82 degrees
Average Winter Temperature : 60.7 degrees

Taxes

◆ Property Taxes
The unincorporated areas of Orange County have an average millage rate between 19.0 and 20.0 per $1,000 of assessed property value. The City of Orlando has a millage rate of 21.0, which provides revenues for both county and municipal services.

County millages for the incorporated cities, which range from 14.6 to 16.1, are combined with the following municipal millage rates: Apopka - 3.5359; Belle Isle - 3.4168; Eatonville - 6.6950; Edgewood - 3.4; Maitland - 3.9; Ocoee - 4.0; Windermere - 2.0; Winter Garden - 3.804; Winter Park - 3.728.

◆ Sales and Use Tax
Orange County collects a 6% sales and use tax levied by the State of Florida.

Voting and Elections

To facilitate voter registration, Orange County offers numerous voter registration sites throughout the area. To obtain the locations of the participating banks and businesses offering this service, call the County Supervisor of Elections.

Supervisor of Elections, 119 W. Kaley Street, Orlando, FL 32806.

Orange County. There are six county commissioners and a county chairperson elected for a four-year term of office. The commissioners are elected by the residents of the district in which they reside. The chairperson, however, is elected at-large by the entire county. *Ph. 836-2070.*

Orlando. The City of Orlando is governed by six city commissioners and a mayor/commissioner for a four-year term of office. Each of the six districts elects a commissioner who must reside in that district; the mayor is elected at-large. The elections occur on the first Tuesday, after the first Monday, in September. If run-offs are necessary, they take place on the first Tuesday, after the first Monday, in October. *Ph. 246-2251.*

Note: Both city and county elections are held every two years, at which time half of the district seats become available.

Neighboring Municipalities have a mayor/council form of government. Contact the municipality for specific election dates which vary from city to city.

Pet Registration

All dogs and cats over four months of age must be inoculated for rabies. Pet owners must show proof of vaccination each year in order to register their pets and obtain a county license tag. Dogs are not allowed to roam, but cats have more freedom. If a cat, however, poses a nuisance such as property damage, soiling property or unwelcome visitations, the county will investigate and intervene to curb the behavior. Dogs must be on a leash, unless in clear sight of the owner and responsive to voice commands. When you purchase or adopt a dog, you must also buy a pooper-scooper. Violations can lead to citations if pet owners do not comply with county regulations.

Orange County Animal Services plays an active role in controlling the animal population through its spay and neuter clinic and encouraging all animal owners to spay and neuter cats and dogs by reducing fees for license tags. They also have an adoption program for stray, homeless, or unclaimed animals. Community education programs, which focus on issues related to animal care, are offered free of charge. *Ph. 352-4390.*

The Orlando Humane Society is a private, non-profit organization which shelters unwanted pets and finds adoptive parents for orphaned animals. Their unusually high adoption rate is a reflection of their proactive approach and innovative strategies. Five to six days a week a mobile adoption unit brings 'adoptable' animals to various sites in the community. *Pet Smart*, a warehouse of pet supplies, provides the Humane Society with off-site adoption centers at their locations. *Pet Talk*, a bimonthly newsletter, discusses pet news, programs and upcoming events. There are many volunteer activities for those who wish to become involved with the Society. *Ph. 351-7722.*

Transportation

Air Travel

ORLANDO INTERNATIONAL AIRPORT
One Airport Boulevard
Tampa, FL 32827-4399
Main Number: *Ph. 825-2001*
Information Center: 7 am - 11 pm, 7 days a week: *Ph. 825-2352*
Passenger Page Service & 24 Hr. *Ph. 825-2000*
Parking Information: *Ph. 825-2458*

As one approaches the Orlando International Airport, a subtropical setting of lush foliage and waterways comes into view. The interior was designed to simulate a Florida landscape with its use of plants, skylights and wide, open areas. Dramatizing the space and presenting a venue for public art is a major collection of large-scale paintings, sculptures and fiber works. Orlando International Airport is one of the state's largest public art galleries of contemporary fine art. Todd Warner, a Florida artist, was commissioned to design an identification system for the parking garages. Different Florida critters come to life with artistry and humor on each of the levels of the garage, providing a quick and easy association for locating parked cars. Inside the terminal, the space is designed for efficiency. Walking distances are minimized. A traveler walks less than 850 feet before moving sidewalks, escalators or elevators lend an assist. A central landside terminal services three airside boarding centers. The automated transit system connects the landside building to each of the airside terminals with high-speed elevated trams.

The Orlando International Airport, which opened in 1981, is ranked as the 18th busiest airport in the United States and 28th in the world. It is one of the major hubs, with 23 scheduled airlines and over 40 charters providing direct service to more than 100 cities worldwide. With designs to accommodate future technology and growth, plans have been unveiled for Worldport 2000, a vision of OIA in the 21st century. The next generation of airplanes will be sub-orbital, hypersonic aircraft. A flight from Orlando to San Francisco will take 39 minutes. OIA, in preparing to be a hub for both conventional and sub-orbital flights, has the land to expand its facilities and develop the runways to accommodate future aircraft.

Note: Orlando International Airport is approximately 10 miles from downtown Orlando.

Ground Transportation. Airport Limousine *(Ph. 423-5566)* and Transtar *(Ph. 856-7777)* provide a full range of transportation services, including stretch limos, luxury sedans, shuttle vans and buses. Ashtin Leasing, Town & Country and Yellow Cab provide taxi service.

Public Transit. Buses depart from the airport en route to the downtown bus terminal beginning at 6:30 am and continue until 11 pm. Airport service from the downtown terminal begins at 5:45 am and continues until 10:45 pm. Service is hourly, seven days a week. Call for exact schedule. Lynx also has service between the airport and Altemonte Springs. *Ph. 841-8240.*

Amenities. OIA provides many amenities for its passengers, including a bank and 24-hour automatic teller machines; postal service; Western Union and wire transfer; Florida State Lottery; and business centers with conference rooms and fax/copier machines. For the traveler who needs temporary storage space, there are four self service locker locations.

Handicapped passengers have easy wheelchair access, wide elevators, ramps, and wheelchair-height drinking fountains. Special amenities include Braille-signed elevator controls, TDD and amplified telephones, and audio visual information systems.

Major Airlines include:
Aeropostal (Venezuela)
All Nippon Airways, ANA (Japan)
American Airlines
American Trans Air
America West Airlines
Braniff International
British Airways
Comair
Continental Airline

Delta Airlines
Icelandair
LTU (Germany)
KLM (Amsterdam)
Northwest Airlines
TransBrasil Airlines
TWA
USAir
United Airlines
Virgin Atlantic

Commuter Service includes:
Gulfstream International Airlines:
  Daily non-stop flights to Vero Beach.
Paradise Island Airlines:
  Weekly flights to Paradise Islands, Bahamas

Local Transportation

Bus Service. LYNX, a tri-county public transit system, services Orange, Seminole and Osceola Counties with its colorful jewel-toned fleet. The name of the transit system is not an acronym but rather an image, representing the fast moving cat. There are presently 134 buses covering 40 different routes. They operate seven days a week, with a reduced schedule on the weekends. Downtown Orlando, with its 24-bay transit center, is the main terminal.

According to the LYNX five-year plan (1992-1997), the transit system will expand to four times its present size with 500 buses in the system. Anticipating the growth and transit needs of the tri-county area, the five-year plan includes the development of numerous regional transit centers. Within each of these hubs, buses will circulate in the local community and bring passengers to central feeder points. The system is similar to the hub and spoke network employed by the airlines. Express service is also on the drawing board. Commuters will drive to Park 'n Ride points and then board an express bus which travels along the expressway en route to downtown Orlando and major business areas.

If you do not want to drive to work, call LYNX and ask about their computerized van pooling program. It eliminates much of the hassle and expense of driving to work.

FreeBee Downtown Shuttle Service. The FreeBee is a convenient and free way to get around downtown Orlando. Buses run every five minutes on this 15-minute round-trip route. "Buzz" stops are located along Orange Avenue and Rosalind Avenue between Concord and Anderson Streets.

Special Services. There are reduced fares for students, seniors and handicapped people. Ask about the Advantage Pass, which may be purchased monthly.

A+ Link. The A+ Link is a special transportation service for folks who are unable to use the regular bus system due to a documented medical problem. It provides door-to-door service for individuals who need transportation from home to a medical facility. You must call a day in advance to schedule a ride. *Ph. 841-2279.*

Routing Information: A dispatcher is on duty Monday - Friday, 6:30 am to 6:30 pm; Saturday, 7:30 am to 6:00 pm; and Sunday, 8:00 am to 4:00 pm. *Ph. 841-8240.*

Postal Service

The branches and the stations carry on full service postal activities. The annex operations do not have any customer service operations.

Post Offices

Main Office	10401 Tradeport Drive Open: 24 Hours/7 Days	850-6200
Alafaya Annex	1000 N. Alafaya Tr.	384-7175
Azalea Park Branch	501 N. Semoran Blvd. Monday - Friday: 9:00 am - 5:00 pm Saturday: 9:00 am - noon	275-1830
College Park Station	1705 Edgewater Drive Monday - Friday: 8:30 am - 5:00 pm Saturday: 9:00 am - 1:00 pm	425-1525
Colonialtown Station	611 N. Mills Avenue Monday - Friday: 9:00 am - 5:00 pm Saturday: 9:00 am - 1:00 pm	896-2147
Dixie Village Station	2860 Delaney Avenue Monday - Friday: 8:30 am - 5:00 pm Saturday: 9:00 am - noon	843-1088
Downtown Station	46 E. Robinson Street Monday - Friday: 8:00 am - 5:00 pm Saturday: 9:00 am - noon	843-5673

Herndon Station	821 Herndon Avenue Monday - Friday: 8:30 am - 5:00 pm Saturday: Closed	894-3941
Hiawassee Branch	3200 N. Hiawassee Road Monday - Friday: 10:00 am - 6:00 pm Saturday: 9:00 am - noon	293-3296
Lee Vista Annex	6301 Hazeltine Ntl. Drive Monday - Friday: 9:00 am - 5:00 pm Saturday: 9:00 am - noon	240-9496
Lockhart Branch	7214 Edgewater Drive Monday - Friday: 9:00 am - 5:00 pm Saturday: 9:00 am - noon	293-2681
Orange Blossom Station	440 S. Orange Blossom Trail Monday - Friday: 9:00 am - 5:00 pm Saturday: Closed	843-6400
Oriovista Branch	501 S. Kirkman Road Monday-Friday: 9:00 am - 5:00 pm Saturday: 9:00 am - noon	293-6410
Pine Castle Branch	7707 S. Orange Avenue Monday - Friday: 8:30 am - 5:30 pm Saturday: 9:00 am - noon	855-3010
Pine Hills Branch	811 Deauville Drive Monday - Friday: 9:00 am - 5:00 pm Saturday: Closed	293-3274
Sand Lake Branch	10450 Turkey Lake Road Monday - Friday: 9:00 am - 5:00 pm Saturday: 9:00 am - noon	351-9037
Union Park Branch	1801 N. Econlockhatchee Tr. Monday-Friday: 9:00 am - 5:00 pm Saturday: 9:00 am - noon	282-1421
Ventura Branch	7360 Curry Ford Road Monday - Friday: 9:00 am - 5:00 pm Saturday: 9:00 am - 1:00 pm	277-2686

Contract Stations

Call for business hours and the services provided by the contract station beyond routine operations.

Eckerd Drugs CONROY	4792 S. Kirkland Rd.	296-2900
Eckerd Drugs COYTOWN	2519 E. Colonial Dr.	896-7423

Orlando

Liggett Drugs DOVER SHORES	3207 E. Curry Ford Rd.	894-7913
Liggett Drugs FAIRVILLA	1912 Silver Star Rd.	298-8114
Lake Buena Vista Post Office LAKE BUENA VISTA	12541 State Rd. 535	828-2606
Global Books and Video, Inc. LAKE MARGARET	3942 S. Semoran Blvd.	249-1307
Eckerd Drugs MARKET PLACE	7600 Dr. Phillips Blvd.	352-1177
Us Pak N Ship METROWEST	2457A S. Hiawassee Rd.	294-9058
Eckerd Drug MURDOCK	10543 E. Colonial Dr.	277-8781
Global Books and Video, Inc. ROYAL OAKS	136 S. Semoran Blvd.	658-6397
Eckerd Drugs SOUTHCHASE	12339 S. Orange Blossom Tr.	240-2472
Eckerd Drugs SUNCREST	10051 University Blvd.	679-4900
Bealls Dept. Store WESTSIDE CROSSING	5062 W. Colonial Dr.	578-8405
Eckerd Drugs WILLIAMSBURG	5402 Central Florida Pkwy.	239-6065

Newspapers and Magazines

The ORLANDO SENTINEL, a daily newspaper with international, national and local news coverage, is circulated in Orange, Seminole, Lake, Volusia, Brevard, and Osceola Counties. *Orange Extra* is a Thursday and Sunday supplement featuring the community news of Orange County.

Weekly Features
- Monday: *Central Florida Business* is published in tabloid format.
- Thursday: *Transportation*, a consumer section focusing on buying and maintaining cars and boats; *Food*, a section for people who enjoy cooking and eating.

- Friday: *Fantastic Friday*, a sports guide for the weekend and upcoming week; *Calendar*, an arts and entertainment guide for the week (Friday-Thursday).
- Saturday: *Homes*, a section devoted to home improvements, gardening and decorating.
- Sunday: The Sunday edition contains a variety of special sections including *Florida Magazine*.

Special Editions
- *Florida Forecast*, featuring articles on the economy, is a special edition of Central Florida Business published in January.
- *Season Preview* presents the arts and entertainment calendar for the upcoming season. It is usually published in late August/early September, prior to the beginning of the new theater season.
- *Hot Cars*, published in July, features the best cars in the market according to automotive specialists.

Note: Contact the *Orlando Sentinel* for a full listing of their special editions. *Ph. 420-5000.*

◆ Community Publications

APOPKA CHIEF, a community weekly for Apopka and neighboring communities. *Ph. 886-2777.*
THE WEST ORANGE TIMES, a community weekly for West Orange County. *Ph. 656-2121.*
THE OBSERVER, a community weekly for Winter Park and Maitland. *Ph. 628-8500.*
SOUTHWEST BULLETIN, a community news publication for Southwest Orlando, published every three weeks. *Ph. 351-1573.*

◆ Business Publications

ORLANDO BUSINESS JOURNAL is a tri-county weekly publication servicing Orange, Seminole and Osceola counties. In its weekly Focus, it features a particular industry or aspect of business. Once a year, the Business Journal publishes a *Book of Lists* and a *Business Service Guide*. *Ph. 649-8470.*

◆ Ethnic/Religious Publications

HERITAGE JEWISH NEWS: *Ph. 834-8277*
FLORIDA CATHOLIC: *Ph. 423-3438*
ORLANDO TIMES (AFRICAN-AMERICAN): *Ph. 841-3052*
LA PRENSA NEWSPAPER: *Ph. 767-0070*

◆ Special Interest

THE WEEKLY is a human interest and entertainment publication for Orange and Seminole counties. *Ph. 645-5888.*

ORLANDO MAGAZINE is a city and regional publication which profiles life styles and business in the Orlando area. Its monthly format includes newsmakers and public issues; features on health; a home and garden design section; fashion; dining and attractions; and an arts and entertainment calendar of events. A business section features business happenings and trends in the Orlando marketplace.

Orlando Media Affiliates, Inc. also publishes two special editions. LIVING IN ORLANDO, an annual relocation guide, presents an overview of where to live, work and play; OPPORTUNITY ORLANDO focuses on demographics and business relocation. *Ph. 539-3939.*

Library System

Orlando Public Library
101 East Central Blvd.
Orlando, FL 32801
Ph. 425-4694

The Orlando Public Library is the main library of Orange County. There are also eleven branch libraries throughout the county servicing the various communities. The main library is open seven days a week and five evenings during the week. There are six meeting rooms available to non-profit organizations for monthly meetings.

Note: The Orange County Library System has an independent library millage tax which supports its operation. The cities of Maitland and Winter Park support their own libraries and are not part of the county system.

The library offers several interesting programs:
- Mailbox Access to Your Library, commonly known as MAYL, is an innovative program which happens to be 20 years old. In order to accommodate community needs and busy lifestyles, the library will mail books, compact discs or videos to your home. You may request any type of literature, ranging from

British mysteries, American biographies, mythology, popular fiction to current best sellers. Selections, which are sent to your home as instructed – weekly, biweekly or monthly – may be kept for three weeks.
- In order to assist with your selections, the library sends a list of the best sellers and different types of literature which are available at the library. The librarians will also assist with suggestions of books to suit your literary taste and interest.
- The library purchases best sellers in quantity and processes them immediately to be in sync with current literary tastes.
- Framed prints are available for loan and may be checked out for three weeks.
- The Friends of the Library operate a "look and browse" book store on the third floor of the library. Revenues from purchases are applied towards special projects.
- The County Law Library is housed in the Orlando Public Library in lieu of the traditional court house. The purchase of books is supported by court fees.
- Oral History is a special project which involves interviewing older people to preserve the history of the area.
- *Clubs and Organizations in the Greater Orlando Area* is a publication which is funded by the Friends of the Library. This is a great directory for any newcomer.

Health Care

Orlando Regional Healthcare System has a network of hospitals and medical centers providing a variety of medical specialties and services under its umbrella. The following six medical facilities are part of the Orlando Regional Health Care System.

Orlando Regional Medical Center
1414 Kuhl Ave., Orlando
Ph. 648-3806

ORMC, the flagship hospital of the Orlando Regional Healthcare System, is one of the oldest and largest hospitals in Florida. It is a private, not-for-profit, 598-bed full service hospital. Physicians on staff are board certified or in the process of acquiring certification. Also a teaching hospital, it has seven residency programs and two fellowship programs in colorectal surgery and pediatric orthopedics. ORMC is a designated level I trauma center (one of only four in the state) and has a hospital-based helicopter rescue service. A remodeled *cardiology center* with intensive care facilities, a *cardiovascular unit, oncology, orthopedics* (including joint replacement and sports injuries), *rehabilitation*, and a *burn center* are also specialties of ORMC.

Orlando Cancer Center
85 W. Miller St.
Ph. 648-3800

The Orlando Cancer Center is under the aegis of ORMC in partnership with the *M.D. Anderson Cancer Center* at Houston, Texas. Services focus on helping the patient through the medical process, beginning with diagnosis through the various stages of evaluation, treatment, rehabilitation, support networks and educational programs.

Arnold Palmer Hospital For Children & Women
92 W. Miller Street, Orlando
Ph. 649-9111

Arnold Palmer Hospital is a 255-bed facility specializing in *obstetrics* and *gynecological health care* for women as well as *pediatric medicine*. The OB program is very strong with 6,000 babies delivered at the hospital each year. Areas of sub-specialty include a *high risk pregnancy unit* for patients who need intensive care and monitoring during difficult pregnancies; *a pediatric intensive care unit* staffed by pediatric intensivists certified in critical medical care; an *intermediate and regular pediatric care unit; pediatric neurosurgery;* and *oncology*. The hospital philosophy focuses on family-centered care; the family is treated as a unit and all members are given consideration. *Note:* The hospital opened its doors on September 10, 1989, the day Arnold Palmer celebrated his 60th birthday.

Sand Lake Hospital
9400 Turkey Lake Road, Orlando
Ph. 351-8500

Sand Lake Hospital is a 24-hour emergency, medical/surgical facility with 182 beds. Its specialties include *a brain and head injury rehabilitation center; STARTBACK*, an outpatient rehabilitation program; and inpatient mental health. The *center of advanced reproductive technology* is one of the most successful reproduction assisted programs in the country. With a team of specialists and advanced techniques, many patients are provided with alternative fertilization procedures. Sand Lake's other medical specialties include its department of *nuclear and diagnostic medicine and colorectal treatment center.*

Ambulatory Care Center

1414 Kuhl Ave., Orlando
Ph. 841-5274

The Ambulatory Care Center provides comprehensive outpatient diagnostic testing and one-day surgical procedures. Its specialties include endoscopy, cardiology testing, cardiac monitoring, and a women's imaging center.

Lake Buena Vista Walk-in Clinic

Near Walt Disney World Village, off S.R. 535
Ph. 828-3434

If you need immediate medical attention, the Buena Vista Clinic provides emergency care, X-rays, and a pharmacy to fill prescriptions.

ORHS Community Outreach Programs

Healthline is a doctor's referral service which provides background information on physicians. The *55 Plus Program* offers health exams, screenings and seminars. The *Young Hero's Club*, for the two-through-12 generation, promotes health, fitness and safety through its programs and activities. *On Center* is the quarterly newsletter published by the Orlando Regional Healthcare System.

Florida Hospital, Orlando

601 E. Rollins St.
Ph. 896-6611

Florida Hospital, founded in 1908 as a sanitarium, is a community hospital operated by the Seventh Day Adventist Church. With four hospital campuses in the greater Orlando area, a rehabilitation center and eight urgent care walk-in centers, Florida Hospital has the second highest volume of patients in the state. Florida Hospital Orlando, with 801 beds, is the main campus with satellite hospitals in East Orlando, Apoka and Altamonte (Seminole County).

Florida Hospital, East Orlando, located at 7727 Lake Underhill Drive, is a 197-bed facility. *Ph. 277-8110.*

Florida Hospital, Apoka, at 201 N. Park Avenue, is a 50-bed facility. *Ph. 889-1000.*

Florida Hospital Services

The *Florida Heart Institute* is one of the four largest in the country and has been recognized for its heart surgery program. The *Walt Disney Memorial Cancer Institute* at Florida Hospital in Altamonte houses the *Cancer and Leukemia Research Center* and the *Martin Andersen Outpatient Treatment Center.* Other specialties include the *Kidney Stone Center; Organ Transplant Program; Orthopedic Surgery; Neuroscience Center; Psychiatric Center; Diabetes Program; Women's Medicine;* and *Pediatrics.*

Community Outreach Programs
- *The Birth Coordinator Program:* Recognizing individual needs, the birth coordinator helps make the birthing experience a special one for parents. *Ph. 897-1518.*
- *The Stork Line:* The hospital provides a free telephone information line which parents can call before and after birth.
- *Mend 'N Tend:* The Florida Hospital Children's Center offers a day care program for children who are sick with colds and minor illnesses. Trained nurses administer tender loving care and provide the necessary attention.
- *Ask-A-Nurse:* Registered nurses staff a free 24-hour health care information line and provide the answers to health-related problems and questions in a private and confidential manner. *Ph. 897-1700.*
- *Other outreach programs:* Florida Hospital offers a series of health seminars, weight control and nutrition programs, support groups for people with health related issues, life style seminars for seniors, and a wealth of other interesting programs. Call and ask for a calendar of their upcoming events.

Florida Hospital, Southwest Centra Care

Vineland Road
Ph. 660-8118

Southwest Centra Care is a walk-in clinic which provides treatment for colds, fever, broken bones and minor emergencies. An on-site pharmacy, laboratory, and X-ray services are available. The clinic is open seven days a week, from 8 am to 8 pm.

Education

ORANGE COUNTY PUBLIC SCHOOLS
445 W. Amelia Street
Orlando, FL 32801
Ph. 849-3200

The Orange County Public School System has the distinction of being the 18th largest district out of 16,000 in the country and the sixth largest in the state. There are 126 schools in the system, providing an education for approximately 110,000 students in kindergarten through 12th grades. There are 85 elementary schools, 21 middle schools, 13 senior high schools, three exceptional schools for students with special needs, and four vocational-technical centers.

Students from 75 countries speaking 57 different languages bring an international flavor to the classroom. Since 1985, the school population has increased by approximately 33%. In order to accommodate the continuing growth, the district adopted a plan to operate its elementary schools on a year-round calendar. In the *Multi-Track* system, only 80% of the student body is in school at any one time, while 20% of the students are on vacation. Students are in class for 12-week sessions followed by a three-week vacation. This school/vacation schedule is repeated throughout the year. The *Single-Track* system has the same school/vacation schedule, but has 100% of the students in class at the same time, with the entire school closed for each of the three-week vacations. With increases in population, many schools in the single track program will eventually operate on a multi-track system. Year-round education not only provides continuity but is also cost effective. Students attend school 180 days a year-the same number of days as students in the traditional system.

The *Extended Day Program* is a community service which provides child care and enrichment activities for students in grades K-5 before and after school, from approximately 6:45 am to 6:00 pm. There is a sliding fee scale.

Intersessions is a special full-day program for students who can benefit from remediation or enhancement of the school curriculum during the three week vacation period. Hands-on enrichment activities provide fun and enjoyment without the structure of grades.

◆ Special Programs

NEW DIRECTIONS ACADEMY is a new program offering expelled students and juvenile felons a last chance to get an education within the public school system. Many of the classes are computer driven to enable students to proceed at their own pace and even accelerate the pace to complete requirements. They have the opportunity to earn enough credits to transfer back to their previous school or take the high school equivalency examinations.

◆ Magnet Schools

There are five magnet schools providing a specialized program for students with focused interests and/or talents.

- The International Baccalaureate Program is offered at Winter Park High School. It is one of many such programs given throughout the world and is very much respected by the international community. Students must demonstrate high academic performance and ability to be accepted into the program. *Ph. 644-6921.*
- Animal Production at Colonial High School is the focus of this program for students who are interested in agriculture or animal husbandry. *Ph. 277-5431.*
- Engineering And Science Technology at Edgewater High School offers high tech computer skills and concentrated study in engineering and the sciences. *Ph. 849-0130.*
- Center For International Studies at Dr. Phillips High School focuses on global policies and international relationships. *Ph. 352-4040.*
- Allied Health Professions at Apopka High School focuses on health technologies and medical care. *Ph. 889-4194.*

◆ Pilot Programs

Orange County is participating in School Year 2000 to explore more effective educational delivery systems. This initiative is directed towards developing, testing and implementing a technology-based model to prepare students with the skills necessary for the year 2000.

There are several pilot programs that are exploring Alternative Assessment Strategies. Computers, for example, are being used to enter observations about student competencies and development.

Instruments are being created to measure how well students can utilize and integrate information. Letter grade evaluations may be insufficient to evaluate a student's educational development and critical thinking skills.

◆ Technology-Based Programs

- Tech Prep is a program designed to provide students in grades nine-12 with applied academic study leading to post secondary training, community college or the workplace. The curriculum focuses on the integration of science, mathematics, communication and technical course work. The future goal is to implement the Tech Prep program in all high schools by 1995.
- Biz Kids is an innovative program for fifth grade students to experience the application of technology which they have learned in the classroom. Fifth graders from district schools have the opportunity to staff an operating retail drug store equipped with automated point of sale systems, inventory control and sophisticated scanners.
- Chapter 1 is a model technology program involving 19 elementary schools. Comprehensive multimedia equipment have been installed in first, second and third grade classrooms. Each station has an interfaced computer, laser disc player, VCR, fax machine, telephone and high speed data line. Students can communicate with classrooms in other cities and produce live two-way television transmissions via satellite.
- Ventura Elementary has implemented a computer curriculum in all third and fourth grade classrooms. The program is individualized to each child's level and monitors performance. As the student masters the material, the program becomes more challenging.
- Edgewater High School, a science and technology magnet school, has incorporated technology to enhance the basic curriculum. A computer animation course has been added to the art program; science classes apply technology to monitor water quality of local lakes; and sociology and communications students use technology to exchange and share their cultural heritage with Lakota Reservation students in South Dakota.

There are several other schools in the district integrating technology and computer assisted learning into the curriculum. For more information, call *849-3200, Ext. 2583.*

◆ Exceptional Education Programs

One of the primary goals of Orange County educators is 'inclusion' – to ensure that handicapped students receive special services, but are included in mainstream education wherever possible. There are two schools, however, which have been dedicated for the severely emotionally disturbed. The elementary school serves children in grades K-5 and the secondary school serves students in grades six-12. There is also a school for students who have multiple handicaps and need special attention throughout the day. Other programs for students who are gifted, physically impaired, visually impaired or hearing impaired are delivered within the regular system.

◆ Volunteer Programs

- *ADDitions* is a very active group of parents involved in the school system.
- Green Circle, a program facilitated by trained parent volunteers, helps elementary school students understand the similarities and differences between people.
- The Partners In Education (PIE), a group of Orange County businesses, provide tutors, speakers, internships, mentoring and financial assistance to community schools.

COLLEGES AND UNIVERSITIES

The University of Central Florida, located 13 miles east of downtown Orlando, is part of the state university system. It has been cited as one of the top 15 regional schools in the Southeast by *US News and World Report*. Founded in 1963, it has an enrollment of 22,000 students in its various programs. It offers a four-year Baccalaureate degree, Master's degree, and Doctorate in many different disciplines. As Central Florida has grown, the university has developed new programs, research institutes and centers to meet the needs of technology, tourism and business. *Ph. 823-2000.*

Rollins College, situated on the shores of Lake Virginia in Winter Park, was founded in 1885 and is the oldest private college in Florida. Primarily a liberal arts college with a population of approximately 1,400 students, it offers both undergraduate and graduate programs. The Roy E. Crummer School of Business confers an MBA degree; it was ranked as one of the top 10 MBA programs in the South. The Hamilton Holt School at Rollins provides evening and continuing education classes. *Ph. 646-2000.*

Orlando College, founded in 1918, offers a two-year business curriculum in video arts and sciences, business/management, paralegal and computer applications. A four-year program which confers a Bachelor of Science degree is offered in business administration, computer information sciences, accounting, and management/marketing. At the graduate level, students can earn a Masters of Business Administration or a Masters of Public Administration. Orlando College is a commuter school with a north and a south campus serving 2,400 students. *Ph. 628-5870.*

Valencia Community College is a multi-campus college with six campuses, five located in Orange County and one in Osceola County. Offering day, evening and weekend courses to 60,000 students, Valencia also offers courses via cable television. An Associate of Arts degree is available to students who wish to continue their education at a four-year institution. A two-year career program leading to an Associate in Science degree is offered in more than 40 fields, ranging from film production technology and hospitality management to computer integrated manufacturing. *Ph. 299-5000.*

Florida Technical College, in Orlando, is a private two-year college specializing in computer related courses. *Ph. 678-5600.*

The Cultural Scene

Dr. Phillips Center for the Performing Arts

Destined for the demolition block, this old 1930's power plant was given a second life as a cultural center. As a reminder of days past, a power pump, painted vibrant blue, is part of the interior decor. The main hall, which can accommodate 200-250 people, is used by the Orlando Opera Company and the Southern Ballet Theater. *1111 N. Orange Avenue. Ph. 426-1700.*

Orlando Opera Company

The Orlando Opera Company, which had its debut in 1963, is a major cultural institution and one of three state opera companies in Florida. It performs in a seven-county area, presenting 27 performances of six operas annually. Throughout the years, the Company has hosted opera stars of international fame while also developing its young artists.

In 1990, OCC presented the Opera Company of Toulon, France to the Florida community, as part of the state's first international cultural exchange program in opera. The following year, OCC was invited to France and performed the region's first production of the Mikado by Gilbert and Sullivan.

The OCC is committed to developing new talent and community education. A Resident Artist's Program (RAP) develops aspiring new talent while introducing public school children to abridged performances of opera. The operas selected are geared to the students' educational level. The Children's Opera Group (COG) is designed for ages 8-18. They attend various workshops to study performance, interpretation, music and musical writing. Their efforts culminate in staging a full-length opera. *Opera Through The Looking Glass* is a lecture series for adults which relates to the season's performances. The *Opera Study Groups* appeal to more experienced opera patrons who want to enhance their present level of knowledge. *1111 N. Orange Avenue. Ph. 426-1700.*

Civic Theater of Central Florida

The Civic Theater uses three different stages for its various productions. The Main Stage, a 350-seat theater, presents a series of six Broadway shows each season. During the summer, a musical production is presented as an extra. The Second Stage is a smaller theater which can accommodate 120 theatergoers. Five Off-Broadway shows are selected for production on this stage. The third stage has a 400-seat capacity and is dedicated to children's theater. During the school year, five popular children's shows are performed and students in grades K-6 are invited to the theater. Study guides and class discussions are used to complement the production.

The Civic Theater has an Acting Studio for both children and adults. There are three different programs which are available to students. The Acting Studio has six-eight-week workshops given throughout the year. Classes include study in vocal techniques, scene study, monologue, dialects, acting movement along with other areas of instruction for either the novice or more studied actor. The Studio's *Minimesters Program* offers a four-week session. There are also special one-day seminars which focus on special areas of interest. Talent agents are sometimes invited to a Studio workshop to discuss how to prepare for an audition.

The Civic Theater also offers a *Summer Stock Program* for teenagers, 14 through 19 years of age. They become thoroughly involved with every aspect of theater art, from scenery, props, costumes and stagecraft to the actual theater presentation. Their efforts culminate in a major musical production at the theater. *1001 E. Princeton Street. Ph. 896-7365.*

Orlando Museum of Art

Founded in 1924 as a small art center, this is the largest art museum within a 90-mile radius of Orlando. It is a major cultural institution serving a nine county area. As Central Florida grew with the space industry in the 1950s, the community decided it was time to build a new art center. In 1971, it was accredited by the American Association of Museums. During the mid-to-late '70s, Orlando's metropolitan population doubled with the arrival of new industries and along with it, two significant happenings contributed to the museum's growth. A major collection of Pre-Columbian and African art was donated to the museum and the acquisition of an important contemporary American graphics collection was initiated with the assistance of an NEA grant. The museum has continued to expand its collections and facilities.

Today, the museum's large permanent collection is comprised of American 19th and 20th paintings, drawings, sculptures, photographs and decorative arts – and its collection of Pre-Columbian and African art. In addition, OMA has two long term loans: Glimmers of a Forgotten Realm: Maya Archaeology at Caracol and Selections from the Paul and Ruth Tishman Collection of African Art. OMA also showcases national and international exhibitions of excellence and curates many which travel abroad. Whenever possible, the exhibits are enhanced by video introductions, brochures and interpretive labels.

OMA also has a special hands-on program for children in preschool through third grade. They become acquainted with the permanent collections through fun-filled activities. For adults who are interested in vacationing with art, the museum has a travel program of art-related tours in the U.S. and abroad. *2416 N. Mills Avenue, Orlando. Ph. 896-4231.*

Orlando Broadway Series

The Florida Theatrical Association is a national touring company which presents seven Broadway shows each season. The shows selected may be pre-Broadway productions, touring companies of current Broadway shows or shows which have finished their Broadway season. *Ph. 423-9999.*

Charles Hosmer Morse Museum of American Art

The Charles Hosmer Morse Museum houses a major collection of Hugh McKean's collection of Tiffany art. Mr. McKean was a dedicated friend and admirer; as a scholar, he authored a book on Tiffany's art. The Morse Museum has the distinction of having the world's most important and extensive collection of Louis Comfort Tiffany's work. Many of the pieces are from Tiffany's personal collection which he designed and chose to keep for his own enjoyment. The museum collection includes leaded glass windows, glass buttons, favrile glass, pottery, paintings, desk sets and decorative arts. A highlight of the collection is the chapel and furnishings he created for the World's Columbian Exposition in Chicago in 1893. Tiffany was born in 1848 and died in 1933.

On permanent exhibition are Tiffany windows and glass, American art pottery and late 19th/20th-century paintings. The museum was founded by Jeanette Genuis McKean who curated the first major exhibit of Louis Comfort Tiffany's artworks; the museum is dedicated to her industrialist grandfather, Charles Hosmer Morse. *133 East Welbourne Avenue, Winter Park. Ph. 644-3686.*

SAK Theater Comedy Lab

SAK Theater Comedy Lab has been in existence for 15 years. It is an impromptu theater group performing to audience suggestions. Two teams create scenarios using themes prompted by the audience. The teams, which are judged, must both conform to given parameters or guidelines in their respective sketches. It is great theater sport and lots of fun. By a stretch of the imagination, 'SAK' refers to the sac in which props and costumes were carried. *45 E. Church Street. Ph. 648-0001.*

Theater Downtown

Adapted from an old 1920's store with high ceilings and balconies, this is a gem in the rough. As a local community alternative theater producing Broadway, off-Broadway and original works by Central Florida playwrights, it has received high praise from people involved in the performing arts. Through the active support of an all volunteer organization (from production to marketing), it presents a selection of 15 shows during its year-round season. Its main theater seats approximately 120 people. Its lobby theater performs more cutting-edge productions. *2113 N. Orange Avenue. Ph. 841-0083.*

Enzian Theater

The Enzian Theater is an alternative cinema which offers a unique experience for moviegoers. The non-traditional theater house has four tiered levels with tables and plush seating for 250 people. A menu ranging from pizza and beer to elegant gourmet appeals to a variety of tastes.

The Enzian Film Society, which was formed in 1990, presents an annual Florida Film Festival. The week-long cinema festivities are held late spring and feature the best in upcoming domestic, international and independent films. Celebrity actors, directors, filmmakers and producers are invited guests. During the year, the Society sponsors *Meet the Filmmakers*, a lecture series which presents an evening with film professionals discussing various aspects of cinematic production. The programs are open to the public at no cost. Panel discussions and guest speakers are also hosted by the Society following screenings of provocative films. They may focus on contemporary controversial issues dealing with the arts or examine films which have been produced to address inequities in society. *1300 S. Orlando Avenue. Ph. 629-1088.*

Maitland Art Center

The Maitland Art Center was one of five recipients of the Walt Disney World Community Service Awards in the Cultural Category. It is also distinguished by an interesting past and was entered on the National Register of Historic Places in 1982. During the 1930's, Maitland was an artist's colony, developed under the auspices of Andre Smith, artist and architect. Smith integrated decorative murals and carvings of Mayan Aztec motifs into the architectural design of the stucco studios and residency quarters. Its Research Studio housed the studios and living accommodations for emerging artists, such as Milton Avery. Today it is used as studio space for classes and workshops and as a gallery for contemporary American artists and crafts people. The gardens, walkways and courtyards provide a lovely place to stroll as well as an intimate setting for concerts and recitals.

The Maitland Art Center offers a variety of studio classes and workshops to suit the art tastes and ability levels of both adults and children. Lectures and demonstrations are frequently held during the year to complement a special gallery exhibition. The gallery program features changing exhibits as well as a permanent museum collection. The center has a very active volunteer effort which sponsors special events and activities. *231 West Packwood Avenue, Maitland. Ph. 539-2181.*

Orlando Science Center

The Orlando Science Center explores the world of science with hands-on exhibits, demonstrations, special workshops and innovative programs. The *Tunnel Of Discovery* examines four of the physical sciences: electricity; magnetic forces; waves and sound frequencies; light and optical illusions. The visitor is involved in each of the exhibits and learns through experiencing the different phenomena. *Natureworks* features the natural sciences through a look at four different Central Florida habitats. Ecology, conservation and different species of animals, birds and insects are explored through experiment, experience or touch. *Weather Central* is a station with the up-to-date technology for predicting weather and tracking hurricane systems. *Kidspace* is a special area designed for kids, ages two-eight, who want to dive into an understanding of the Waterworks exhibit. The *Carol Wine Observatory* in the courtyard invites any would-be astronomers, with or without telescopes to its *Skywatch.* On Friday evenings, the Science Center sets up its primary telescope and projects video images onto the patio. The *John Young Planetarium* presents celestial shows under a 40-foot dome. Family laser shows are scheduled on weekends and also weekday matinees.

Special traveling scientific exhibits are featured at the Orlando Science Center throughout the year. Beyond the exhibitions, there are innovative community outreach programs to enhance an understanding of science as it influences our daily lives. Science camps, workshops, field trips and travel programs are available for children, families and youth groups. *810 East Rollins Street. Ph. 896-7151.*

The Arts Services Council

This is an information source for non-profit cultural groups. It provides a 24-hour Arts Information Line with a weekly calendar of cultural events and information on art exhibitions and museums. *Ph. 420-2150.*

Events and Attractions

Orlando Shakespeare Festival

The Shakespeare Festival, affiliated with the University of Central Florida, is presented by a professional repertory theater. Every spring, two Shakespearean plays are selected to be performed during the month of April in the Walt Disney Amphitheater at Eola Park. *Ph. 423-6905.*

Note: Special events, such as concerts, film series or political rallies are also held at the Walt Disney Amphitheater, which seats 960 people. Call for a schedule of events.

Fountain View

Fountain View, a two-day Masters' Craft Festival, is a juried fine art craft exhibition held in early April at Eola Lake. Approximately 100 artists throughout the country are invited to exhibit work in two- and three-dimensional media, including ceramics, sculpture and jewelry. Prize money is awarded to the best work in the various categories.

Orlando Sentinel Book Fair

This two-day book fair, sponsored by the Orlando Sentinel in cooperation with the Library Association and the City of Orlando, is held in April at Eola Lake. In addition to approximately 125 booths and vendors selling new and used books, there are workshops for aspiring authors and songwriters, luncheons with celebrity authors, and storytelling sessions.

Orlando Theater Project

The Orlando Theater Project produces the *Fringe Festival* during the last week in April. It is a 10-day event showcasing performing theater arts in five different venues. The festival had its beginnings in Scotland when a group of theatrical performers were not permitted to participate in the Edinburgh Theater Festival. Not easily deterred, they went to the fringe of the city and gave their performances there. The Orlando Festival is modeled after the Fringe Festivals in Canada and is only one of two in the United States. Many of the plays are original, cutting edge productions, although some are established works. Theater performances also include impromptu comedy, music and juggling acts. There are more than

45 different groups which perform during the festival. *Ph. 648-0001.*

Light Up Orlando

Light Up Orlando is a big block party, held in downtown Orlando during the second Saturday evening in November. Various stages for national and local performances are set up within a nine-block closed-off area stretching from Church to Livingston Street. In addition to the evening's featured entertainment, food and drink are available. *Ph. 648-4010.*

Blue Springs State Park

Blue Springs State Park, 30 miles north of Orlando, is the winter home of the manatees. These beloved sea cows may attain a weight of 3,000 pounds. From November through March, they enjoy the warmer 72 degree temperature of the clear spring waters. Visitors are able to watch as many as 50 manatees at play from boardwalk platforms. In the afternoon, as water temperatures warm, manatees leave the spring for a brief time to feed in the St. John River. *2100 West French Avenue, Orange City. Ph. (904) 775-3663.*

Note: Manatees, which are an endangered species, are classified as marine mammals.

Scenic Boat Tour

The Scenic Boat Tours, which depart from Winter Park, are both educational and entertaining. A one-hour narrated tour on a pontoon boat cruises through a beautiful chain of lakes. The captain narrates the history of Winter Park, relating anecdotal stories about the area and the exquisite residences along the shoreline. This showcase of exclusive million-dollar homes is a visual experience which can be seen only from the lake. Tours operate seven days a week, from 10 am until 4 pm, on the hour. *312 E. Morse Blvd. Winter Park. Ph. 644-4056.*

Sea World

Sea World, showcasing marine animals "in their natural behavior," is a favorite of adults and children alike. It features a multimedia production starring the playful Shamu and his family; an ensemble show of dolphins and 'false' killer whales performing and socializing with their trainers; communities of dolphins, sea lions and sting rays which visitors may feed. Other features include *Terrors of the Deep*, an exhibit of different species of sharks; *Penguin Encoun-*

ter, a production casted with hundreds of penguins in an icy, snow-filled naturalistic habitat; and *Manatees, The Last Generation?* starring manatees who have been rescued by Sea World. *7007 Sea World Drive. Ph. 363-2200.*

Walt Disney World

- *Magic Kingdom* celebrates the wonderful world of the imagination as you journey through seven fantasy lands with forty-five adventures and attractions. Disney characters are everywhere.
- *Epcot Center* celebrates technology and people. *Future World's* exhibits and rides transport you on a journey through past achievements and possible advancements in the future. *World Showcase* presents international villages and the architecture, culture and history, reflecting many different nationalities from around the world.
- *Disney-mgm Studios* is an operational television and motion picture studio. The theme park has attractions, rides and recreations from the movies. Guided tours provide a look into backstage production facilities. *Lake Buena Vista. Ph. 934-7639.*

Note: If you are planning to use any (of the many) theme parks on a regular basis, call and ask about yearly passes and resident discounts.

Don't Miss

Park Avenue. Winter Park, with its upscale and charming shopping district, was originally established as a winter resort at the turn of the century. A quiet, yet undisputed wealth, is evidenced by its lakefront homes and fashionable Park Avenue, the site of elegant boutiques, fine dining, and unique museums. Stately awnings and moss-draped trees lining the avenue create a sense of the old world. *Ph. 644-8281.*

Renninger Antique Center. Mt. Dora, a quaint and charming city in Lake County, is well known for its antiques. Several times a year, the Renninger Antique Center invites dealers from the U.S., Canada and Europe to participate in a three-day weekend show. The Extravaganza Antique Show is held during the third weekend of November, January and February; 1,200 dealers set up booths and tents outside and inside with displays of antiques. From March through October (excluding July), 350-500 dealers participate in a two-day Antique Fair held during the third weekend of the month.

If you want to do some weekend antiquing, take a drive to Mt. Dora. *Ph. (904) 383-8393.*

Note: There is an admission charge for the Extravaganza Antique Shows, but the Antique Fairs are free to the public.

Monday At Webster. Webster is an old farming community which is approximately 50 miles west of Orlando. During the week, the people of Webster clean out their farmhouses and barns and bring old and used items to the flea market. If you enjoy sifting through other people's cast-aways and looking for appealing little treasures, visit Webster's – but only on Monday!

Tubing At Kelly Park. For the adventuresome or those who want to submerge in cool waters on a hot day, a visit to Kelly Park is the thing to do. You can have fun tubing, snorkeling and/or swimming in the cool spring waters which originate from a cave and flow downstream for 3/4 of a mile. A lazy current of water guides the inner tube down the course. A boardwalk brings you back to the beginning of the run. If you do not have your own inner tube, you may rent one outside of the park. Kelly Park is six miles north of Apoka on Kelly Park Road. *Ph. 889-4179.*

Note: You may be fortunate to find a memento at the bottom of the spring. Prehistoric sharks' teeth have been flushed out and discovered there.

Recreation

Professional Sports

Florida Citrus Bowl Stadium. The Citrus Bowl seats more than 72,000. It hosts the annual New Year's Day 'Comp USA' Citrus Bowl game. Pre-season NFL games and UCF's college football season are played here. *1610 W. Church Street. Ph. 423-2476.*

Tinker Field. The Orlando Cubs, an AA team for the Chicago Cubs, plays its summer season from April through September at Tinker Field. *287 S. Tampa Avenue. Ph. 872-7593.*

The Orlando Arena. The Orlando Arena can accommodate 15,500 fans. It is home to the Orlando Magic NBA franchise from November through April. *Ph. 649-BALL.*

The Orlando Predators, a member of the Arena Football League, uses the facility during the summer. *Ph. 87-ARENA.*

The Arena also hosts the McDonald's American Cup Gymnastic Competition and several home games for the Tampa Bay Lightning hockey team. *600 W. Amelia Street. Ph. 849-2001.*

Parks and Lakes

There are three public parks with lakes and water activities in the city of Orlando.

Lake Eola, a downtown park which is easily accessible, offers a serene respite for anyone living, working or even shopping in the city. During the day, joggers, speed walkers and strollers circle the scenic path around the lake. Paddle boats offer another venue for recreation if you prefer to be on the water. Business people may be seen with brown bag lunches or sitting at the small outdoor cafe. Many, who are young at heart, enjoy feeding the ducks and other water birds or visiting the gold fish pond. If you're young in age, a children's play area is also located in the park. On scheduled evenings, a dazzling water and light show takes place in the middle of the lake. Lake Eola is on Rosiland Avenue at Washington Street. *Ph. 246-2827.*

Lake Ivanhoe Plaza Park, situated on 4.5 acres, is in the northern part of downtown Orlando. It is an active, scenic park with playground facilities, picnic tables, volleyball courts, boat ramp, fishing, recreational boating and water skiing. A boardwalk overlooking the lake provides a good view of the various water activities. During the year, water skiing competitions entertain the many park visitors.

Turkey Lake Park is in the southwest part of Orlando at 3401 Hiawassee Road. The largest of the city parks, it is an enormous playground for all ages. There are bicycle trails and nature/hiking trails; four boardwalks with lake overlooks; a frisbee golf course, softball field and swimming pool; a children's fully equipped playground and an area with farm animals. The lake, approximately 600 acres in size, is shaped like a turkey with inlets and coves. Most of it is surrounded by a shoreline of trees and bushes. Fishing enthusiasts can indulge their passion along a 200-foot fishing pier; if successful, there is a special area to clean the day's catch. Amenities also include picnic facilities and shelters as well as campsites for those who want a weekend away from home.

230 Orlando

Directory of Services

9-1-1 Emergency Only POLICE • SHERIFF • FIRE • MEDICAL • RESCUE

AGENCY	DESCRIPTION	ORANGE (407)
ALCOHOL & DRUG ABUSE	Intervention & Referral AA	800-821-4357 647-333
CRISIS HOTLINE	24 Hour Help Line	847-8811
ABUSE CENTER: SPOUSE ABUSE, INC.	Women in Distress	886-2856
POISON CONTROL & INFORMATION CENTER		800-282-3171
SENIOR SUPPORT HELP NOW	Telephone Reassurance & Support 24 Hour	648-4357
TEEN HOTLINE		644-2027
TIME/TEMPERATURE		646-3131

County Services

AGENCY	DESCRIPTION	ORANGE(407)
GOVERNMENT CENTER	201 S. Rosalind Avenue	836-7700
ANIMAL CONTROL BOARD OF EDUCATION		352-4390 849-3200
COUNTY COOPERATIVE EXT. SERVICE		836-7570
COUNTY COURTHOUSE		836-2055
EMERGENCY MGMNT	Disaster Readiness Training & Evacuation Information	658-6911
FIRE PREVENTION		658-6901
FL. HIGHWAY PATROL	All Interstate Roads & Turnpikes	897-5898
GARBAGE COLLECTION		836-7001
LIBRARY		425-4694
LICENSES	Auto Tag Parking Permit - Handicapped Boating Registration Fishing & Hunting	836-4120 836-4120

Directory of Services 231

BOARD OF EDUCATION		849-3200
COUNTY COOPERATIVE EXT. SERVICE		836-7570
COUNTY COURTHOUSE		836-2055
EMERGENCY MGMNT	Disaster Readiness Training & Evacuation Information	658-6911
FIRE PREVENTION		658-6901
FL. HIGHWAY PATROL	All Interstate Roads & Turnpikes	897-5898
GARBAGE COLLECTION		836-7001
LIBRARY		425-4694
LICENSES	Auto Tag	836-4120
	Parking Permit - Handicapped Boating Registration Fishing & Hunting	836-4120
MASS TRANSIT	Bus Route Information	841-8240
MOSQUITO CONTROL		352-4370
PARKS AND RECREATION		836-4290
PASSPORT INFORMATION		850-6335
PROPERTY APPRAISER		836-2144
SHERIFF		657-2500
TAX COLLECTOR		836-2700
TRAFFIC VIOLATION INFORMATION		836-2360
VOTER REGISTRATION		836-2070
WATER/SEWER	24 Hour/Emergency	836-7030 352-4300

Human Services

AGENCY	DESCRIPTION	ORANGE(407)
AMERICAN ASSOC. OF RETIRED PERSONS (AARP)	Florida State Headquarters Provides source for local contact	813-576-1155
AMERICAN RED CROSS	Hurricane Shelter Information Disaster Relief, Blood Banks, Educational Programs	894-4141

CHILD CARE	Information & Referral Sources for day care services	894-8393
INFORMATION & REFERRAL	Connects You with the Appropriate Person or Agency Who Can Answer Your Question or Assist You With A Particular Need	897-6464
HANDICAPPED/DISABLED SERVICES	Easter Seals Society	628-6800 896-2293
HEALTH DEPARTMENT		836-2600
I R S	Location & Hours of Local Offices Tax Information Tax Forms	800-829-1040 904-354-1760 800-829-3676
PARENT RESOURCE CTR	Parenting Programs & Support Network for Families	425-3663 644-KIDS
SENIOR CITIZEN SERVICES COUNCIL ON AGINIG	Information/Assistance Programs for Seniors	425-7873
SOCIAL SECURITY		800-772-1213
SOCIAL SERVICE TRANSPORTATION	Reduced Fares, Dial-A-Ride Transport for Seniors & Special Groups	841-2279
UNITED WAY	An Excellent Resource of Community Information	246-1500
VETERAN'S ASSISTANCE		836-7150
VOLUNTEER CENTER	A Clearinghouse for Volunteer Positions	896-0945
RETIRED SENIOR VOLUNTEER PROGRAM (RSVP)		422-1535
WOMEN'S RESOURCE CENTER		426-7960

City Numbers

GOVERNMENT CENTER Help Desk	Orlando City Hall 400 S. Orange Avenue	246-2121 246-2600
CITY CLERK		246-2251
POLICE (Non Emergency)		246-2414
FIRE (Non-Emergency)		246-2141
DRIVER'S LICENSE		856-6500
ELECTRICAL SERVICE	Florida Power Corporation Orlando Utilities Commission	629-1010 423-9100

GARBAGE COLLECTION	246-2314
LIBRARY	425-4694
PARKS & RECREATION	246-2287
TELEPHONE COMPANY Southern Bell	780-2355
VOTER'S REGISTRATION	836-2070
WATER & SEWER	246-2213
Emergency/After Hours	246-2151

Civic Organizations

Greater Orlando Chamber of Commerce	425-1234
Downtown Development Board	246-2555
Economic Development Commission of Mid-Florida	422-7159
Visitor Information Center	363-5872

Sarasota

In many ways, Sarasota is similar to other cities along the Gulf Coast. It has sun, beaches, palm trees and recreational activities of all kinds. But yet, it is also different. Sarasota, often referred to as the "Athens of the West," is a cultural Mecca. For those seeking an energetic and enriched cultural environment, Sarasota is a very special place. It is the home to many artists, authors, poets, performing artists, actors and musicians. They bring their ideas, talents and creativity to the galleries, stages and concert halls – all enthusiastically supported by Sarasotans.

Its cultural presence is rooted in its history. Sarasota became noticed with the arrival of Bertha Honore Palmer, wealthy widow of Chicago businessman, Potter Palmer. She invested in considerable land holdings and businesses in Sarasota. Finding the area to be endowed with great natural beauty, she built an opulent estate along the bayfront. She attracted many of her wealthy friends to the area including one in particular, John Ringling. In 1927, he established a winter residence in the heart of Sarasota. With him, came his passion for Italian Renaissance and Baroque works of art, which he would ultimately bequeath, along with other collections, to the public. Sarasota flourished as John Ringling invested in building and beautifying his adopted city.

While known for its culture and recreational activities, Sarasota is seeking to build a vital business community. Its main industries are agribusiness, tourism and retirement-affiliated services, but it is also attracting light manufacturing, high-tech and service fields as well. Today, the county boasts over 50 firms which employ 40 persons or more. A welcoming business climate, affordable housing, the breadth of its art community, and leisure activities offer new Sarasotans a very distinct and enriching life style.

Demographics

Sarasota County includes the cities of Sarasota, Venice, North Port, Longboat Key and the unincorporated areas of Sarasota County. Approximately 98% of Siesta Key is included in unincorporated Sarasota County while the remaining 2% (at the northern tip of the island) resides within the City of Sarasota.

◆ Size

Sarasota County, with its 35 miles of Gulf beaches, spans 573 square miles; 80% of the county is unincorporated (470.5 square miles). The City of Sarasota encompasses 24 square miles; Longboat Key is 4.26 square miles (approximately 50% of Longboat Key is in Sarasota County and 50% is in Manatee County); Venice is 7.9 square miles; and North Port is 68 square miles.

◆ Population

As of the 1990 census, the total population of Sarasota County was 277,776. The City of Sarasota had a population of 50,740; Longboat Key had 3,563; Venice had 17,216; and North Port had 12,558.

Age Demographics in Sarasota County

Under 18	16%
18-24	6%
25-44	24%
45-59	15%
60-74	25%
75 and over	14%

The median age in Sarasota County is 49; in Longboat Key it is 68; in Venice it is 68; and the median age in Northport is 50.

◆ Climate

Elevation: 18 feet
Annual Rainfall: 57.11 inches
Average Summer Temperature: 80 degrees
Average Winter Temperature: 61.5 degrees

Taxes

◆ Property Taxes

The Sarasota County millage rate is 14.240 mills per $1000 of assessed taxable value. Municipalities within the county are required to add additional millage: City of Sarasota - 6.518 mills; Venice -3.806 mills; North Port - 4.600 mills; Longboat Key - 2.2142.

◆ Sales and Use Tax

Sarasota County collects a 7% sales and use tax. 6% is levied by the State of Florida and 1% by the county.

Voting and Elections

Sarasota County

Sarasota County residents elect a board of commissioners from five districts for a four-year term of office. A recent referendum provides for single-member district elections; only voters living in a district may vote for a candidate seeking election to represent that district. The five county commissioners appoint a chairperson for a one-year term. Every two years, either two or three of the district seats are up for election.

Sarasota County Elections Office, 100 S Washington Blvd., Sarasota, FL 34236. *Ph. 951-5307.*

In the City of Sarasota, residents elect a city commission which has five members for a four-year term. Three of the commissioners are elected by district and two are elected at-large. The general municipal election takes place on the second Tuesday in March of each odd year. The mayor and vice-mayor are elected yearly by their fellow commissioners. A city manager, who is hired by the commissioners, administers the daily operations of the city. *Ph. 954-4115.*

Neighboring Municipalities

Longboat Key. Longboat Key residents elect seven commissioners, five of whom must live in the district which they represent while two are elected at-large. The commissioners serve a two-year term. The mayor and vice-mayor are elected by their fellow commissioners for one year. Elections take place on the third Tuesday in March. *Ph. 383-3721.*

Venice. The residents of Venice elect a mayor and six council members at-large for a three-year term. They may serve three consecutive terms of office. Two seats become available every year. Elections take place on the first Tuesday, after the first Monday, in December. *Ph. 485-3311.*

North Port City Commission. The governing body of North Port has five commissioners elected at-large for a four-year term. They may serve two consecutive terms of office. Each year, a chairperson is elected by fellow commissioners. Elections take place every odd year on the first Tuesday after the first Monday in November. *Ph. 426-8484.*

To facilitate voter registration, Sarasota County offers numerous voter registration sites throughout the area. To obtain a listing of participating banks, libraries and agencies offering this service, call the County Supervisor of Elections.

Pet Registration

Beginning at four months of age, dogs and cats are required to have an annual rabies vaccination and be licensed with the county. Sarasota County has a containment ordinance which is enforced with fines. Pets must be contained on one's property; they are not allowed to stray and visit your neighbors for a friendly little chat. Even if accompanied by an adult, they are not permitted on the Sarasota public beaches. Pooper-scooper ordinances and enforcement are decided upon by the cities.

The Humane Society is a volunteer organization which serves as an adoption center for pets. Its quarterly newsletter, *Advisor*, publicizes educational and special events. *Ph. 955-4131.*

Transportation

Air Travel

SARASOTA/BRADENTON INTERNATIONAL AIRPORT
6000 Airport Circle
Sarasota, Fl 34243
Communications Center - *24 Hr. Ph. 359-5200*
Passenger Page Service: *Ph. 359-5200*
Parking Information: *Ph. 359-5390*

Sarasota/Bradenton International Airport opened its new $56.6 million dollar terminal in 1989. Its tropical feeling is reflected in the 12-foot waterfall, exotic tropical plants, and saltwater aquarium which is located in the main lobby. Recently, it received status as a US Customs Port of Entry, inviting and processing arrivals from other countries. A new Federal Inspections Facility will process international flights as well as clear overseas cargo. Presently, international arrivals are from charter and tour companies; however, construction plans are in process to accommodate regularly scheduled international passenger service to gateways in Europe. SRQ (the government designation for Sarasota/Bradenton International Airport) is one of the state's most modern airports; it has been praised for its accessibility, cleanliness and convenience.

The Sarasota/Bradenton International Airport is five miles from downtown Sarasota.

Amenities. There is an automatic teller machine near the ticketing wing on the first floor lobby. A full service post office, also located on the first floor lobby, is open Monday-Friday, 9 am-12 noon and 1 pm-4:30 pm. Saturday hours are from 9 am-noon.

Parking. If you find yourself without enough money to pay for parking, you will not have to 'beg' to get out of the parking lot. Visa, MasterCard or a local check with identification are accepted at the cashier's booth.

If you plan to park your car for an extended period of time, inform the airport parking authorities of your intentions.

Ground Transportation. Airport Operations provides information on taxis, shuttles, limousines and charter buses servicing the airport. *Ph. 350-5225.*

Public Transit. Sarasota *(Ph. 951-5850)* and Manatee *(Ph. 749-7116)* counties provide public transit from the airport. Both ground transportation and public transit are located at the west end of baggage claim.

Major Airlines include:
American Airlines
Continental Airlines
Delta Airlines
Northwest Airlines
TWA
United Airlines
US Air

Commuter Service includes:
Air Sunshine: Service to Ft. Lauderdale. *Ph. 800-432-1744.*
American Eagle: Service to Miami. *Ph. 800-443-7300.*
US Air Express: Service to Orlando, Daytona Beach, Jacksonville. *Ph. 800-428-4322.*

Note: If you are a passenger or picking up a guest at the airport, an automated flight information system allows you to check on the arrival or departure status of any flight – before you leave for the airport. *Ph. 359-5436.*

Local Transportation

Bus Service. Sarasota County Area Transit (SCAT) operates 17 bus routes in urban parts of Sarasota County. Daily service is available Monday through Saturday, 6 am through 7 pm. There is no service on Sundays or major holidays. If you need assistance with routing information or bus schedules, call the SCAT information line. *Ph. 951-5851.* It is in service from 5:30 am to 7 pm, Monday through Saturday. You may request a schedule from them or obtain one on any of the SCAT buses.

If you are disabled, 65 years of age or older, or under 18 years of age, you can obtain a gold card which entitles you to half fare. You must show proof of age or certification of a handicap verifying that you are unable to drive a car. A number of buses are now equipped with lifts to accommodate wheelchairs. Call SCAT for additional information.

Senior Friendship Centers, Inc. provide door-to-door transportation service Monday through Friday for those who need assistance or are without any alternate means of transportation You must call 24 hours in advance to schedule a trip. *Ph. 955-2122.*

SCAT's Silver Card: If you are unable to use SCAT's bus service due to a physical disability, you can qualify for a Silver Card which entitles you to door-to-door transportation at a reduced cost. *Ph. 955-0304.*

Intra and Intercounty Systems. If you need to take more than one bus to reach your destination, request a transfer from the driver when you pay your fare. Or, if you are planning to continue your trip into Manatee County, also request a transfer.

Sunday Beach Special. There is free bus service to and from Siesta Beach on Sundays. Call the SCAT information line for departure locations and time schedule.

Sarasota Trolley. The Sarasota open air trolley has become a colorful part of downtown Sarasota and is one of the best buys in town. On weekdays, you can travel its 30-minute route through downtown Sarasota for only 25 cents. On Saturdays, the fare is reduced to a nickel. Hours of operation are from 9:45 am to 4:45 pm, every 30 minutes.

Note: Whether boarding a bus or trolley, you will need the exact fare. Drivers are not equipped to provide change.

Postal Service

The City of Sarasota has one main post office and two branch offices.

Post Offices

Main Office	1661 Ringling Blvd. Monday-Friday: 8:30 am - 5:00 pm Saturday: 9:00 am - noon	952-9720
Gulf Gate	2875 Ashton Road Monday - Friday: 8:30 am - 4:30 pm Saturday: 9:00 am - noon	924-8116
South Gate	2155 Siesta Drive Monday - Friday: 8:30 am - 4:30 pm Saturday: 9:00 am - noon	955-9355
Sawyer Court Annex (only customer-notified parcels & mail; no window service)	4041 Sawyer Court Monday - Friday: 10:00 am - 4:30 pm Saturday: 10:00 am - 1:00 pm	924-5956

Contract Stations

Contract Stations, located in business establishments, are extensions of the post office and provide full postal operations. It is always best to call, however, if you need a special service. Hours may vary; call for specific hours of operation.

Airgate	60000 Airport Circle	351-7360
Beneva Village	3406 Clarks Road	922-6601
Crescent Beach	6595 Midnight Pass	349-4343
Downtown Station	1461 Main Street	366-1997
East Avenue	1039 N. East Avenue	954-5573
Forest Lakes	3644 Webber Street	921-6645
Fruitville	4904 Fruitville Road	378-2881

Gold Tree	75 S. Tuttle Avenue	366-0090
Lockwood Ridge	3251 17th Street #60	955-7943
Midtown	1281 S. Tamiami Trail	365-9116
Newtown	1922 Martin Luther	953-5434
Northside	50 Trail Plaza	351-6672
Palm Plaza	4402 Bee Ridge Road	377-0101
Pinecraft	1240 Yoder Avenue	957-0644
St. Armand	421A St. Armand's Circle	388-2824
Siesta Branch	5124 Ocean Blvd.	349-1111
Sarasota Commons	935 N. Beneva Road #601	365-3725
Sarasota Square	8201 S. Tamiami Trail	921-7741
South Side	1905 S. Osprey Avenue	955-0147
South Trail	2184 Gulf Gate Drive	922-0765

Newspapers and Magazines

The SARASOTA HERALD TRIBUNE is a daily newspaper with international, national and local coverage. *Florida West* is the local section with listings of events, meetings and support groups. *Ticket*, the entertainment supplement, is printed on Fridays. *Ph. 953-7755.*

THE PELICAN PRESS, a weekly newspaper for Thursday readers, presents in-depth coverage of local news in Sarasota County. It features political, social and cultural happenings in the area. *Ph. 349-4949.*

SARASOTA MAGAZINE, a monthly publication, focuses on people, places and events in Sarasota. Many of its feature articles focus on important city issues, prominent personalities and other newsworthy happenings. Its calendar of cultural events is a useful guide to the arts in the city. *Ph. 366-8225.*

SCENE MAGAZINE, issued monthly, features social, civic and cultural events. In addition to its cultural calendar, there are updates on business, medical and real estate news. *Ph. 365-1119.*

BUSINESS MAGAZINE is a bimonthly publication focusing on the Sarasota, Venice and Bradenton areas. It highlights what's happening in the business community, business personalities, and special business features. *Ph. 378-9048.*

Library System

Selby Public Library

1001 Blvd. of the Arts.
Sarasota. *Ph. 951-5501*
Reference assistance: *Ph. 364-4411*

Selby Public Library is the main library of the Sarasota County Library System. Highlights include:

- *Framed art prints*, which are available on loan for eight weeks; they can be renewed for an additional period of time.
- *The Mertz 16 millimeter collection of motion picture films* is available for loan along with a projector to show them. These films have large screen capabilities for group viewing and do not require public viewing rights.
- *Computers* may be used on the library premises. A printer is available but bring your own paper.

The **Ann Marbut Environmental Library**, one of the five branch libraries, has a unique focus. It has been acclaimed for its extensive collection of environmental literature and commitment to promoting environmental sensitivity. You can find literature on air quality, water quality, recycling, insect control, marine life, as well as EPA technical documentation. *Ph. 924-9677.*

Call the main library to learn of special and ongoing community programs at the five branch libraries throughout Sarasota County.

Health Care

There are three full-service hospitals in Sarasota County.

Sarasota Memorial Hospital

1700 South Tamiami Trail
Sarasota. *Ph. 955-1111*

Sarasota Memorial Hospital, an 863-bed acute care facility, is a fully accredited and certified public hospital offering a wide range of medical/surgical services. It is recognized as one of the largest hospitals in Florida. Approximately 90% of Memorial's physicians are board certified.

It provides full *cardiac care* (including cardiac surgery), a strong inpatient and outpatient *oncology unit* and an *obstetrics program* with a *neonatal intensive care unit*. On the hospital campus, there is also a *Sports Medicine Center* offering physical therapy, rehabilitation and reconditioning. A *Sports Medicine Hotline* (*Ph. 957-7600*) answers questions about training and conditioning, injury prevention and injury management. If you can't sleep, a new *Sleep Disorder Center* monitors sleep patterns. Other specialized services include *New Dawn*, which provides information, support and treatment for chemical dependency. *Lakeside Pavilion*, located on Clark Road, is a psychiatric treatment facility which also offers many community programs. *Ph. 921-8888*.

Community Programs

Kids Under The Weather is a special program for children between the ages of three months to 12 years. If you are a working parent and your child has the sniffles or a stomach ache, Sarasota Memorial Hospital will lend a helping hand. Pediatric nurses at the hospital provide tender loving care to children who are not feeling well and need to be looked after. Kids must be picked up at the end of the day. *Ph. 957-7500*.

Senior Care Advisor is a unique Sarasota Memorial program designed for seniors. If you are a senior, an advisor will assist with problem solving, finding answers to questions, and locating resources in the community. *Ph. 953-1999*.

Doctor's Hospital of Sarasota
2750 Bahia Vista Street
Sarasota. *Ph. 366-1411*

Doctor's Hospital is a 168-bed private medical/surgical hospital. In 1982, it was purchased by the Hospital Corporation of America. It has modern facilities, comprehensive services, and a staff of approximately 320 physicians. Outpatient affiliates provide specialty services, such as nuclear medicine, radiology and a center for breast care. The *Eye Surgery Center*, located within the hospital, allows patients to be admitted directly to the center on an outpatient basis. The most modern technology in stretcher design results in less body movement and consequently less stress on the eye following surgery. Their *Respiratory Therapy Department* offers a wide variety of heart/lung diagnostic procedures and services. Serving the community 24 hours a day, seven days a week, their *Emergency Treatment Center* is staffed by physicians qualified in emergency medicine. In the summer of 1994, a new hospital facility with additional private rooms is expected to be completed.

Venice Hospital

540 The Rialto
Venice. *Ph. 485-7711*

Venice Hospital is a private, not-for-profit, hospital with 342 beds. Its nationally accredited cancer program has a 40-bed unit devoted to it. The *Heart Institute* provides comprehensive outpatient and inpatient diagnostic services as well as a critical care unit well staffed by cardiologists. Modern facilities include a new *Pediatric Unit* and a new *Emergency Care Center* for acute care illnesses and injuries as well as minor emergencies. Its *Physical Medicine And Rehabilitation Program* has been nationally acclaimed. *Easy Street* is a re-creation of a little town, similar to a movie set, contained within the hospital to assist rehabilitation patients relearn basic mobility skills. It simulates the outside world with a full-scale apartment, grocery store, gas pump, and even an ATM machine.

Venice Hospital also sponsors *Connections*, a community service and resource program. It locates people in the community who provide services related to home, medical, legal or personal needs. *Ph. 483-7567.*

Education

SARASOTA COUNTY SCHOOL BOARD

Administrative Office and Information
2418 Hatton
Ph. 953-5000

◆ Sarasota County Public Schools

The Sarasota County Public School System has 19 elementary schools, six middle schools and five senior high schools.

Special Programs and Highlights. Sarasota County has developed some outstanding innovative curricula for exceptional and nontraditional students with special needs.

- *Pine View School for the Gifted* is a non-districted school for grades 2-12. It is a dedicated facility, with full-time faculty and advanced curriculum, for gifted learners. Challenging and stimulating programs have been designed to meet the special needs of these exceptional students.
- *Booker High School* offers specialized programs in the Visual and Performing Arts. Students must audition to be accepted into one of the five disciplines: art, dance, music, radio/television, and theater. During the morning hours, students follow a regular academic schedule; in the afternoon, the program focuses on intensive study in their major area. Most of the 250 students who are enrolled in the program continue their professional preparation at universities and professional schools.
- *Bay Haven School of Basics Plus* opened as a magnet elementary school requiring a contract commitment which includes parental involvement. The mission of the program is to ensure competencies in language arts, math, social studies, science, fine arts, foreign language and physical education. Bay Haven is the only elementary school offering foreign language study.
- *Oak Park* was established for exceptional students in the fall of 1993. The program was developed to meet the special needs of the physically handicapped, the medically fragile, the severely emotionally disturbed, and the mentally retarded. Students may be enrolled at the age of three and continue until they have completed program requirements or reach 22 years of age. Oak Park's mission is to provide an environment for students to develop their potential and become functioning members of society. They receive a level of support, assistance, and physical care not available within the traditional school. An academic curriculum includes math, language arts, science and social studies; vocational programs offer culinary arts, floral design, woodworking and basic mechanical repair in a sheltered workshop setting and experiential job training; classes in home living skills and community-based instruction provide experiences, behaviors, and skills critical for everyday living. Reflecting the philosophy of the school is Oak Park's motto: "Diversity: Our Cause for Celebration."
- *New Directions High School*, recognized as a model school, offers an alternative educational program for students considered to be at risk of dropping out of school. Since instruction is based

on developing competencies, it is non-graded and students work at their own pace in individualized programs. In order to complete the necessary academic requirements, they attend classes for a half-day with three 50-minute academic periods. During the second half of the day, they are enrolled in either a credit-earning vocational education program or approved and monitored employment situations. Emphasis is placed on helping students develop the necessary employment skills to qualify and succeed in the job market. Its primary mission, however, is to assist students in securing a high school diploma. Many of the graduates continue their education at colleges throughout the country.
- *Martin Luther King Academy* offers a unique non-traditional educational opportunity to students who are over-age and behind in their academic credits, many of whom would otherwise remain dropouts. The GED Exit Option allows them to earn a high school diploma through computer-assisted instruction. The King program combines this option with counseling and work experience. This innovative program is being used in only six states and only 20 of the 67 school districts in Florida.
- *Computer laboratories* can be found in every school while state grants are making it possible to provide a high-tech classroom with modern telecommunications equipment in selected schools. Students are being afforded the opportunity to speak with other students around the world.
- Sarasota County was recognized nationally for implementing innovative *art instruction* in the public school system. All schools have teams which provide specialized art instruction in art classrooms and interdisciplinary art activities in other classes.

COLLEGES AND UNIVERSITIES

Within Sarasota and nearby Bradenton, a selection of various college and university programs are available.

The **University of Sarasota** offers graduate programs in business administration and education for working professionals. Classes are scheduled evenings and weekends. *Ph. 355-2906.*

The **University of South Florida** at Sarasota offers two distinct educational programs on the same campus:

The University Program offers junior and senior level study in the liberal arts, education, business and engineering. Graduate programs in education as well as graduate studies in some of the social and behavioral sciences are also available. *Ph. 359-4220.*

New College is the state's honor college. Its unique four-year liberal arts academic program is individually tailored to each student. It includes tutorials, independent study, and off-campus special projects and internships. Its innovative curriculum focuses on fulfilling a personalized academic contract rather than the traditional core course approach. Letters of evaluation are used in lieu of grades. *Ph. 355-2991.*

Florida State University offers two graduate programs at the Asolo Center for the Performing Arts.

- FSU Asolo Conservatory of Motion Picture has received recognition for its two-year graduate program in film, television and the recording arts.
- The Asolo Acting Conservatory is renowned for its three-year graduate program. In the third year, students perform on the main stage of the Asolo theater. Graduates in both programs receive an MFA degree.

Manatee Community College has two campuses. The north one is located in Bradenton *(Ph. 755-1511)* and the south campus is in Venice *(Ph. 493-3504).* Manatee Community offers a two-year liberal arts program for transfer to a four-year school.

The **Ringling School of Art and Design** is a nationally recognized institution offering a four-year degree program in five art disciplines: fine arts, computer graphics, graphic design, illustration, and interior design. *Ph. 351-4614.*

There are also several special community programs sponsored by *The Ringling School of Art and Design* through their Continuing and Professional Education Department. *Ph. 359-7577.*

- The *Pre College Perspective* is a one-month summer campus program offered to high school students in grades 10-12. The focus is on gaining an exposure to the various art disciplines offered at the college as well as building a portfolio. In addition to accepting local applicants, students come from many different states and other countries.

- The *Summer Art Camp* offers a half-day program for students in grades 1-12. Children may attend for either a three- or six-week session.
- The *Youth Program* is held on Saturday mornings for students in grades 1-12 during the fall, winter and summer seasons.
- *Spring Art Week* is a one-week campus program for adults which takes place during the college spring break. Small, studio-based workshops are available in a variety of art disciplines, such as painting, printmaking, collage, computer animation, and photography.
- The *Community Art Adult Program* offers approximately 30 different classes featuring many art disciplines, ranging from the purely creative to technology-assisted art. There are six-week sessions during each season, as well as weekend workshops.

Sarasota Institute of Lifetime Learning. SILL, a non-profit, volunteer community organization, presents a lecture series on the arts, society and international issues. During January through March, a variety of stimulating themes are presented in a six-week mini-course format. Experts in the various subjects are invited as guest lecturers. After the presentation, the audience is usually invited to participate in a question and answer session. For information, call the Selby Public Library. *Ph. 951-5501.*

Friends of Selby Public Library offer a lecture series beginning in January. A broad spectrum of subjects in the arts and humanities are presented by guest speakers. *Ph. 365-5228.*

Longboat Key Adult Education Center offers classes in the visual arts, literature, cinema, writing, music appreciation, and more. *Ph. 383-8811.*

The Cultural Scene

The Ringling Estate

John and Mabel Ringling, who settled Sarasota in the 1920s, played a significant role in the cultural life of Sarasota. The Ca'd'Zan, the Museum of Art, the Circus Gallery and the Asolo Theater are a major part of the Ringling legacy and share space on the Ringling grounds. *5401 Bayshore Road.*

The **Ca'd'Zan** (House of John), the winter home of John and Mabel Ringling, was built in 1925. The 30-room mansion, overlooking

Sarasota Bay, was modeled after the Doge's Palace in Venice, Italy. Its opulent grandeur, decor and art reflect the Ringling taste for European treasures.

The **John and Mabel Ringling Museum of Art**, Florida's official state art museum, is located on the Ringling estate overlooking Sarasota Bay. It houses a nationally acclaimed collection of Renaissance and Baroque art, including five large oil paintings by Peter Paul Rubens, as well as a contemporary collection of art. *Ph. 355-5101.*

The **Asolo Theater**, also on the Ringling grounds, was purchased in Asolo, Italy (a hill town near Venice) and shipped to Sarasota. This 18th-century rococo-style Italian playhouse was the first home to the Asolo Theater Company. The theater is presently being used for special community events and meetings. *Ph. 351-8000.*

The **Asolo Center for the Performing Arts**. This is the present home to the Asolo Theater Company. Although the building has a Renaissance design in harmony with the Art Museum, the interior is from the Dunfermline, a Baroque Opera House in Scotland, originally built in 1903. Purchasing the dismantled interior from storage, it was reconstructed for the Asolo in 1987. The Asolo Theater Company, which has received national recognition, is the official theater company of Florida. It stages eight productions each year. On selected evenings during the season, the audience is invited to attend "Playtalks." Following the theater performance, the actors and the audience engage in a lively analytical discussion of the play. If you want to speak the native tongue, pronounce it "Ahs-lo."

The Asolo Center for the Performing Arts is a non-profit, independent institution which hosts and provides outstanding cultural programs throughout the year. It also houses the two Florida State Conservatories for acting and film production. *5555 N. Tamiami Trail. Ph. 351-8000.*

Van Wezel Performing Arts Hall

Its shell-shaped architectural design and bayfront location make it a landmark in Sarasota. The blueprints are the work of noted Taliesin Associated Artists of the Frank Lloyd Wright Foundation. Locally, it is known as the "purple palace." In fact, Mrs. Wright was instrumental in selecting this vibrant color. Its interior design and engineering provide ideal visual and acoustical conditions. During season, touring theater productions, dance and musical performances, and concerts by popular artists and internationally acclaimed performers are presented on stage. *777 N. Tamiami Trail. Ph. 953-3366.*

Sarasota Opera Association

The Sarasota Opera House, formerly the historic A.B. Edwards Theater, had its beginnings in the Ringling era and attracted many famous vaudeville acts. In 1982, the Sarasota Opera Association purchased it and began a decade of restoration. It is now home to Sarasota's professional opera company. They perform four operas during the two-month winter season beginning in February. *61 N. Pineapple Avenue. Ph. 366-8450.*

Sarasota Youth Opera Company

The Youth Opera Company offers a program of vocal and stage training coupled with actual performances. Auditions are held early in September.

Sarasota Ballet of Florida

The much-acclaimed Sarasota Ballet is the resident company of Sarasota and Manatee counties. Its exciting repertoire includes excerpts and single acts from historic classics, neo-classic ballets in the tradition of George Balanchine, beautiful contemporary works, as well as full-length ballets. Its season, which begins in September, includes a series of six productions performed at the Sarasota Opera House and the Van Wezel Performing Arts Hall. The Company has been invited to participate in a cultural exchange program with the Bolshoi Ballet. *Ph. 954-7171.*

The Sarasota Ballet has a very strong educational commitment to the community. It offers a four-week *Summer Intensive Workshop* which includes ballet, jazz, modern, choreography and production. Although there are auditions, it is open to most students who have had dance training. Three levels of classes (beginners, intermediate and advanced) are taught by an international faculty of dance. The *Apprenticeship Program* offers students, who are recommended from area dance schools, the opportunity to receive extra training from the Russian ballet masters at the Company. They may audition to perform in some of the productions. *Dance the Next Generation,* a partnership with the University of South Florida, is an innovative program which has received high acclaim from the school system. The Sarasota Ballet Company targets schools with minority populations and students at-risk for dance scholarships. The program focuses on children at the third-grade level who demonstrate the motivation and commitment to learn ballet and have the appropriate physical attributes necessary for a dancer. Fifty students each year are awarded a seven-year scholarship. Students are taught by the same ballet masters as the ballet company. If they complete the seven years with the Sarasota ballet and maintain a good academic standing, they are offered an academic scholarship at USF.

Florida West Coast Symphony

The Symphony performs a series of classical programs, pops and children's concerts from October through May. It is also the official orchestra which accompanies the Sarasota Ballet. Beginning in 1949 as a community orchestra, it has become the resident symphony for Sarasota and Manatee counties. During the season, it performs at the Van Wezel Performing Arts Hall with a symphony of 80-100 musicians. The exciting musical season includes a series of six concerts featuring classical masterpieces; six concerts by the chamber orchestra which combine classical and pops in their themed "Enchanted Evenings" series, and four pops concerts.

During the first three weeks of June, the West Coast Symphony sponsors the *Sarasota Music Festival*. Master musicians, teachers and performers are invited from countries throughout the world to teach classes and present seminars to students with exceptional musical talent. Performing at the festival, this elite gathering presents the best in music.

The Symphony also sponsors *Summer at the Symphony*, a three-week instructional program for winds, brass and percussion instruments. Another three-week program is devoted to the strings.

Five youth orchestras are under the auspices of the Symphony. It is open to all levels of students who wish to participate. They rehearse at the Symphony Center, which is the rehearsal home of the West Coast Symphony. During the Spring, the youth orchestras are invited to perform at the Van Wezel. *Symphony Center, 709 Tamiami Trail, N. Ph. 953-4252.*

Jazz Club of Sarasota

The Jazz Club hosts concerts and jazz jams during the year. They also sponsor lectures, educational programs and community events. Founded in 1980, they have dedicated themselves to the mission of preserving and promoting jazz music as America's art form. Attracting a large membership, the club keeps jazz very 'visible' and alive in the Sarasota community throughout the year. The primary style of music is Mainstream Jazz from the 40's and 50's. During the year, they sponsor seven concerts, inviting well-known artists from around the country. The performances are held at the Van Wezel Performing Arts Hall. Jazz jams are held twice a month for both professional and amateur musicians at Holley Hall in Symphony Center. From October through April, the club sponsors free *Jazz at Noon* programs at various locations in the city. As part of its educational program, *Inside Jazz*, a series of six jazz lectures, is presented by well-known musicians and educators. Beginning in November, monthly lectures are held on Saturday mornings, from 10 am till noon. They are free to the public. *Ph. 366-1552.*

The *Sarasota Jazz Festival* is hosted by the Jazz Club in the beginning of April. Jazz enthusiasts look forward to this four-day festival featuring the legends of jazz. In addition to mainstream jazz, musicians play a repertoire which includes blues, big band and Latin music. There are featured artists as well as musicians playing in combos and ensembles.

The Florida Studio Theater

The Florida Studio Theater is a small, professional equity theater with a contemporary focus. During the year, it stages four Mainstage Productions for its winter program and three during the summer season. Some plays are selected for the eight-week *Reading Series* which is held during the fall and summer. Actors perform the plays every Sunday – with script in hand.

The Florida Studio Theater hosts the *New Play Festival* during the month of May. The first two weekends are devoted to young playwrights, 8th grade and below. Every style of theater is represented by the young playwrights. From the thousands of entries (each play is five pages or less), one hundred are selected to be performed by professional actors with full staging. The last three weekends are devoted to adult playwrights. Three new plays are selected and performed by studio professionals. After each show, the audience is invited to participate in a discussion. *1241 N. Palm Avenue. Ph. 366-9017.*

Sarasota Film Society

The Society showcases cinema screenings of current international and independently produced American films. On occasion, revivals are brought to the screen. A new three-theater cinema was dedicated to the film society in the summer of '93. During the first week of November, the Society sponsors the Cine-World Film Festival, a gourmet film fest featuring the best of new releases from different countries around the world. *Ph. 388-2441.*

Sarasota Arts Council

The Council serves as a liaison between the visual, literary and performing arts communities and area residents. It provides information on cultural happenings throughout the county. *Ph. 351-6433.*

Events and Attractions

Sarasota French Film Festival

Contemporary French films are featured by this five-day cinema celebration during the second week in November. The newest and best of French cinema, many of them U.S. premieres, are previewed each day, beginning at 10 am and continuing into the evening hours. After each screening, the audience is invited to remain for a discussion of the film with either its producer, director or actors. Seminars and a critics' panel provide insights into French cinema, enhancing the experience through their analysis and commentary. The social highlight of the festival is a black tie gala on Friday evening. This annual event is sponsored by the Asolo Center for the Performing Arts in collaboration with the State of Florida and the French government. *Ph. 351-9010.*

The Medieval Fair

This four-day extravaganza in March is hosted by the John and Mabel Ringling Museum of Art on the museum grounds. A 14th-century market place offers a selection of food appealing to the medieval palate of hungry travelers. Juried, handmade craft items, using only materials available in the 14th century, are for sale. A human chess match with a period theme and an authentic full-armored joust on draft horses provide medieval entertainment. *Ph. 359-5733.*

Mote Marine Laboratory/Aquarium

The aquarium has a 135,000-gallon shark tank, in addition to showcasing a variety of sea creatures in other aquaria. Guided tours, of approximately 45 minutes, describe marine life in the gulf and bay waters and discuss research presently being conducted at Mote Laboratories. Mote Marine also offers a Monday night seminar series on marine life featuring the communities and culture of sea animals and plants. The program begins in January with research highlights from the previous year and continues with guest lecturers and films through May. Mote's quarterly newsletter presents interesting articles and upcoming events. *1600 Thompson Parkway. Ph. 388-4441.*

The Marie Selby Botanical Gardens

Noted for its unparalleled and exquisite collection of orchids, the Gardens also specialize in bromeliads, exotic tropical plants, hundreds of plant varieties, and lovely gardens.

This Sarasota botanical treasure is renowned for its showcase of epiphytic plants from rain forests around the world. Epiphytes, such as orchids and bromeliads, extract their nutrients and water from the air rather than the soil. In addition to the epiphytes, there are many other botanical delights to be enjoyed. Eleven acres of walkways include the Tropical Display House with a lush jungle environment and rich display of color; the Waterfall Garden with cascading waters, lily pond, Japanese carp, and surrounding tropical plants; the award winning Hibiscus Garden with spectacular large blossoms and vibrant colors; the Giant Banyan Grove; and the Tropical Food Garden with fruity tropical edibles.

During the year, the Marie Selby Botanical Gardens offers classes and seminars in horticulture, botany, organic gardening, landscaping, nature art, and cooking with herbs as part of its educational focus. Quarterly newsletters, plant fairs, festivals and holiday celebrations are part of its active program of community involvement. It has a large volunteer organization attracted to the rewards of working in this environment. Within the international community of botanists, it has become a world renowned research center. *811 South Palm Avenue. Ph. 366-5730.*

Myakka River State Park

Myakka Park was originally a cattle ranch owned by Mrs. Potter Palmer at the turn of the century. It presently has the distinction of being Florida's largest state park (as measured by land mass), approximately 45 square miles. Within the park, wildlife and birds roam freely. An Interpretive Center showcases the animals and birds encased in their natural habitats. A 39-mile loop for hiking, with camping sites along the way, attracts campers and backpackers. Bicycles are available for rent. For the less energetic, there is a 1/2-mile self-guided walk along a scenic nature trail. A bird walk for observing waterfowl, fresh water fishing, and canoeing are along the Upper Lake. From November through April, park rangers lead guided walks through the less traveled areas. Sunday mornings attract novice bird watchers to the park's *Beginning Birding* program. The lakes are filled with alligators but, according to the rangers, they've been rather well-behaved. The *Wilderness Preserve*, which has 75 acres of undisturbed land, remains as a vision of old Florida. Only 30 people per day are allowed to visit in order to preserve its natural state. *9 Miles East of I-75 on State Road 72 (Stickney Point Road), Exit 37. Ph. 361-6511.*

The *Myakka Safari Tour* cruises the Upper Lake in *Gator Gal*, one of the largest air-boats. A narrated 45-minute water tour describes the waterfowl, alligators and wildlife of Myakka Lake State Park. A narrated Tram Tour visits the interior of the park's wilderness areas where visitor vehicles are not permitted. *Ph. 365-0100.*

Lipizzan Stallions

The Herrmann family's association with the Lipizzan stallions dates back to Austria, about three hundred years ago. Their Myakka ranch is presently a breeding ground and training center for showcasing the famous Lipizzan stallions which travel around the world. The Lipizzans were bred as war horses for high ranking officers before the use of gun powder. Being regal in stature, they were shown for their particular grace and skill in Austrian high society. They are best known for their ballet-like maneuvers, "airs above the ground," used during combat to defeat foot soldiers. Leaping into the air with all four legs above ground, the different "airs" have been set to music as the stallions perform their graceful movements. During their training season, the first Thursday in January through the last Saturday in March, the Lipizzans perform at home to prepare for their tour. *32755 Singletary Rd., Myakka City. Ph. 322-1501.*

Don't Miss

St. Armand's Circle. St. Armand's Circle, with its elegant shops, restaurants, lovely courtyards, patios, and landscape design, is a delightful way to spend the day – even if just to stroll and window-shop. Always a hub of activity, enjoy a patio lunch while people watching.

Shelling on Siesta Key. Shelling is a pastime enjoyed by both novices and collectors as they stroll the Siesta Key beaches looking for the colorful and unusual treasures deposited along the shores. As a matter of fact, when you walk along the beach, you will be walking on the 'whitest and purest sand in the world.' In 1987, Siesta Beach competed in the Great International Sand Beach Challenge. Its 99% pure quartz sand qualified it for top honors.

Warm Mineral Springs. If you're feeling a little stiff and sore, relief is only 12 miles south of Venice (on US 41). Florida's only warm mineral springs provides millions of gallons of 87° water, rich in mineral content, to soothe those aches and pains. The spring-fed lake has a special area for bathing. For more privacy, individual hot tubs with mineral spring water are also available. If you need some additional attention, a masseuse/masseur offer a relaxing massage. To complete your relaxation therapy, bring a chair or spread a blanket on the grassy area near the water. A snack bar offers a light lunch menu. *Ph. 426-1692.*

Recreation

The Grapefruit League

The Chicago White Sox has its spring training camp at the Ed Smith Stadium, which is also home to the Sarasota White Sox. *12th Street and Tuttle Avenue. Ph. 954-SOXX.*

Golf Courses

There are more than 30 public, semi-private and private golf courses in Sarasota County. Contact the County Dept. of Parks and Recreation for locations.

Note: John Hamilton Gillespie, a Scottsman, is credited with establishing the nation's first golf course in downtown Sarasota in 1886.

Beaches

The Sarasota County Department of Parks and Recreation regulates county and city beaches. Parking is free at all beaches/parks, but overnight parking – from midnight to 6 am – is not permitted. Water temperature in the Gulf during the winter months may dip into the low 60's, whereas in late July and August it may reach 90°. Sarasota County has 35 miles of Gulf beaches. Some have a more primitive, secluded setting while others are more developed and offer numerous amenities. Pets are not permitted on any of the beaches.

Lido Beach, 1/2 mile southwest, of St. Armand's Circle, 400 Ben Franklin Dr., Sarasota
Amenities: Observation deck, playground; picnic facilities; snack bar; cabana rentals.

North Lido, 1/4 mile northwest of St. Armand's Circle
A private setting; use caution as the currents can be swift.

South Lido
Southern tip of Lido Key
Expansive views of the city and the Gulf.
Amenities: Grills; playground; nature trails; observation tower and deck.

Siesta Beach, 948 Beach Road, Siesta Key
Amenities: Playground; fitness trails; softball field; volleyball courts; tennis courts; picnic facilities; snack bar; cabana rentals. For beach conditions and water temperatures on Siesta Key, contact the Siesta Public Beach station. *Ph. 349-7981.*

Turtle Beach, 8918 Midnight Pass Rd., South end of Siesta Key
A quieter beach; the sand is a bit coarser, but great for shelling. No food concessions on beach but private restaurants are located across the street.
Amenities: Boat ramps; playground; horseshoe courts; volleyball; picnic facilities.

Nokomis Beach, Casey Key Rd. west of Albee Rd. Bridge
A family oriented beach.
Amenities: Boat ramps; boardwalk and deck; dune walkovers; picnic facilities; snack bar.

North Jetty, Southern tip of Casey Key
A favorite for fishing.
Amenities: Volleyball courts; horseshoe courts; picnic facilities; snack bar.

Venice Beach, 100 La Esplanade, Venice
There is a diving reef 1/4 mile offshore.
Amenities: Volleyball courts; picnic facilities; snack bar.

Caspersen Beach, 4100 Harbor Dr. S., Venice
South of Venice Fishing Pier. A secluded beach in a natural setting.
Amenities: Boardwalk; nature trail; great shelling beach; picnic facilities.

Manasota Beach, 8570 Manasota Key Rd., Manasota
Situated between the Gulf and the Intracoastal waterways.
Amenities: Boat ramp & dock; picnic facilities.

Blind Pass, 6725 Manasota Key Rd., Manasota
Located one mile north of the Charlotte County line.

Fishing Piers

New Pass Sarasota Fishing Pier
Turtle Beach Fishing Pier
Venice Fishing Pier
North Jetty

Surfing Beaches

North end of Siesta Beach
Jetties at Venice Inlet, 1 mile north of Venice Beach
North Jetty Park, across the Inlet
Manasota Beach, 1 mile north of lifeguard tower
Blind Pass, 4 miles south of Manasota Beach

Snorkeling Beaches

Crescent Beach, south of Siesta Beach, extends for 1 1/2 miles to Point of Rocks
North Jetty Beach
Venice Beach along rocky areas

Public Swimming Pools

There are 2 fresh water swimming pools in Sarasota. Call to find out fee schedules.
Lido Beach (Tuesday-Sunday). *Ph. 388-3626*
Arlington Aquatic Complex. *Ph. 364-4855*

Directory of Services

9-1-1 Emergency Only	POLICE • SHERIFF• FIRE• MEDICAL• RESCUE	
AGENCY	**DESCRIPTION**	**SARASOTA (813)**
ALCOHOL & DRUG ABUSE FIRST STEP	Intervention & Referral Drug & Alcohol Rehab.	800-821-4357 366-5333
CRISIS CENTER	24 Hour Help Line:	364-9355
ABUSE CENTER	Women in Distress Safe Places & Rape Crises	365-1976
POISON INFORMATION CENTER		800-282-3171
SENIOR SUPPORT	Telephone Reassurance & Support Senior Friendship Center 24 Hour Hotline	955-2122
TEEN HOTLINE		364-9355
TIME/TEMPERATURE		953-2900

County Services

AGENCY	DESCRIPTION	SARASOTA (813)
GOVERNMENT CENTER COUNTY COURTHOUSE	2000 Main Street	364-4417
PUBLIC INFORMATION	Information & Referral	364-4455
ANIMAL CONTROL		951-5550
BOARD OF EDUCATION		953-5000
COUNTY COOPERATIVE EXTENSION		951-4240
COUNTY COURTHOUSE		951-5000
EMERGENCY MGMNT	Disaster Readiness Training & Evacuation Information	366-6000
FIRE PREVENTION		951-4215

FL. HIGHWAY PATROL	All Interstate Roads & Turnpikes	483-5911
GARBAGE COLLECTION		378-6188
LIBRARY		951-5501
LICENSES	Auto Tag	951-5600
	Parking Permit - Handicapped	951-5600
	Boating Registration	951-5600
	Fishing & Hunting	951-5600
MASS TRANSIT	Schedules	951-5851
MOSQUITO CONTROL		951-5556
PARKS AND RECREATION		951-5572
PASSPORT INFORMATION		951-5206
PROPERTY APPRAISER		951-5650
SHERIFF		951-5800
TAX COLLECTOR		951-5600
TRAFFIC VIOLATION INFORMATION		951-5102
VOTER REGISTRATION		951-5307
WATER/SEWER		378-6100
Emergency/After Hours		378-6100

Human Services

AGENCY	DESCRIPTION	SARASOTA (813)
AMERICAN ASSOC. OF RETIRED PERSONS (AARP)	FL State Headquarters Provides local chapter contacts	576-1155
AMERICAN RED CROSS	Hurricane Shelter Information Disaster Relief, Blood Banks, Educational Programs	379-9300
CHILD CARE OF SOUTHWEST FL.	Information & Referrals on Licensed Child Care Centers & Registered Care Providers	366-2047
FIRST CALL FOR HELP Information & Referral	Connects You with the Appropriate Person or Agency Who Can Answer Your Question or Assist You	366-5025
HANDICAPPED/DISABLED SERVICES		951-5800
HEALTH DEPARTMENT		954-2900

I R S	Location & Hours of Local Offices Tax Information Tax Forms	800-829-1040 904-354-1760 800-829-3676
NEWCOMERS CLUBS	The Sarasota Herald Tribune publishes a Clubs Directory in *September*. The Chamber of Commerce also has a listing of contacts and phone numbers.	955-8187
SENIOR CITIZEN SERVICES	Information / Assistance Programs for Seniors	955-2122 365-2800
SOCIAL SECURITY		800-772-1213
SOCIAL SERVICE TRANSPORTATION	Reduced Fares, Dial-A-Ride Transport for Seniors and Special Groups	955-2122 955-0340
UNITED WAY	An Excellent Resource for Community Information	366-2686
VETERAN'S ASSISTANCE		951-5498
VOLUNTEER CENTER OF SARASOTA	A Clearinghouse for Volunteer Positions	953-5965

City Numbers

GOVERNMENT CENTER Information Desk	SARASOTA CITY HALL 1565 First Street	365-2200
CITY CLERK		954-4160
POLICE (Non Emergency)		366-8000
FIRE (Non Emergency)		364-2215
DRIVERS LICENSE		361-6222
ELECTRICAL SERVICE	Florida Power & Light	379-1424
GARBAGE COLLECTION		365-7651
LIBRARY		951-5501
TELEPHONE CO.	GTE New Service GTE Billing	800-483-4200 800-483-3200
VOTER'S REGISTRATION		954-4115
WATER AND SEWER Emergency/After Hours		954-4197 955-4838

Civic Organizations

Greater Sarasota Chamber of Commerce	955-8187
Greater Sarasota Committee of 100	955-8187
Longboat Key Chamber of Commerce	383-2466
Siesta Key Chamber of Commerce	349-3800
Convention and Visitors Bureau	957-1877

Tampa

Tampa is best described as a multi-faceted city – from its brick-lined streets in the colorful Latin Quarter to its tall modern skyscrapers in the growing downtown business sector. A world class airport, major highways, white sandy beaches, cultural activities and professional sports all contribute to its attractiveness as a place to live.

But beneath the brick, steel and asphalt of this modern city lies the real charm of Tampa: its rich blend of multicultural and ethnic diversity. The cultural heritage of its Cuban, Spanish, Italian, German, African-American and English populations continue to influence government, education and the arts. Historically, it began in 1885, when Don Vicente Martinez Ybor (pronounced Ee-bore), a prominent cigar manufacturer and Cuban exile, decided to move his factory to Tampa. Other manufacturers soon followed creating jobs for nearly 12,000 people. An influx of Cubans, Spanish, Italians and Germans came to Tampa to work in the cigar industry. As Tampa became the "World's Largest Manufacturer of Havana Cigars," a spirited Latin community also emerged. Henry B. Plant, railroad magnate, also played a major role. He extended the railroad to the mouth of the Hillsborough River and created the steamship lines from Tampa to Key West, thus linking it with Havana, Cuba. The cigar industry remained alive until the emergence of Fidel Castro and the Cuban embargo.

Today, many of the abandoned cigar factories of Ybor City have been converted into commercial ventures, ethnic boutiques, and art galleries. Artists have converted some of the factory space into living quarters and studios. Restaurants and nightclubs have also proliferated in this colorful section of the city.

Tampa's rich ethnic history and its dynamic commitment to cultural growth continue to receive many positive reviews. New waterfront construction is presently underway with plans for an $84 million dollar aquarium, scheduled to open in 1995. Its business focus, favorable tax climate, airport, harbor, and highway networks have been instrumental in attracting business to the area. A modern, multi-use convention center, attracting national and international business guests, has added to Tampa's stature. And, of course, Tampa's proximity to the Gulf cities of St. Petersburg and Clearwater make weekends fun with excursions to the different beaches.

Demographics

The Metropolitan Statistical Area (MSA) for Tampa/St. Petersburg consists of four counties: Hillsborough County, Pinellas County, Pasco County, and Hernando County.

Tampa's neighbors, St. Petersburg and Clearwater are located in Pinellas County.

◆ Size

Hillsborough County includes the three cities of Tampa, Plant City and Temple Terrace. The county has an area coverage of 1,072.5 square miles. Tampa covers approximately 10% of the county with 109.9 square miles. Plant City comprises 19.3 square miles and Temple Terrace 4.6 square miles. Unincorporated areas span 938.7 square miles.

◆ Population

In the 1990 census, Hillsborough County had a population of 834,054 people; Tampa had 280,015 residents; Plant City had 22,754; and Temple Terrace had 16,444. The remaining 514,841 people live in unincorporated areas.

◆ Age Demographics in Hillsborough County

Under 18	24.3%
18-24	10.7%
25-44	34.1%
45-59	14.4%
60-64	4.2%
65 plus	12.2%

Tampa's residents are among the youngest in Florida. The median age in Hillsborough County is 33.4; the median age in Tampa is 33.7; the median age in Plant City is 32.6; and the median age in Temple Terrace is 33.2.

◆ Climate

Elevation: 121 ft.
Annual Rainfall: 48.48
Average Summer Temperature: 81.5 degrees
Average Winter Temperature: 60.4 degrees

Taxes

◆ Property Taxes
Hillsborough County has an average millage rate of 25.0654 per $1,000 of assessed property value. The City of Tampa has an average millage rate of 26.5423. Tampa Palms residents voted an extra assessment of 2.600 mills for community use and maintenance. The City of Temple Terrace has a millage rate of 23.9632; and Plant City has an average millage rate of 23.7582.

◆ Sales and Use Tax
In addition to the 6% sales and use tax levied by the State of Florida, Hillsborough County collects an additional 1/2% tax which helps to provide services for the indigent.

Voting and Elections

Hillsborough County
The seven county commissioners who govern Hillsborough County serve a four-year term of office. Four are elected from single-member districts and three are elected at-large. Every two years, either three (or four) of the seats are up for election.

County Elections Office, Hillsborough County Courthouse, 419 Pierce Street, Rm. 195, Tampa, FL 33602-4062, *Ph. 272-5850*

Tampa. Residents of Tampa elect a mayor and seven council members to govern for a four-year term of office. Four members are elected from single-member districts and three are elected at-large. Elections are scheduled for the first Tuesday, after the first Monday, in March; "runoffs" occur the last Tuesday in March, if necessary. The election year is one year off the standard cycle; the next one is scheduled for 1995.

Plant City. Residents in Plant City elect a mayor for a one-year term and five city commissioners for a three-year term of office. City commissioners are elected on the first Tuesday, after the first Monday, in April; "runoffs" occur on the third Tuesday in April, if necessary. The next election is scheduled for 1996. The mayor is elected from the body of commissioners on the first Tuesday, after the first Monday, every May.

City of Temple Terrace. Temple Terrace residents elect a mayor and five council members at-large for a four-year term. The primaries are held on the first Tuesday, after the first Monday, in September; "runoffs" are held on the first Tuesday in October, if necessary. Municipal elections are scheduled on the same day as the general elections in November. Every two years, two (or three) of the council seats are up for election.

To register to vote, call the County Elections Office to obtain a list of the 50 branch registration offices around the county.

Pet Registration

All dogs and cats over four months of age must be vaccinated for rabies and licensed. After inoculation, make sure that you have a vaccination certificate for your pet; most veterinarians will provide the necessary tags. If your pet is spayed or neutered, licensing fees are reduced. The City of Tampa requires that dogs be leashed while away from home; pooper-scooper laws are also in effect.

Although most public beaches do not allow pets, if you want to take your dog to the beach, there are two areas which residents suggest. One, commonly known as "Dog Beach," is located on the west side of Courtney Campbell Causeway en route from Tampa to Clearwater. Dogs must be leashed while walking the beach. At Belleair Beach, south of Clearwater on the Intracoastal Waterway (444 Causeway Boulevard), your dog can go for a swim or play in the water.

The Humane Society of Tampa. This is an active organization which provides many services to the "animal community." They assist in humane pet euthanasia; shelter unwanted pets; sponsor a pet adoption program; and operate a lost & found clearinghouse. Their *Purina Pets for People* program matches people over 60 with loving animals over one year of age. They provide referrals to appropriate agencies and individuals who can help with pet-related problems. *Making Tracks* is their quarterly newsletter.

Transportation

Air Travel

TAMPA INTERNATIONAL AIRPORT
4510 Airport Blvd.
Tampa, FL 33614
Communications Center - 24 hours
Aviation Authority: *Ph. 870-8700*
Monday - Friday, 8:30 am - 5:00 pm
Information Line: *Ph. 870-8770*

After-Hours and Weekends:
Passenger Page Service: *Ph. 870-8770*
Parking Information: *Ph. 870-8718*

Tampa International Airport has received world acclaim from the International Airline Passengers Association; it is ranked first in the United States and second in the world. Its modern facilities, innovative features and efficient servicing of passengers has made it a model airport. Automatic shuttles move passengers between airside boarding terminals and the main landside terminal. A monorail connects the long term parking area to the landside terminal.

Tampa International Airport is five miles from downtown Tampa, in the northwest corner of Hillsborough County.

Amenities. Services include a bank, currency exchange, foreign language assistance, medical provisions, nursery, and handicap facilities.

Parking. If you plan to park your car for an extended period of time, inform the airport parking authorities of your intentions. Cars parked for more than 45 days are considered abandoned.

If you find yourself without enough money to pay for parking, you have some alternatives. Visa, MasterCard or a local check with identification are accepted at the cashier's booth.

Ground Transportation. In addition to rental cars, taxis and limousine services, there are contract shuttle vans which service three different geographical areas. The vans, which are scheduled to meet each arriving flight, are located at a courtesy vehicle waiting area in each of the four quadrants of the terminal. Call airport parking for more information. *Ph. 870-8718.*

Public Transit. The Route 30 Town N' Country bus line travels to and from Tampa International Airport from early morning to early evening hours. It departs from downtown Tampa at the Marion St. Transit Parkway. Buses run frequently, arriving and departing from the airport approximately every 30 minutes. Call Hartline for route and schedule information. *Ph. 254-4278.*

Major Airlines include:

Air Canada	Condor	Northwest
American	Continental	Sun Country
American Trans Air	Delta	TWA
American West	Lauda Air	United
Canadian International	Martinair Holland	US Air
Cayman Airways	Midwest Express	US Air Express
Comair		

Sea Travel

The Tampa Port, an active industrial facility, also has cruise lines departing from its harbor. Cruise lines offer weekend voyages to the Gulf of Mexico and one-week cruises to Mexico and the Caribbean.

Local Transportation

Bus Service. Hillsborough Area Regional Transit (HARTline) operates a fleet of 172 buses traveling 44 routes throughout the county. A limited number of buses travel into Pinellas County. During the weekday business rush hour, there is express service to downtown Tampa. Drive to any of the 20 Park 'N Ride facilities to board an express. Local service provides transportation to area malls, government buildings, attractions, museums, and sporting events. Buses operate seven days a week, with reduced service on weekends. During weekdays, buses run from 4 am until 11 pm. If you need assistance with routing information or bus schedules, call HARTline. Schedules are available at HARTline's Operations Facility; Northern Terminal; Marion and Kennedy Information Center; Hillsborough County Courthouse; city halls and other public buildings. *Ph. 254-4278.*

Seniors, disabled and young people may qualify for discount fares with proper identification. HARTsaver Passes are also available with substantial discounts for frequent users. Many of the buses are equipped with lifts to accommodate wheelchairs.

The Marion Street Transit Parkway spans nine city streets in downtown Tampa, from Tyler Street at the northern end to Whiting Street at the southern end. It is the cornerstone of the transit system and also the location of the Northern Terminal. The Transit Parkway is the hub and converging point for 30 different bus routes in the system. Automobiles are only permitted use of the Parkway streets during the weekends and from 7 pm to 6 am on weekdays. The Bay Area Commuter Services, Inc. (BACS) offers a Regional Commuter Assistance Program for Hillsborough, Pinellas, Pasco and Hernando counties. They answer questions and offer solutions for transportation problems in the Tampa Bay region. *Ph. 282-2467; 800-998-RIDE.*

Postal Service

Post Offices

Main Post Office	5201 Spruce Street (adjacent to the airport) 24 hr. service/7 days a week	877-0635
Carrollwood Branch	12651 N. Dale Marby Hwy. Monday - Friday: 8:00 am - 7:00 pm Saturday: 8:00 am - 2:00 pm	961-2962
Commerce Station	925 S. Florida Ave. Monday - Friday: 8:30 am - 6:00 pm	221-3126
Downtown Station *(Finance Unit)*	401 S. Florida Ave. Monday - Friday: 7:00 am - 5:00 pm Saturday: 8:00 am - noon	221-3002
Forest Hills Station	11800 N. Florida Ave. Monday - Friday: 8:30 am - 6:00 pm Saturday: 8:30 am - noon	933-8187
Hilldale Station	3201 W. Hillsborough Ave. Monday - Friday: 8:00 am - 6:00 pm Saturday: 8:00 am - 2:00 pm	876-9147
Interbay Station	4520 Oakellar Street Monday - Friday: 8:00 am - 6:00 pm Saturday: 8:00 am - noon	831-7963
Peninsula Station *(Finance Unit)*	1002 S. Church Street Monday - Friday: 8:00 am - 6:00 pm Saturday: 8:00 am - 1:00 pm	286-7599

Tampa

Port Tampa Station	6801 S. Westshore Blvd. Monday - Friday: 8:00 am - 6:00 pm	839-9315
Produce Station	2901 E. Hillsborough Ave. Monday - Friday: 8:30 am - 5:00 pm Saturday: 8:30 am - noon	239-2633
Seminole Station	5206 N. Florida Ave. Monday - Friday: 8:30 am - 5:00 pm Saturday: 8:30 am - noon	232-0171
Sulphur Springs	6706 N. Nebraska Ave. Monday - Friday: 7:30 am - 5:00 pm Saturday: 7:30 am - 1:00 pm	238-5000
Temple Terrace (Finance Unit)	9748 N. 56th Street Monday - Friday: 8:30 am - 6:00 pm Saturday: 8:30 am - 1:00 pm	988-4776
Town N' Country Station	7521 Paula Dr. Monday - Friday: 8:00 am - 6:00 pm Saturday: 8:00 am - 1:00 pm	885-6296
West Tampa Station (Finance Unit)	1802 N. Howard Ave. Monday - Friday: 8:30 am - 5:30 pm Saturday: 8:30 am - 12:30 pm	253-3062
Ybor Station	1900 E. 12th Ave. Monday - Friday: 7:30 am - 5:00 pm Saturday: 7:30 am - noon	248-2543

Note: Finance Units offer retail postal operations, but no carrier service.
Zip Code Information: 872-3636
Passport Operations and Processing: Main Post Office and Carrollwood

Contract Stations

The contract stations in Tampa perform basic postal services. Most, however, cannot accept and process international parcels and packages. Several contract stations have authorized US postal boxes for rent.

		PO Boxes
Davis Island Pharmacy Davis Island Station	232 E. Davis Blvd., 254-1888	No
Westshore Pharmacy West Shore Station	3206 S. Westshore Blvd., 837-9095	No
North Dale Branch	3887 Northdale Blvd., 963-0577	Yes
My Pharmacist Bearss Plaza Station	14936 N. Florida Ave., 961-6546	Yes
Eckerd Drug Store East Fletcher Branch	13528 University Plaza, 971-8719	Yes

Eckerd Drug Store Terrace Area Branch	8925 Terrace Plaza, 988-5214	No
Beauty Express II Sable Park Branch	9720 Princess Palm Ave., Suite 122, 621-1953	No
Check Casher of Tampa Clair Mel City Branch	7613 E. Causeway Blvd., 623-2393	No
Lawrence Plaza Broadway Station	5006 E. Broadway Ave., 248-5560	Yes
Hensel's Clock Repair Palma Ceia Station	2707 S. Macdill Ave., 839-2900	Yes
Alicia's Gift and Accessories Citrus Park Branch	5353 Ehrlich Road, 962-3598	No
Univ. of So. Florida Campus	4202 E. Fowler Ave., 974-2606	No
Univ. of Tampa Campus Univ. Of Tampa Station	401 W. Kennedy Blvd., 253-3333	No
Eckerd Drug Store Twin Lakes Station	8434 N. Armenia Ave., 933-6702	No
Bealls Dept. Store West Waters Branch	7039 W. Waters Ave., 885-5319	No
Gift and Parcel Center Tampa Palms Station	15307 Amberly Drive, 979-1880	No

Newspapers and Magazines

The TAMPA TRIBUNE is a daily newspaper with international, national and local coverage. The circulation areas are divided into zones; Hillsborough County has five zoned sections, each providing local news coverage and community announcements of activities and meetings. *Friday Extra!* is the weekly arts and entertainment magazine.

In October, the *Tampa Tribune* publishes *Discover Tampa Bay*, a special edition for newcomers as well as established residents. Contact the *Tampa Tribune* at the end of September for the exact date of publication. *Ph. 272-7711.*

The ST. PETERSBURG TIMES, a daily newspaper with international, national, and local coverage, is circulated in the five counties of Pinellas, Hillsborough, Hernando, Pasco, and Citrus. The various editions include a regional section with coverage of state and community news and issues specific to each county. Human interest theme sections feature different topics each day of the week, such as *Parental Guidance, Connections* (People and Relationships), *Days Off* (Local Trips and Things To Do), *Landscape*, and the *Floridian*. Ph. 273-4414.

Throughout the year, the *Times* prints a series of special sections to meet different interests within the community. *Back To School* is a parent's guide to the school year. Bus schedules, starting times, holiday dates, important school phone numbers, and school updates are printed in this issue. Look for it in August, usually one week before school begins. *Fun Book*, published in October, is for the newcomer and seasoned resident as well. A descriptive and demographic overview of the various counties in the Tampa Bay Area, places to visit, attractions, events, cultural activities and entertainment are featured in this edition. *Hurricane Preparedness* is the focus of this special section which rolls off the press, June 1 (just in time for hurricane season). *Healthwise* is printed the second Wednesday of each month; and *Seniority* (for youngsters 55 and older) is printed the last Tuesday of each month. Ph. 273-4414.

The TAMPA BAY MAGAZINE focuses on the lifestyles and happenings in the Tampa Bay area. Monthly articles feature people in the community, coverage of the arts, events, interesting places, and leisure activities. Each edition also has a dining guide and restaurant reviews. Ph. 855-1874.

There are several publications in the Tampa Bay area which have a particular focus:

Community: BRANDON NEWS, CARROLLWOOD NEWS, NORTH TAMPA INDEPENDENT, APOLLO BEACH NEWS, PLANT CITY COURIER, TEMPLE TERRACE BEACON.

Business: TAMPA BAY BUSINESS JOURNAL, MADDUX REPORT.

Ethnic: EL SOL DE LA FLORIDA, LA GACETA, JEWISH PRESS OF TAMPA.

Special Interest: HOSPITAL NEWS GULF EDITION, CREATIVE LOAFING (which has a Greenwich Village flavor).

TAMPA BAY NEIGHBORHOODS is a comprehensive guide to Tampa's finer neighborhoods and communities. It is published by Smith and Associates. Contact the Chamber of Commerce for available copies.

Library System

The Main Library
900 Ashley Street
Tampa, FL
Ph. 273-3652

In addition to the Main Library of the Tampa Hillsborough County Library System, 16 branch libraries serve the various communities of Hillsborough County.

Besides the standard fare of talking books and story hour for toddlers, the County Library System sponsors some unique programs for all to enjoy. Its *Storytelling Festival*, featuring young storytellers, has become an annual event. Hundreds of children (primarily elementary school students) are selected to tell a three-five-minute story; the storytellers perform in the various classrooms of Hillsborough High School. Anyone else who wants to participate may do so at the 'Swapping' area of the festival grounds; just pull up a bale of hay and start talking. Nationally acclaimed storytellers are invited as guest speakers. A parade of book characters dress in costume, which old and young alike enjoy. The festival, held on the third Saturday in April, is co-sponsored with the City of Tampa.

In October, the library sponsors *In Celebration of Hispanic Heritage*. Events include Hispanic tales and puppet shows for children; presentations of book reviews, film, music, folk dance, arts and crafts. The cultural influences and the heritage of different Hispanic countries are featured during the month.

Saluting Afro-Americans is celebrated in February. Guest speakers share their experiences and present programs on African-American culture and history. For children, there are tales, films and puppet shows; for adults, there are book reviews, African-American stories with musical accompaniment, films, fashion shows, cuisine, as well as displays of fine art, photographs, and collectibles.

May is celebrated with *Asian/Pacific American Heritage Month*. Programs, symposiums and activities are featured at the various libraries.

In addition to celebrating diversity, the library presents programs which serve a wide range of interests. Contact the Main Library for its calendar of monthly events as well as its scheduled toddler and children's activities.

Health Care

There are 54 hospitals and medical centers within the four-county Metropolitan Statistical Area. The Greater Tampa Bay area has become a magnet for attracting an elite core of physicians, research scientists, and health care providers of national and international acclaim. Within Hillsborough County, there are 21 hospitals. The wealth of medical specialties in an area this size is outstanding; residents have a broad spectrum of medical services available to them.

Tampa General Hospital
Davis Island
Tampa, FL
Ph. 251-7000

Tampa General Hospital, the state's second largest regional medical center, provides acute care and specialized medical services. It is also the primary teaching hospital for USF School of Medicine. In recent years, it has received international recognition. Its specialties include *open heart surgery, laser cardiac angioplasty* (second hospital in the state to provide this technology); *heart* and *kidney transplant programs; rehabilitation technologies; neonatal intensive care* for high risk mothers and babies; and a *Level 1 Trauma Center* with trauma specialists available 24 hours. Its *Regional Burn Center* is also highly acclaimed.

A new *Children's Medical Center*, a 32,000-square-foot hospital within a hospital, provides more than 26 pediatric specialty services.

St. Joseph's Hospital

3001 W. Dr. M. L. King Jr., Blvd.
Ph. 870-4848

St. Joseph's Hospital and Health Care Center is a not-for-profit general medical/surgical facility. It is the sixth largest hospital in Florida, housing 883 beds. Its specialties include *cardiology care and surgery; oncology care* and a state of the art *Radiation Therapy Center* which uses computer-operated equipment to deliver treatments developed by modern technology; a *Neuroscience Institute* which focuses on a range of problems from sleep disorders to diagnosing Alzheimer's disease; a *Pediatric Hospital* dedicated to children's diseases and health care; and a new *Women's Hospital* specializing in complete obstetrics and gynecology, infertility clinics, and neonatal intensive care. A 24-hour *Level 2 Trauma Center* is also on site.

St. Joseph's Hospital is also involved in various community outreach programs.

- *Ask-A-Nurse* is a 24-hour phone support system for medical inquiries. Registered nurses are available to answer health and medical questions. *Ph. 870-4444.*
- Cancer Help Link is a 24-hour phone support system staffed by oncology nurses who respond to questions about cancer. *Ph. 870-4123.*
- *SeniorCare*, a support network for seniors, offers open forums and educational programs. *Ph. 870-4400.*

University Community Hospital

3100 E. Fletcher Avenue
Ph. 972-7202

University Community Hospital is a not-for-profit 424-bed full service facility. Its Centers of Excellence include the *Pepin Heart Centre* which provides a full range of cardiac services and open heart surgery; the *Women's Center*, offering obstetric and gynecological services, including the highly praised program which allows the new baby to room-in with Mom; the *Center for Cancer Care*, with a full range of treatment modalities; and the *Diabetes Treatment Center*, specializing in both inpatient and outpatient programs. *Ph. 800-326-4325.*

The **University of South Florida's Health Science Center** includes the Colleges of Medicine, Nursing and Public Health. *Ph. 974-3300.*

Hospital and Medical Clinics Affiliated with the University

- *H. Lee Moffit Cancer Center* is a 162-bed private, not-for-profit, cancer care and research facility affiliated with the University Health Sciences Center. In 1989, it opened a *Bone Marrow Transplant Center* with a 20-bed unit; it is one of only three in the nation. *Ph. 972-4673.*
- *Shriner's Hospital For Crippled Children* is a pediatric orthopedic hospital specializing in bone deficiency treatments; its research center studies bone and cartilage growth and bone joint diseases. *Ph. 972-2250.*
- *USF Psychiatry Center.* Alzheimer's research is currently being conducted at the Center by noted research scientists; there are plans for a multi-disciplinary aging center which will include biological research in Alzheimer's disease, Parkinson's disease and other brain disorders. *Ph. 972-3000.*

Other Medical Centers Affiliated with the University

- *Brain Tumor Treatment Center*
- *University Diagnostic Institute*
- *Comprehensive Breast Cancer Center*
- *Suncoast Gerontology Center*
- *USF Diabetes Center*
- *Center For Swallowing Disorders*

The Health Science Center receives various grants from government, business and health organizations to help support its recognized research efforts. Projects underway include a study to test a high-tech small and efficient heart pump and the use of interferon in attacking brain cancers.

Education

School Board of Hillsborough County

901 E. Kennedy Blvd.
Tampa, FL 33601
Ph. 272-4055

Hillsborough County has the third largest public school system in the State of Florida. There are 159 public schools for students in grades K-12; 109 elementary schools, 22 junior schools, four middle schools, 14 senior high schools, and 10 school centers for students with special needs. Hillsborough County Public Schools provides exceptional student programs for the disabled, impaired and academically gifted. The School Board is in the process of restructuring its single grade centers and junior high schools to a middle school system. The conversion is expected to be completed by 1998.

An adult education program, which is provided at four post-secondary adult centers, offers skills training and enhancement. Continuing education courses are held at 240 locations throughout the county.

The school district, parents, businesses and the community at large are very involved in the education of its students. It is said that in many tribal societies, it takes an entire village to raise a child; similarly, Hillsborough residents believe that it takes a whole community to educate one.

Teachers. The Board of Education designates time for in-service teacher training to present innovative strategies for more effective communication and cooperation in the classroom. Previous training programs have included: *Creating Culturally Sensitive Classrooms*; *Students Under Stress*; *Tactics for Teaching Thinking*; and *Motivating Student Behavior*.

Students. Hillsborough County is also proud of its 512 seniors who were named Florida Academic Scholars in 1992, ranking the county number one in the state. In August 1991, Florida's Commissioner of Education presented Hillsborough County with the Commissioner's Award of Excellence for its superior educational programs.

◆ Special Programs

The Hillsborough Education Foundation, Inc. has an independent board of directors not affiliated with the school system. It sponsors special programs not funded by the state or federal government by generating financing from individual benefactors and business partnerships. The Foundation, in partnership with the Chamber of Commerce, sponsors *The Great American Teach-In*. This special event, which takes place on a Saturday during American Education Week, provides a forum for volunteers to teach either an hour or all day. The program has been a large success attracting people from different walks of life, including celebrities. *Horizons to Success* provides student scholarships, based on need, to encourage students to complete their education. Hillsborough County has made great strides and has an impressive record in delivering programs to enhance equal opportunity education in the community. The drop-out rate of Hillsborough students decreased to 2.6% in 1992; this is below the state's drop-out rate and the lowest among Florida counties with school districts of equal size.

Personalized Education Program is for fourth, fifth and sixth graders who lack appropriate behaviors, academic skills, and study habits to achieve in school. PEP provides a highly motivating learning environment designed to increase academic success with the acquisition of basic skills.

Business Partnership Program: Individual businesses select a school to support in their community. This may be done in various ways: financial contributions, equipment, physical enhancement of the school, sponsorship of events, student scholarships or personally providing knowledge and expertise, instruction, tutoring or mentoring.

Guidance Mentoring Program: Students at-risk are connected to people in the business community who become their mentors.

GPA (grade point average) Incentive Program: This provides financial incentives to students who must work after school. The GPA Employer Program heightens the sensitivity of employers by informing them of how they can help students create more of a balance between work and school. Employers provide monetary rewards to employed students who improve their grades. This initiative, set in motion by the Hillsborough Educational Foundation in conjunction with the Chamber of Commerce and business community, has helped students at-risk to remain in school and improve grades.

◆ Summer Programs
- *Extended School Year*, a summer school program, allows students to complete requirements for advancement to the next grade.
- *Summer Program for the Academically Gifted* is an extension of the school curriculum, but with an emphasis on enrichment activities.
- *Summer Science/Mathematics Camps* provides programs for students in grades three through five who are not eligible for the Extended School Year Program or the Summer Program for the Academically Gifted. Problem solving skills and scientific inquiry are practiced in hands-on investigations.

- *Summer Creative Arts Program* is designed for students with an interest and talent in art, drama, dance, writing, and music. The various workshops are experientially focused.

◆ Magnet Programs

The Academy of Health Professions opened its doors in August, 1991 at Tampa Bay Technical School. Created in cooperation with area colleges and health care providers, the Hillsborough County School District designed this magnet program for students interested in the medical and health care professions. In addition to the required basic core academic courses, a large variety of medical/health care programs are tailored to each student's interests, from neurosurgery to nutrition.

The International Baccalaureate Program is a magnet program offered at Hillsborough High School. With its rigorous academic focus, it is only offered to highly motivated students in the 11th and 12th grades who fulfill academic requirements. Students must complete written examinations in each of six areas and submit an extensive essay in order to satisfy diploma requirements. An IB diploma is recognized world-wide and ensures admission at renowned universities.

The Lee Elementary School and the Middleton Middle School are new magnet schools offering students intensive study in high technology and computer programs.

◆ Other Special Programs

Nature's Classroom is an outdoor educational program for every sixth grader. Students spend a week on-site at Nature's Classroom learning camping, boating, archery, gunnery, hiking, and developing survival skills. There is also an emphasis on science and plant/animal identification.

Environmental Studies Center Program for grades three-six combines classroom study with a field trip to explore Florida's marine environment.

Computer Learning. In the Hillsborough School System there are more than 11,500 computers for instructional use. Elementary school students receive computer instruction weekly; most seventh grade classrooms provide nine weeks of computer instruction. High school students may select courses ranging from a basic introductory elective to an AP computer science course.

Chamberlain High School is one of the state's five model technology schools to install high technology in order to assess its effect on the teacher/learning process. State-of-the-art computer equipment, laser disc technology, and active video instruction are being used interactively in various areas of study. As we advance into the year 2000, this cutting-edge technology may be the new road to learning.

Advanced Placement. Hillsborough County Public Schools offers advanced placement college courses to qualifying high school juniors and seniors.

Dual Enrollment Program. The Hillsborough School System and Hillsborough Community College offer dual enrollment classes at 13 senior high schools. Students may earn both high school and college credit simultaneously.

UNIVERSITIES AND COLLEGES

The University of South Florida, only 33 years old, is the second largest of Florida's state universities, with a population of 33,000 students. The sprawling green campus at Tampa is the main headquarters for the University. USF offers a large number of advanced degrees, including Ph.D. programs in the sciences, humanities and engineering; MD. degrees; Ed.D. degrees in various fields of education as well as Master's degrees in a broad range of subject areas. Its undergraduate program has a multitude of offerings. USF is an active partner in the business community and home to medical clinics, research centers, and hospitals. It also plays a vital civic and cultural role in the community, underwriting various public programs.

The University of Tampa is a private, liberal arts institution with a student body of 2,400. Thirty-six different areas of study are offered to undergraduates. It is a residential school located on the grounds of the old H. B. Plant Tampa Bay Hotel with its charming Victorian architecture and silver minarets. Its College of Business, College of Liberal Arts and Sciences, Center for Quality, and Center for Ethics have prominent programs which have been recognized in the educational community. The University also offers an MBA program and has an Evening College.

Hillsborough Community College is the sixth largest of the 28 community colleges in Florida. Its campuses in Brandon, Dale

Mabry, Plant City and Ybor City offer A.A. and A.S. degrees. The College has nearly 40 different A.S. degree programs for students who wish to pursue a career upon graduation. Areas of study range from ornamental horticulture to fire science technology. Employment needs are often identified by people in the Tampa business community, resulting in new courses and programs. The Associate in Arts curriculum offers a general academic education, preparing students for transfer to four-year institutions. HCC has also become recognized for its non-degree programs including community education classes and workshops. *Ph. 253-7000.*

Tampa College is the oldest business college in Florida. In addition to the main college, which is located in Tampa, there are campuses in Clearwater, Brandon and Lakeland. There are 1,400 students enrolled in undergraduate and graduate programs. Associate degrees are awarded in accounting, marketing and management, computer information sciences, commercial art, criminal justice, paralegal and medical assisting. Students may also enroll in a four-year bachelor's degree program in any of the above studies, with the exception of paralegal, medical assisting and commercial art. Tampa College also offers a Master's degree in business administration. For working students, evening and Saturday courses are available. Life experiential credits are given to qualifying students. *Ph. 879-6000.*

Florida College is a private college with two divisions. The Junior College offers an Associate of Arts degree which includes bible study as part of its liberal arts curriculum. The Bible and Religious Education Division offers an advanced degree beyond the two-year program. Florida College is located in Temple Terrace. *Ph. 988-5131.*

The International Academy of Merchandising and Design offers both Associate and Bachelor degrees in interior design, fashion design and merchandising management. There are both full and part-time programs available. The main campus is in Chicago, with affiliates in Montreal, Toronto and Tampa. *Ph. 286-8585 or 800-ACADEMY.*

The Cultural Scene

Tampa Bay Performing Arts Center

The Tampa Bay Performing Arts Center is situated on a scenic nine-acre site east of the Hillsborough River in downtown Tampa. The largest performing arts house south of the Kennedy Center in Washington, DC, it was designed with three different theaters. Festival Hall, the largest, accommodates 2,493 with seating arranged in the horseshoe shape of classical theater. Major productions of opera, music and ballet, as well as Broadway musicals are performed in Festival Hall. The Playhouse, more intimate in design, is a three-tier theater with 960 seats and is well suited to staging dance, drama and smaller musical performances. The Jaeb Theater, a 300-seat black-box performing house, stages experimental theater, cabaret, and television production. TBPAC has become a venue for award-winning Broadway musicals and dramas, popular artists, symphonic music and recitals. It has a *Kid Time Series* which features entertaining and enlightening theater for children. The *H.O.T.* (Humanities Outreach in Tampa Bay) program allows teachers to augment their curriculum with on-site visitations during current productions. *1010 North W.C. MacInnes Place. Ph. 222-1000.*

Ruth Eckerd Hall

Ruth Eckerd Hall, which accommodates 2,182, is housed in the Richard B. Baumgardner Center for the Performing Arts. The Frank Lloyd Wright Foundation, architects for this project, incorporated both graceful lines and open spaces in its modern design. The versatile performance schedule includes renowned opera, dance and symphonic companies and virtuosos from around the world; special performances by popular artists; concerts by country & western vocalists, folk singers and jazz artists; comedy; and popular Broadway musicals and theater. A schedule of educational and entertaining children's theater is also produced during the year. Pre-performance luncheons and dinners are served for selected performances in the Margaret Heye Great Room, an elegant dining and banquet room. Theatergoers are also invited to behind-the-scenes discussions with performers and production staff prior to selected performances. *1111 McMullen-Booth Road, Clearwater. Ph. 791-7060.*

Bayfront Center

The Bayfront Center houses an 8,400-seat Arena for large events and the Mahaffey Theater, which can accommodate nearly 2,000. The Mahaffey is an elegant European-style theater with box seating on either side. Its season includes concerts, opera, ballet, plays and theater productions, as well as special performances by popular artists. *400 1st Street South. St. Petersburg. Ph. 892-5798.*

The Tampa Bay Area has a resident orchestra and ballet troupe which perform at the three Performing Arts Centers in the Bay Area.

The Florida Orchestra

Designated as a "Major Cultural Institution," this is considered one of the finest regional orchestras in the country. The 88-piece symphony performs a varied repertoire, including *Masterworks, Super Pops, Champagne and Coffee Series, Concerts in the Park*, and programs for children. *Ph. 286-2403.*

The Bay Ballet Theater

Formed in 1992, this is a versatile company engaging audiences with its classical as well as modern performances. From October through May, it performs seven different ballets under the artistic direction of Christopher Flemming, a former member of the New York City Ballet. *Ph. 221-7553.*

Tampa Theater

This is an elegant movie palace which dates back to 1926. Its classical Mediterranean style, opulent interior flourishes, and starlit ceiling were left in place during its restoration in the 1970s. Foreign and art films are featured as well as Disney classics. Bringing to mind a memory of earlier cinema days, an organist plays the pipe organ before the Saturday matinee. Cartoons are shown with weekend serials. *711 Franklin Street. Ph. 223-8981.*

The Tampa Players

In existence since 1926, the Tampa Players became a professional theater company in the early 1980's. The Players present contemporary and classical dramas, some of which are world premieres of new works. *601 Harbour Island Blvd., South. Ph. 221-9192.*

Stageworks

Stageworks is a small, private, non-profit theater. It is committed to showcasing new works by Florida artists and producing enduring works by minority artists, with an emphasis on social issues. When not performing in residence, the company tours nationally and internationally. *University of Tampa. Ph. 251-8984.*

Florida Dance Festival

Produced by the Florida Dance Association, this is an annual Tampa event hosted by the University of South Florida. During one week in June, classes and workshops in all styles of dance are offered to hundreds of professional and student dancers from Florida and around the United States. Students may enroll in studio classes ranging from modern, jazz, ballet, tap, and street dance to more ethnic ones, such as Spanish, Classical, Indian, and African. Nationally acclaimed and professional dancers perform every night, showcasing a broad range of styles. *Ph. 305-974-1537.*

Summer Concerts

Two summers concerts, Summer Jazz and *Summer Blues*, are held in Centennial Park, Ybor City. Corner of 18th & 19th Sts. and 8th & 9th Aves.

Summer Jazz Concerts. Beginning in May and continuing through September, summer jazz concerts are held on the third Friday night of each month. Bring a blanket or chair and enjoy the sound of jazz under the stars. Local food venders and restaurants serve culinary delights under the pavilion. Contact the Ybor Chamber of Commerce for more information. *Ph. 248-3712.*

Summer Blues Series. If you are more of a blues lover, park concerts are held the last Sunday of each month at 3 pm, March through August. *Ph. 248-6097.*

Olde Hyde Park Village Live Music Series. The open air concerts at Hyde Park offer a venue of music including reggae, blues, rhythm and blues, and jazz. The concerts are presented from May through October on the last Wednesday of each month at 6 pm. You can sit and enjoy the music relaxing in the village park or listen to the sounds from one of the patio restaurants. *Swan & Dakota Aves. Ph. 251-3500.*

Salvador Dali Museum

After a nationwide search for a permanent site to house their vast collection of Dali's work, Eleanor and A. Reynolds Morse selected St. Petersburg. The Morses, long-time close friends of Dali, assembled their private collection during a period of 45 years. The museum, which is dedicated to Salvador Dali, has the world's most comprehensive collection of his work from 1914 to 1980 and presents a retrospective of his evolving styles. Docents are available to conduct tours of the museum. Scheduled lectures, films and workshops are open to the public, as well as special programs for children. *1000 Third Street S., St. Petersburg. Ph. 823-3767.*

Tampa Museum of Art

The Tampa Museum of Art, which opened in 1979, curates one of the finest collections of Classical Greek and Roman antiquities in the country. It has 7,000 works of art in its permanent collection as well as presenting changing exhibits from around the world. As part of its community outreach program, there are seminars, slide lectures, demonstrations and educational programs for children. *Focal Point* presents an in-depth look at selected artwork from the permanent collection on the third Tuesday of each month. The Museum *Walking Tour*, scheduled on the second Saturday of each month, explores Tampa's architecture and outdoor public art. *601 Doyle Carlton Drive. Ph. 223-8130.*

Museum of African-American Art

This is the only dedicated African-American art museum in Florida and one of only 10 such museums in the country. It is the permanent home of the Barnett-Aden Collection which presents a historical and cultural perspective of black artists from the 1800s to the present. Featured in the exhibit are master artists from the Harlem Renaissance period and Work Progress Administration. Many of the works were painted by underground artists reflecting significant periods throughout their history. It is a powerful and provocative exhibit. *1308 N. Marion Street. Ph. 272-2466.*

Henry B. Plant Museum

In 1891, business tycoon and railroad magnate Henry B. Plant opened the Tampa Bay Hotel. The 511-room structure was modeled after the Alhambra in Spain. After his death, it was purchased by the city and operated as a hotel until 1930. In 1933, the hotel became home to the University of Tampa and the Henry B. Plant Museum was established in the south wing. Plant's legacy is displayed in the historic room settings which showcase the elegance and wealth from this turn-of-the-century hotel. Its furnishings, objects, art works and fashions of the era are exhibited in the Museum. *401 W. Kennedy Blvd. Ph. 254-1891.*

Annual Victorian Christmas Stroll

Designers decorate this wonderful Victorian museum and transform it with candles, wreaths and "1900" holiday touches to enhance the Christmas spirit. Performers in elegant costume re-create the mood of the era with music and dance.

Museum of Science and Industry (MOSI)

The Museum of Science and Industry is a scientific playground to explore how things work in the world around us through hands-on activities and interactive exhibits. There are over 300 exhibits from which to choose as you embark on a self-guided tour through the museum. Investigate *Earthworks* and travel through the lightning lab, experience a hurricane with 74 mph winds, or walk through a simulated aquifer. Afterwards, visit the *Communications Gallery* to broadcast the evening news or get on board the *GTE Challenger Learning Center* for a simulated space mission.

New construction is underway which will triple the size of the present MOSI and make it the largest science center in the Southeast. New additions will include outdoor environmental discoveries and exciting new explorations into Florida, earth, space and health. It will also house the only Omnimax Theater in Florida. The domed screen employs the largest film frames in cinematic history, the most advanced projection systems, and high fidelity six-channel sound technology. The viewer, surrounded by a domed screen in seats tilted back at a 45-degree angle, is swept into the action of the film. No, you are not in a dentist's chair! You are at the movies. *4801 E. Fowler Avenue. Ph. 985-5531.*

Great Explorations

The Great Explorations Museum is a hands-on museum for people of all ages who enjoy - not just looking - but touching, moving and exploring things that arouse their curiosity. There are six exploration areas, including a *Think Tank,* which involves a series of brain teasers and problem-solving games and a *Body Shop* with a series of physical tests that measure strength and flexibility. Its special exhibits are very innovative and exciting. The Museum's calendar of events includes many special ongoing programs. *1120 4th Street South, St. Petersburg. Ph. 821-8992.*

Arts Council of Hillsborough County

This organization publishes *Arts News* three times a year and *ArtsNews Calendar*, six times a year. The *Calendar* provides a comprehensive listing of arts events for the family as well as festivals, dance, film, literary arts, theater, visual arts and lectures/workshops. *Ph. 229-2787 (ARTS).*

Artsline is a 24-hour up to date phone recording. *Ph. 229-6547.*

Pinellas County Arts Council publishes listings of theater, music, dance, museums, galleries, cultural activities and special events. *Ph. 449-2787.*

Events and Attractions

Gasparilla Pirate Festival

The legendary José Gaspar, aka Gasparilla, is Tampa's patron pirate of the seas. The roguish and colorful exploits of Gaspar who, according to legend, was a young, well-educated Spanish aristocrat-turned-outlaw, are celebrated the first Saturday in February. The Shipwreck Ball begins the festivities on Friday evening with a contest for the most dazzling and original costumes. On Saturday morning, Ye Mystic Krewe of Gasparilla (a band of 700 swashbuckling pirates) set sail on the José Gasparilla, a fully rigged pirate ship which is a replica of one used by 18th century pirates. They are accompanied by rowdy crews on pleasure craft who join the flotilla. Explosions from cannons and muskets reverberate through the air as the pirates sail the Tampa waters to invade the city. Arriving at the Convention Center on Harbour Island, Tampa is officially under siege as they disembark and release a battalion of balloons into the air. Following the invasion, the pirates lead a lavish parade with colorful floats and marching bands along Bayshore Boulevard into downtown Tampa. The revelry continues with the Pirate Fest at Franklin Street Mall. Mimes, jugglers, magicians and clowns provide family entertainment while music played on different stages accompanies the dancing in the streets. The festivities culminate at Harbour Island with an extravaganza of fireworks lighting up the skies. *Ph. 241-4500.*

Ybor City Fiesta and Illuminated Night Parade

The week following the Gasparilla Pirate Invasion, the Ybor City Fiesta continues the festivities with a gala multicultural street festival celebrating the history of Ybor City. Ethnic foods, crafts, sidewalk entertainment and music highlight this spirited street party. Following the Fiesta, the Krewe of the Knights of Sant'Yago sponsors an evening parade with Gasparilla floats, decorated cars, marching bands and outlaw pirates. The streets come alive as the skies are illuminated with a dazzling display of color and costumes reminding many of Mardi Gras.

Gasparilla Distance Classic

The Gasparilla Distance Classic takes place during a Saturday in February. It has been ranked in the top 10 races in the country by Runner's World and *Running Times* magazines. Runners from across the country compete in this premier running event. People of *all* ages participate with varying levels of ability. Most of the Gasparilla Distance Classic is routed along the picturesque Bayshore Boulevard, overlooking Hillsborough Bay.

The different divisions include a 15K Men's/Women's Course; a 15K Wheelchair Competition; and a 5K All Runners Course. Prize money is awarded to the top 10 overall finishers in the 15K men's and women's competition; top finishers in the wheelchair division also receive cash prizes. Recognizing the different age levels of the participants, awards are presented to the first five runners who complete the course in each of the age groups. The youngest runners are in the 14-and-under group; the oldest are in the 75-plus bracket, with a few in their 90s. In the 5K competition, the top 10 finishers are awarded prizes. Call for registration information. *Ph. 229-7866.*

Gasparilla Sidewalk Art Festival

The Gasparilla Art Festival is Tampa's premier show for area art lovers. It is an annual juried two-day art festival with 300 selected works from artists working in various media. Serious buyers, "lookers," and art buffs are treated to a spectacular display of ceramics, hand-crafted jewelry, photography, glass sculpture, and paintings. The art show, part of the Gasparilla festivities, takes place in the early part of March in downtown Tampa.

Guavaween

A Latin-style Halloween celebration in Ybor City, Guavaween pays homage to the mythical Mama Guava. Tampa was humorously dubbed the *Big Guava* (after New York became the Big Apple) in memory of the unsuccessful exploits of a Spanish food broker who came to Tampa with the intention of planting acres of guava. Guavaween festivities include a parade, art shows, costume contests and an outrageous street party.

Harbour Island Christmas Tree Lighting Ceremony

Harbour Island, a mixed use development with boutiques, galleries, and eateries on the waterfront, can be reached by a monorail system. One of several annual events, the Christmas Tree lighting ceremony takes place the Friday after Thanksgiving. The evening begins with the lighted boat parade, followed by a Christmas concert on the waterway. The crowning event is the lighting of the 50-foot tree. *Ph. 980-2626.*

Florida Strawberry Festival

Plant City, the *Winter Strawberry Capital* of the world, holds its annual festival the last Thursday in February through the first week in March. It is a family event with enough different activities to capture anybody's fancy. *Ph. 752-9194.*

- Horticulture exhibits and livestock shows.
- A pioneer village with an old operating log cabin post office and early settlers demonstrating the skills and crafts of the time.
- A sample field to demonstrate the art and technique of planting and harvesting strawberries; strawberry eating and stemming contests; booths with strawberry shortcakes, jams and any other strawberry recipe imaginable (including fresh strawberries).
- Craft booths and demonstrations.
- A youth parade and diaper derby.
- Continuous entertainment highlighted by well-known stars from Nashville performing country and western music.
- The crowning of a Strawberry Festival Queen; in the junior division, a princess, duchess and baroness are selected to become junior royalty.

Busch Gardens

Busch Gardens is an African theme park with zoological habitats, animal exhibits in naturalistic environments, amusements, and live entertainment. Featured habitats include the *Serengeti Plain*, open grasslands with 800 African animals moving in herds across the plain; the *Myombe Reserve*, a lush habitat with gorillas and apes roaming through shrouds of mist; and *Nairobi Field Station Animal Nursery*, a field hospital for nursing and recovering animals.

Safari Programs include a *Photo Safari* aboard an open truck into the Serengeti Plain and *Senior Safari*, a close-up look at zoo animals in Busch country Africa. *Junior Zookeeper*, a program for 4-5 year olds, teaches the daily care of animals. The *Zoo Camp* is both a fun and educational experience for youngsters in kindergarten through ninth grade. It offers insights into the many roles a present day zoo must play in animal conservation and preserving life.

Authentic African villages, action-packed rides (such as *Kumba*, the largest and fastest roller coaster in the Southeast and the *Congo River Rapids* white water rafting experience), and on-going live entertainment have helped make Busch Gardens a popular family attraction. *3000 E. Busch Blvd. Ph. 987-5082.*

Don't Miss

Ybor City. A 90-minute (free) walking tour of historic Ybor City includes the famed cigar factory and hand-rolled cigar demonstrations. Tours are usually scheduled on Tuesday, Thursday and Saturday. For reservations, call the Chamber of Commerce. *Ph. 248-3712.*

Ybor City Gallery Walks. Twice a year, in November and April, galleries and artists' studios are open to the public on Saturday evening from 4-10 pm. Many of the artists provide refreshments and will personally discuss their work. A directory of artists and galleries, as well as street maps, are pre-printed for the event.

John's Pass Village. A charming turn-of-the-century fishing village, John's Pass has a 1,000-foot boardwalk, more than 100 boutiques, eateries and fresh seafood (its specialty). Boat rentals, parasailing, and jet skiing are available at the beach. *284 1/2 - 128th Avenue, Madeira Beach. Ph. 393-7679.*

Note: In October, the John's Pass Annual Seafood Festival features a potpourri of fresh seafood from local waters.

Tarpon Springs. Located on the northern boundary of Pinellas County, this Greek sponging village has existed since the turn of the century. Visitors can experience the old world charm of the Aegean, dine on Greek food, and watch divers combing the waters for sponges.

Special Events
In March, sample a taste of the Mediterranean at the *Greek Wine and Food Festival.*

A Tampa Must! Jog or walk along Bayfront Boulevard. It hugs the waterfront and offers a scenic and soothing background for any kind of exercise.

Recreation

Baseball

Beginning in March, the Grapefruit League comes to town. The Tampa Bay area has several major league spring training camps as well as a minor league team in residence.

Cincinnati Reds
Plant City Stadium, Plant City, *Ph. 752-REDS*

Philadelphia Phillies
Jack Russell Stadium, Clearwater, *Ph. 442-8496*

St. Louis Cardinals
Al Lang Stadium, St. Petersburg, *Ph. 893-7490*

Baltimore Orioles
Al Lang Stadium, St. Petersburg, *Ph. 893-7490*

Toronto Blue Jays
Dunedin Stadium, Clearwater, *Ph. 733-0429*

New York Yankees (Minor League)
New York Yankee Complex, Tampa, *Ph. 875-7753*

Hockey

Professional hockey has made a home in Tampa with the purchase of the NHL franchise, the Tampa Bay Lightning. During the October-through-April season, there are 41 home games played in Exposition Hall at the Florida State Fairgrounds. *Ph. 229-8800.*

Football

The Tampa Bay Buccaneers have a following of loyal football fans with four pre-season games in August and early September and eight home games, September through December. The Buccaneers play in the 72,000-seat Tampa Stadium. *Ph. 879-BUCS.*

The Hall of Fame Bowl, the NCAA famed post-season college football game, is traditionally played on New Year's Day at Tampa Stadium. *Ph. 874-2695.*

Soccer

The Tampa Bay Rowdies, Tampa's professional soccer team, competes May through August at the Tampa Stadium. *Ph. 877-7800.*

Golf

Arnold Palmer has established his headquarters at the Saddlebrook Golf and Tennis Resort. Classes for golfers at different levels are offered at the Academy; there are one- , three- , and five-day instructional programs. On the grounds, there are two championship Palmer-designed golf courses and 45 tennis courts. Saddlebrook is 12 miles north of Tampa. *Ph. 393-1111.*

Hall Of Fame Golf Course
2222 N. West Shore Blvd.
An 18-hole, 6263-yard course with par 72. Facilities include a driving range, putting green, club rental, lessons, and pro shop. *Ph. 876-4913*

Rocky Point Golf Course
4151 Dana Shores Dr.
An 18-hole, 5986-yard course with par 71. Facilities include a putting green, club rental, lessons, pro shop and snack bar. *Ph. 884-5141*

Rogers Park Golf Course
7910 N. 30th St.
An 18-hole, 6215-yard course with par 72. Facilities include a driving range, putting green, club rental, lessons, and pro shop. *Ph. 234-1911*

Babe Zaharias Golf Course
11412 Forest Hills Drive
An 18-hole, 6200-yard course with par 70. Facilities include a putting green, club rental, lessons, pro shop and snack bar. *Ph. 932-8932.*

University of South Florida Golf Course
4202 Fowler Avenue
An 18-hole, 6809-yard course with par 71. Facilities include a putting green, club rental, lessons, pro shop and snack bar. *Ph. 974-2071.*

Tennis Anyone!

The Tennis Complex at Hillsborough Community College has 16 hard surface and 12 clay courts. Call for hours of operation and availability. *Ph. 870-2383.*

Watering Holes

Lithia Springs, located on the Alafia River, has a natural spring which attracts swimmers because of the constant 72-degree water temperature. Park amenities include a bath house, playground, and picnic facilities, as well as camping sites. *Ph. 744-5572.*

Beaches in Hillsborough County

E.G. Simmons, 2401 19th Ave, NW Ruskin
A county park with a beautiful waterfront view and beaches for swimming and sunbathing.
Amenities: Boat launch; fishing pier; campgrounds; picnic facilities.

Ben T. Davis Beach, Courtney Campbell Causeway, Tampa, *Ph. 223-8018*
A city beach with 1 1/2 miles of beachfront along Tampa Bay. At the east end, there is approximately 1/4 mile of sandy beach which narrows at the west end. Parking is metered on the main beach road but free parking is available along the service drives. There are city-sponsored recreational events at the beach. Call for the schedule.
Amenities: Fishing pier; volleyball courts; picnic facilities; snack bar; cabana rentals.

Davis Island Beach, 900 Maritime Drive, Tampa
This no-frills beach is located on a small inlet of Hillsborough Bay, close to downtown Tampa. It is a small beach ideal for sunbathing. Free parking.
Amenities: Boat ramp.

Picnic Island Beach, 7404 Picnic Island Blvd.
Picnic Island Beach, located at the southern tip of the Tampa peninsula, has about 1/2 mile of beachfront as well as surrounding mangroves and sand dunes. Free parking.
Amenities: Fishing pier; playgrounds; boat ramp; picnic facilities.

Beaches in Pinellas County

Fort DeSota Park, 3500 Pinellas Bayway S., Tierra Verde, *Ph. 866-2662*
A county park covering seven miles of waterfront with two beaches. The North or Gulf Beach has a natural lagoon; the East or Bay Beach is an open expanse with fine textured sand.
Amenities: Fishing pier; campgrounds; play area; picnic facilities; snack bar.

St. Petersburg Beach
Upham Beach: Access at 68th Ave.
County Park Beach: Access at 46th Ave.
Pass-A-Grill Beach: Access at 21st - 1st Ave.
Ph. 363-9200
St. Pete's shoreline has a wide expanse of coarse white sand beaches. Parking is all metered.
Amenities: Water sports and rentals; snack bar; cabana rentals.

Treasure Island, Begins two blocks north of 107th Ave., *Ph. 360-3278*
The municipal beach of Treasure Island is operated by the municipality of St. Petersburg. It is considered to be the widest and least crowded of the city beaches. It has dressing rooms with hot and cold showers.
Amenities: Volleyball courts; picnic facilities; snack bar; cabana rentals.

Madeira Beach, 128th - 155nd Avenue, *Ph. 391-9951*
There is metered parking at the beach; picnic facilities; snack bar; cabana rentals.

Reddington Shores, 174th - 183rd Avenues, two miles north of Madeira Beach, *Ph. 397-5538*
No food concessions on the beach, but there are restaurants across the street on Gulf Blvd. Free parking.
Amenities: Fishing pier.

Indian Rocks Beach, 27th Ave. - White Hurst Ave., *Ph. 595-2517*
The beach spans about 2 1/2 miles.
No food concessions on the beach, but there are restaurants across the street on Gulf Blvd.

Clearwater Beach
An expansive eight mile stretch of beach with four beach areas: North Beach, Rockaway Beach, Main Beach and South Beach, *Ph. 462-6893*.
Most "action" is at the Main and South Beaches. Rest rooms are at Palm Pavilion and the Main Beach concession hut. Clearwater Beach is known for its miles of soft white sand. There is metered parking, as well as parking lots. It gets crowded early in the day.
Amenities: Water sports and rentals including water bikes, catarmarans and wind surfers; snack bar; cabana rentals.

Note: There are 28 miles of beaches along the St. Petersburg/Clearwater coastline. In some areas where there has been erosion, the white fine sand has been mixed with sea shells, creating a coarser texture. The Gulf of Mexico is a low energy body of water providing swimmers with calm conditions. Jet skis, speed boats, and even motorized rubber boats are off-limits in the gulf waters.

Directory of Services

9-1-1 Emergency Only   POLICE • SHERIFF • FIRE • MEDICAL • RESCUE

AGENCY	DESCRIPTION	HILLSBOROUGH(813)
ALCOHOL & DRUG ABUSE	Intervention & Referral	800-821-4357 238-9505
CRISIS HOTLINE	24 Hour Help Line	238-8821
ABUSE CENTER: THE SPRING	Women in Distress; Shelter for Abused Women	621-7233
POISON CONTROL & INFORMATION CENTER		800-282-3171 253-4444
SENIOR SUPPORT: *ELDER HELP LINE*	Telephone Reassurance & Support	653-7709
TELEPHONE SUPPORT FOR LATCH KEY CHILDREN: *PHONE FRIEND*		681-6543
TIME/TEMPERATURE		976-1111

County Services

AGENCY	DESCRIPTION	HILLSBOROUGH (813)
GOVERNMENT CENTER	601 E. Kennedy Blvd.	272-5900
ANIMAL CONTROL		744-5660
BOARD OF EDUCATION		272-4000
COUNTY COOPERATIVE EXT.		774-5519
COUNTY COURTHOUSE		223-7811
COUNTY ROAD DEP'T.	Information about streets, roads & access roads	272-6760
EMERGENCY MGMNT	Disaster Readiness Training & Evacuation	996-3911
FIRE PREVENTION		774-5638
FL. HIGHWAY PATROL	All Interstate Roads & Turnpikes	272-2211
GARBAGE COLLECTION		744-5650
LIBRARY		273-3652
LICENSES	Auto Tag Parking Permit - Handicapped Boating Registration Fishing & Hunting	272-6020 272-6020 272-6040 272-6040
MASS TRANSIT	Bus Route Information	254-4278
PARKS AND RECREATION	24 Hr. Information Line Parks Recreation	229-7529 223-8230 223-8615
PASSPORT INFORMATION		877-0662
PROPERTY APPRAISER		272-6100
SHERIFF		247-8000
TAX COLLECTOR		272-6000
TRAFFIC VIOLATION INFORMATION		229-2437
VOTER REGISTRATION		272-5850
WATER/SEWER	Northwest Central South	554-5010 744-5600 671-7604

Directory of Services 297

Human Services

AGENCY	DESCRIPTION	HILLSBOROUGH (813)
AMERICAN ASSOC. OF RETIRED PERSONS (AARP)	Florida State Headquarters Provides source for local contact	576-1155
AMERICAN RED CROSS	Hurricane Shelter Information Disaster Relief, Blood Banks Educational Programs	251-0921
CHILD CARE	Information & Referrals on Licensed Child Care Centers & Registered Family Care Providers	272-6487
INFORMATION & REFERRAL SVCS: HILLSBOROUGH INFORMATION LINE	Connects You with the Appropriate Person or Agency Who Can Answer Your Question or Assist You With A Particular Need	272-5900
HANDICAPPED/ DISABLED SERVICES	Self Reliance Easter Seals	977-6338 236-5589
HEALTH DEPARTMENT		272-6200
I R S	Location & Hours of Local Offices Tax Information Tax Forms	800-829-1040 904-354-1760 800-829-3676
NEWCOMERS CLUBS	New Tampans Tampa Newcomers, Inc.	961-4129 886-1135
SENIOR CITIZEN SERVICES	Information/Assistance	653-7709
SOCIAL SECURITY		800-772-1213
SOCIAL SERVICE TRANSPORTATION		
SHARE A VAN ANGEL WINGS OASIS	Reduced Fares, Dial-A-Ride Transport for Seniors and Special Groups	272-7272 251-0921 229-5553
UNITED WAY	An Excellent Resource for Community Information	228-8359
VETERAN'S ASSISTANCE		272-5700
VOLUNTEER CENTER	A Clearinghouse for Vounteer Positions	221-8657
RETIRED SENIOR VOLUNTEER PROGRAM (RSVP)		272-5031
WOMEN'S RESOURCE CENTER:		251-8437

City Numbers

GOVERNMENT CENTER Information Desk	Tampa City Hall 315 East Kennedy Blvd.	223-8211
CITY CLERK		223-8396
POLICE (Non Emergency)		273-0770
FIRE (Non Emergency)		227-7015
DRIVER'S LICENSE		272-3770
ELECTRICAL SERVICE	TECO: Tampa Electric Co.	223-0800
GARBAGE COLLECTION		878-1111
LIBRARY		273-3652
PARKS & RECREATION		223-8615
TELEPHONE COMPANY	GTE	800-483-3200
VOTER'S REGISTRATION		272-5850
WATER AND SEWER Emergency/After Hours		223-8811 223-8764

Civic Organizations

Greater Tampa Chamber of Commerce	228-7777
Committee of 100: Economic Development for Tampa Bay	276-9404
Tampa/Hillsborough Convention & Visitors Association	223-1111

Consumer Tips

Shopping is a favorite pastime in many Florida communities. As a newcomer, you will probably be making many purchases. Protect yourself.

Retail and Services

Credit Cards: You are not obliged to provide a retailer with your address and phone number when using a credit card. Once the merchant has received authorization, the card issuer assumes full responsibility for payment.

Personal Checks: A merchant may ask to see additional identification, but it is within your rights not to permit copying of credit card numbers. A merchant may not use your credit card if a check bounces.

For more information, contact the BankCard Holders of America, 560 Herndon Pkwy., Herndon, VA 22070. If you are having "credit card problems," contact the Federal Trade Commission, Regional Office in Atlanta, GA. Ph. 404-347-4836.

Refund Policy: Ask about store policy regarding refunds in advance of any purchase. Certain retailers may only give you a store credit, instead of a cash refund – even if it is returned the next day. If you have a problem with a defective item which has been special ordered, call the Division of Consumer Affairs for advice.

Limited Warrantees: Reputable companies who offer warrantees for mechanical or electrical products will often honor their commitment for replacing a faulty item. However, the consumer may have to pay labor charges. With any warrantee or guarantee, find out whether or not it includes any labor fees that may be incurred in the repair. The cost of the product being replaced may be nominal in comparison to hefty labor costs.

Business Licenses: If you are transacting business with an individual who does not have a retail establishment, ask to see his/her business or occupational license, which is required for every business. The business license may be issued either by the state or county.

If you are planning to do any home remodeling, check the credentials of the general contractor or subcontractor (updated business license, liability insurance and absence of complaints). If state licensed, call the Construction Industry Licensing Board. *Ph. 904-359-6310.*

It is generally a good idea to get three estimates for any given job. You will have a better idea of what the job should cost.

Some South Florida businesses are short-lived – here today and gone tomorrow. If a business does not have established credentials, use caution. If scheduling home remodeling or ordering a custom-made product, negotiate a minimum deposit and arrange a payment schedule based on stages of completion.

Small Claims Court. If a merchant or contractor fails to honor an agreement, there is some recourse – Small Claims Court. You may have your day in court – without the assistance of an attorney – for claims up to $2,500. You can obtain filing forms and instructions at the County Courthouse.

Consumer Check On Charities: It is difficult today to identify bonafide charities. If you have never heard of the charity, it is reasonable to request some printed materials describing the organization prior to making a donation. Or, you can call the Department of Agriculture and Consumer Services. A charity must register with the Division of Consumer Services and file a copy of its financial statement with them. *Ph. 800-FLA-HELP.*

Automobile Protection

Lemon Law: Buyers of new cars and motorcycles are protected by the Motor Vehicle Warranty Enforcement Act. Any new vehicle that is purchased must conform to the manufacturer's warranty. If the problem is not repairable within a specified amount of time, the buyer must be given some *lemon aid*: a new car or full refund. Contact the Division of Consumer Services of the FL Dept. of Agriculture and Consumer Affairs. *Ph. 800-327-3382.*

Motor Vehicle Repair Act: If any automotive repair exceeds $50, obtain a written estimate from your mechanic. The final bill may not exceed 10% of the original written estimate without your consent.

Automotive Consumer Action Program: This is an innovative program designed to help resolve differences between the consumer and the new car or truck dealer. It is sponsored by local automobile dealers and manufacturers participating in AUTOCAP in conjunction with the Better Business Bureau.

Consumer Aids

	Better Business Bureau/Council	Consumer Protection	Occupational, Business, Licenses	Small Claims Court
Brevard	BBC: 268-2822	633-2050	264-6910	264-5350
Broward	BBB: 524-2803	357-6030	765-4400	765-4575
Collier	BBB: 334-7331	800-435-7352	643-8431	774-8106
Dade	BBB: 625-0307	375-2222	375-2569	375-5775
Hillsborough	BBB: 854-1154	272-6750	272-6040	276-8100
Orange	BBB: 621-3300	800-435-7352	836-5650	836-2065
Palm Beach	BBB: 276-9848	355-2670	233-5525	355-2500
Sarasota	BBC: 366-3144	800-435-7352	378-6126	951-5214

Note: For condominium inquiries, information or complaints, contact the hotline, Ph. 904-488-0725.

A Written Agreement

Transacting business on a handshake is fine when everything proceeds well and there are no complications. All too often, however, what one says is not necessarily what the other person hears, creating misunderstandings down-the-road as to what was promised in the original verbal agreement. In order to avoid unnecessary frustration and heartache (remember, you're in Florida to enjoy yourself), use this written agreement – or vary it to suit your own needs. It helps to define what the expectations are on both sides.

Company _____

Contact _____

Address _____

Phone # _____ Best Time to Call _____

License # _____

Customer _____

Address _____

Phone # _____ Best Time To Call _____

The following service is to be performed: _____

The following materials will be used on the job (if applicable):

_____

Work is scheduled to begin on ____. Estimated completion is ____.

The agreed upon price is _____

A deposit of _____ has been given towards purchase price.

Merchant Signature/Date _____

Customer Signature/Date _____

Purchasing Your Florida Home

Before purchasing a home in Florida, consider the variety of living styles and decide which one is best suited to your needs.

Private Home Ownership. Perhaps the most universally familiar, "fee simple" private home ownership permits the most autonomous style of living. There are no common areas owned by the residents living within the community. The home owner has full responsibility for maintaining his/her property and securing any necessary services. At the same time, there are no community restrictions pertaining to landscaping, exterior care and design, or pet ownership.

Communities With Homeowner Associations. Another type of home ownership involves a relationship among a community of homeowners. A Homeowners' Association (HOA) is a non-profit corporation in which homeowners own and share responsibility for common areas in the village or community in which they live.

Homeowners vote for a board of directors which governs the membership. The HOA bylaws specify the number of directors, term of office, and responsibilities; the declaration of covenants and restrictions codifies the rules and regulations and details the do's and don'ts.

Residents pay monthly maintenance dues which support expenditures for common areas and services. Special assessments may be levied if a majority of homeowners vote for non-budgeted improvements or repairs.

HOA responsibilities vary, depending upon the community. Some homeowner associations may assume full landscaping responsibilities for individual homes, selecting one company to service the entire community. Others may only assume responsibility for common areas. Homeowner documents may call for uniformity in streetscape, prohibiting or restricting exterior property changes, such as alterations in patios, doors, windows, awnings, or driveways. It is very important to be aware of homeowner responsibilities, restrictions and the role the association plays within the community.

For many, the benefits of a HOA community outweigh any negatives. The rules and regulations of homeowner associations convey a certainty that the community will establish a uniformly high standard of property maintenance. Not all homeowners want the responsibility of landscaping, planting new shrubs, mowing lawns – or worrying about the height of their neighbor's grass! The value of the neighborhood will not diminish because of lax neighbors. Issues within the community are likely to foster a camaraderie as neighbors work to resolve common problems.

Presently, no state agency regulates homeowners' associations or monitors the documents prior to a developer selling the first home in a homeowner association community. One may generally assume that the particular association has followed proper legal procedure. Nevertheless, it is important to have an attorney look over the documents prior to the agreement of sale.

Homeowner Associations Exist in the Following Types of Communities

Country Club Communities

Within a country club community, there are many different styles of residential living which may include large single homes, zero lot villas or multiplex living – depending upon the grand scheme of the master developer. Often, individual developers/architects will purchase a tract of land and design a residential homeowner village within the country club community.

Country club communities are set up as a corporate enterprise with a board of directors. When there are many homeowner villages within the country club community, each village pays a pro-rated share to the larger community association to support the common grounds and services, such as landscaping, maintenance and gatehouse security.

The Country Club. Homeowners who want to use the country club facilities must purchase a bond or equity membership to "buy in" and also pay annual dues. Amenities usually include golf and/or tennis, swimming, a main clubhouse, and dining facilities. Newly built or remodeled country clubs may offer health and fitness facilities as well. Country club special assessments may be levied for capital improvement projects. In addition to initial equity, yearly dues and possible assessments, members frequently have an obligatory annual food quota or minimum that they must use in one of the dining facilities.

Different categories of membership are usually offered at a country club. Social membership, the least expensive, includes the use of the swimming pool, fitness facilities, social activities, and dining; tennis membership offers all of the social benefits, plus the use of the tennis courts; golf membership, the most expensive, includes both tennis and social memberships, as well as access to all club golfing facilities.

You may choose to live in a country club community, but not belong to the country club. However, resale becomes more difficult without equity membership, especially if there is a waiting list for membership.

Consider the following issues before selecting a country club community.

• Facility Use
Residence and membership in a country club community is expensive. If you do not plan to use the facilities on a regular basis, this may not be the best choice of living styles. Although there are many other factors which enter into a decision, this should be an important consideration. There are other alternatives for participating in occasional exercise and sports which are not as costly.

• Dining Obligations
If you enjoy eating in different restaurants and dining out at your own convenience, a yearly obligation to support the club's dining room, separate from membership dues, may not fit your lifestyle. You must honor the financial commitment even if you do not enjoy the menu selections or the chef's cooking. This yearly obligation may prove to be burdensome for people who are seasonal residents.

• Control
Golfers, who pay more for equity and yearly dues, usually have more votes per member and greater control over club policies. It is advisable to find out what the voting ratio is for different levels of equity as it relates to club improvements and expenditures.

Despite the cautions and considerations, many people enjoy country club living. It offers a self-contained community with opportunities to socialize with others through various activities sponsored by the country club. For retired men and women, country club living is an adult camp with a wealth of daily activities – and plenty of playmates!

Homeowner Communities With Amenities

Another type of homeowner lifestyle offers country club amenities, but it is not a country club community. The common areas which homeowners own not only include the entranceway, lakes, walkways, but also amenities such as tennis courts, swimming pool, and/or clubhouse. The monthly maintenance fee covers all common and shared areas and facilities. Some people prefer a homeowners' community with amenities because it has more of a neighborhood intimacy and doesn't require the same economic outlays as a country club residence.

Gated Communities

Some communities with homeowners' associations exist only to maintain common grounds and offer protection from outsiders entering the community. Some gated communities have staffed gatehouses, while others are automated with an entry code. If security is of primary importance, find out how frequently the automated gates malfunction.

Condominium Ownership

By definition, a condominium is any dwelling that has stacked units which are owned by the residents. Residents own a pro-rated share of the common elements. Condominiums are regulated by state law. The condominium documents, which must be filed with the state, govern the condominium. Before a developer sells the first unit of a condominium, the state must review the documents.

If purchasing a resale unit, the condition of the building and property – its structure, roof, sprinkler system, and landscaping – is an important issue. Find out if there is a future timetable for major repairs. Depending upon the size and type of building, assessments for these can be hefty.

Condominium living requires certain courtesies for high density living. Residents are subject to a number of rules which try to guarantee the privacy, welfare and rights of others. Consideration and respect may be difficult issues to define or negotiate, given the close proximity of neighbors.

If you wish to own a condo unit, but prefer fewer people in your living environment, look for a smaller building. However, it may not have the same social amenities or sponsor the variety of activities as a larger condo. When special assessments are needed, the financial burden may be considerably higher since there are fewer people to absorb the cost.

People who often gravitate to condominium living enjoy the freedom from home maintenance obligations and hassles. In condominiums which attract a large number of retired people, social committees may be actively at work planning a schedule of different activities. In many condos, there are separate card rooms and meeting rooms. Some social committees take recreation very seriously and plan outside activities such as day trips and evening jaunts to local theaters.

Caution: You're Making a Big Investment

It is very easy to get "caught up" in the excitement and anticipation of purchasing a home without giving this important decision the full attention it deserves. Some people take less time to purchase a home than to purchase a pair of shoes.

A Look at the Community. Invest the time to take a macro look at the community rather than a micro look at the house. Although you may be spontaneously attracted to a particular home, communities have different personalities and styles. Are residents full time or seasonal? Does the community attract a certain age group? Are residents from different parts of the country or from a particular region?

With an emphasis on the environment, ask the realtor or property developer about the source of drinking water, where garbage is deposited, whether or not there are any industrial plants in the surrounding area. Are there environmental issues that might be of concern at a later date? Find out the zoning codes for empty lots near your home. Are there properties close by which have been zoned for hotels, hospitals or high density complexes?

Protecting Your Investment. Even if you feel that you have found the "perfect" home in the "ideal" community, it is wise to hire a general contractor or engineering consultant to assess the adequacy of the electrical and plumbing systems, such as water pressure in upstairs/downstairs bathrooms, pool/spa pumps, sprinkler systems, wiring systems, etc.

Review a prepared check list with the engineering consultant to ensure that potential problem areas are assessed and nothing is omitted. It can be costly to deal with home repairs which should have been negotiated prior to settlement.

Check to see if the air conditioning system is sufficient for the square footage of the house. In South and Central Florida, the air conditioner is engaged most of the year. With temperatures frequently leaping from hot to hotter during a prolonged summer season, cool air is intimately tied to your sense of well being, temperament, and happiness.

When purchasing a new home to be constructed, give due consideration to upgrades. Ask about alternatives in air conditioning, plumbing, flooring and windows. The time to upgrade these items is prior to construction, not after installation. Determine whether the electrical outlets on the blueprints are in convenient locations throughout each room.

Check the landscaping plantings to ensure that invasive trees are not planted too close to your property. Many developers are fond of ficus trees for their quick growth and full foliage. Ficus trees are invasive plants that can wreak havoc on your plumbing system because of their expansive root system.

If you are dealing with a large developer, don't assume that the agreement of sale is standard and therefore flawless. There may be certain items which need inclusion to represent your interests in an equitable way. Involve a real estate attorney before you sign the agreement of sale. Most negotiations take place before signing – particularly with a home to be constructed. Specify in writing what was promised; the developer's word, no matter how sincere, is not sufficient.

In Florida, you do not have the option of holding any escrow funds at settlement. All money must be passed over to the owner/developer of the purchase property. Document the items that the developer must attend to and create a timetable for completion.

Consider a Rental. Although few of us are willing to heed this advice, renting a home for a year does give you a transition period to explore the different areas and lifestyles. Although living in an oceanfront community provides many pleasures to those who enjoy the beach, there are some disadvantages: the corrosive effects of the salt air on furnishings and automobiles, strong winds during hurricane season, and hampered access due to bridge openings. If you are attracted to intracoastal living, consider the gasoline fumes, noise and congestion from boats cruising the waterways. Be aware of the frequency of bridge openings with any property on the east side of the Intracoastal. Inland living poses a different set of problems, such as more intense heat, mosquitoes and greater distance to the beach.

Renting prior to purchasing will give you the opportunity to experience the wonderful and not so wonderful aspects of an area, without a serious financial commitment. During the rental period, you will have the time to get the inside scoop on real estate and life style in a variety of communities.

If you have any questions regarding Florida's rental agreements, contact the Division of Consumer Services.

Helpful Hints For The Tropics

Auto Care

Automobile Maintenance

Your automobile is also in a new environment and will require some special attention due to the tropical sun, heat, rain and salt air.

A thorough maintenance check of all operating systems in April or May should help eliminate those miserable breakdowns during the intense summer heat. A November recheck should replace fluid losses and heat-damaged belts and hoses.

Check the cooling system regularly as well as your automobile battery, which is more prone to corrosion and damage in the summer heat.

The engine requires a higher viscosity (heavier weight) motor oil to compensate for Florida's hotter temperatures. A high grade SAE 10W-30 or 40 weight oil is recommended for year-round use by most manufacturers. The oil should be changed every 3,000 to 5,000 miles and kept filled to capacity.

Due to the heavy Florida downpours, windshield wipers are called upon to do extra duty and may need to be replaced more often. Rainnex is a recommended product, especially for those downpours. It is a clear, rub-on windshield treatment which prevents the hazing effect of heavy rain.

Tire Talk

Tires will need additional care and attention. Most road beds are made of coral rock, a plentiful but sharp abrasive material which, unfortunately, causes wear and tear on tires. The Florida road heat shortens tire life as it softens the rubber. Proper wheel alignment and tire pressure are essential.

Sudden rain and frequent summer downpours can produce slick roadways in an instant. Poor tire tread facilitates hydroplaning, the loss of traction as the tire rides on a layer of water. There are specially designed tire treads available to reduce hydroplaning.

Exterior Care

Florida pollutants (such as salt water, abrasive coral dust, insecticide sprays, and the infamous acid rain) along with the sun and heat can damage your automobile's exterior – causing oxidation and fading of paint.

The quality and frequency of care will depend upon where you and your automobile reside. If you live near the ocean, rinse your car daily with clear water and use a mild detergent twice a week to remove the salt residue. If unattended, the salt in the surrounding air will corrode metal parts and paint, resulting in rust. If you live further away from the ocean, wash your car once a week.

If the paint on your automobile is dull, it may only need a good wax rather than a new paint job. During extreme summer heat, waxing every two months is suggested. During the cooler weather, waxing every three months is adequate. There are professional detailers who deep clean the dirt and grime lodged within the paint pores. A good waxing or a coat of acrylic Teflon will seal the paint from the elements. There are also free lance detailers who will come to your home and wash, wax and clean the interior of your car. This is one of the many home services you may enjoy using here – but, always ask for ID and references.

A Few Cautions

Do not park your car near sprinkler systems. This untreated water is unsoftened. It may damage the paint as well as deposit unwanted water spots on your car.

Bugs are certainly not pleasant while alive, but they may create even more problems when they die on your car. Their body acid can eat through the paint. Remove them immediately using water and a mild car soap. Love bugs, in particular, can be a big annoyance – especially during their mating seasons in May and September. Before traveling in more populated love bug areas, apply non-stick Pam to the front of your car (not windshield) and chrome trim to facilitate easy removal. Love bugs may also clog radiators, causing overheating. Inexpensive bug screens will protect your radiator.

Auto Window Tinting

Auto window tinting has several purposes: it reduces sun glare and heat build-up; filters approximately 98% of UV light; reduces night glare from headlights; and protects upholstery from fading and cracking.

There are three different strengths of tint, each gauged by the amount (%) of light they allow through the glass. The darkest tint is 20%, allowing only 20% of light to pass through; the medium tint is 35%; and the lightest tint is 50%.

By Florida law, the front windows can be tinted no darker than 35%. Only the top six inches of the windshield can be darkened to a maximum of 20%. The rear passenger windows and back window can be tinted no darker than 20%.

Whereas there is less heat penetration with tinted windows, any heat that does penetrate will be trapped in a parked car. Do not expect miracles.

There are two different types of film: regular (standard) and metallic. The latter allows greater energy efficiency and has more color stability. If you intend to keep your car for more than two years, the metallic film is recommended.

Bubbling, rippling and peeling may occur from inferior adhesives or if the film is not properly applied. The *manufacturer's warranty* is most important if replacement is necessary.

Maintenance: Clean tinted windows with a damp cloth. *Do not use ammonia or any ammonia product; it will turn your treated windows purple.*

Farewell Snowbirds

If you're leaving Florida for a few weeks or a few months, there are certain guidelines you should follow in closing your home.

A Few Weeks

Leave your air conditioner on, although you may want to raise the temperature. Ensure that there is enough cool air circulating throughout your home. Consider purchasing a humidistat which signals your thermostat when there is a certain level of humidity in the air. Your air conditioner will go on only when the humidity level is too high.

Unplug all major appliances. Although a surge protector reduces the risk of a blow-out in an electrical storm, there is always the possibility of fire during a severe storm.

Raise the temperature in your refrigerator-freezer. If you are going to be away for a brief period of time, leave only a minimum amount of "unspoilable" foods in the event of a prolonged power failure. Do not leave an empty refrigerator on; storage of some food is necessary for effective power usage. If you're going to be away for only a few weeks, store dry products in the freezer.

Hint: Put rolls of scented toilet tissue on your refrigerator shelves to absorb odors. Ground vanilla beans, baking soda, charcoal and mesquite also are absorbing agents.

Ask a friend or neighbor to flush your toilets once a week. Uncirculated water will leave a sediment ring from mineral deposits in the water. If your toilets cannot be flushed on a regular basis, dissolve 1-2 cups of Clorox into the water and seal the bowl with a plastic wrap to slow evaporation.

If you do not want any pests and critters making a guest appearance through the drainage system, keep toilet lids down and use stoppers in all sinks and basins.

A Few Months Or Longer

If you're going to be away for a few months or more, unplug your refrigerator and leave the door open.

Shut off the main water supply to your house. Any substantial water leak will invite mildew and mold from floor to ceiling, creating a tropical forest in every nook and cranny.

Caution: If you do not unplug your refrigerator, be sure to turn off the automatic ice maker. The motor will burn out if no water is going through the system.

Before shutting off the main water valve, make sure you aren't shutting down the water in your sprinkler system as well.

Empty all food storage cabinets. Do not leave any dry foods, such as cereals, flour, corn or oat products, in the cupboards. Leave kitchen drawers and cabinets slightly ajar for maximum air circulation.

Garbage Disposal: Run two trays of ice cubes through the system and then sanitize it with a solution of baking soda and water.

Dishwasher: Remove any food particles and then run it through a short cycle.

Leave bedroom doors/closets open and dresser drawers slightly ajar. Strip the beds, vacuum and lightly sponge the mattress with a solution of 50% rubbing alcohol and 50% water.

Do not use any plastic to cover and protect the furniture from dust. It will only trap moisture and create mildew problems. Place the sofa pillows loosely on the sofa for maximum air circulation.

If you would like your plants to remain healthy and happy in your absence, create a terrarium for them. After a big drink of water, enclose them in an air-tight plastic bubble. You will probably need a roll of plastic (for your larger plants) in addition to a heavy duty stapler. Your plants will be self-sufficient until your return.

If this seems like a tedious process, a house sitting service might well suit your needs. They will check your home once a week (or as instructed) to ensure that everything is operating properly. With T.L.C., they will inspect for leaks, run your disposal, flush your toilets, water your plants and oversee that services are being provided in your absence, such as pool maintenance, landscaping and pest control.

Florida Pests

There are many other living things, besides our beautiful tropical plants, that you probably didn't bargain for when you decided to take up residence here. Some are actually quite beneficial, while others are nuisance pests which can cause discomfort. But, since they were here first, you must be the one to learn the art of peaceful coexistence.

Cockroaches

The tropical palmetto is none other than the homely cockroach. They forage for food at night, eating anything in their path. Although harmless, they can carry bacteria and spread disease through their droppings. If you have an infestation, it is important to get professional help. Do not be surprised by their size! The American cockroach, for instance, measures from 1 1/2-2 inches; Florida homes also host the German and brown-banded variety, smaller in size, measuring about 5/8 of an inch.

Fleas

Fleas love warm temperatures! Dogs and cats are particularly susceptible to hosting the flea and transporting them into the house. If you are in a new construction site, fleas may attach themselves to boots or shoes and piggyback into your home. Once inside, they will feed on human hosts as well as animals. They breed in floor cracks, baseboards and carpets. A flea will usually attack its human host at the feet, ankles or legs. The bite appears on the skin as a small red dot and may cause intense itching and discomfort for many days.

Note: Do-it-yourself products are available in several forms, but are not recommended if severe infestation is evident in your home. Any treatment must combine agents to kill the adult flea and also inhibit the larva from hatching.

Do not use a borax solution on any carpeted area. It kills the carpet as well as the fleas.

Sand Flies (Biting Midges)

Sand Flies are minute insects that bite. Since they are not seen but rather felt, they have been dubbed "No See Ums." The adult is less than 1/16th of an inch. They are often found near beaches, streams and ponds. They can cause itching, irritation and discomfort for days. If you are planning dinner with a lakeside view, protect yourself. For most people, over-the-counter repellents containing diethyl toluamide (DEET) will offer protection for several hours. Check with your pharmacist for product recommendations and use as directed.

Fire Ants

The imported South American fire ant which ranges in color from red to brown is most unfriendly and should not be disturbed. They make their nests in low mounds of sand above the ground. Thousands of them may live in one mound. If a fire ant is disturbed, powerful jaws attach to the skin and stingers release a toxin which can cause tissue swelling and severe itching. While some may not experience any symptoms, others may go into shock. It can be extremely dangerous if you are stung by several of them at one time. Fire ants may also enjoy patio or poolside living. If you see reddish ants by the pool, they may very well be fire ants. Use caution and do not walk barefoot. And beware of fire ant mounds while gardening! Wear shoes while walking around in your yard.

Mosquitoes

Mosquitoes are difficult to control. They breed in ponds and lakes of stagnant water. During the rainy season, they are out in full force. If you are being enveloped by swarms of them, call your County Mosquito Control Agency. Upon citizens' requests, they will spray neighborhood areas. In your own backyard, drain excess standing water from flower pots and plant containers. The water stagnates and can become a nesting place for them.

Fighting Back: Remember citronella! The "citrosa" plant, a genetic hybrid of citronella grass and scented geranium, is being used to keep mosquitoes from invading our space. It exudes a lemony citronella scent which repels mosquitoes within a 20-foot diameter. Plant one citrosa every 5-10 feet around a yard or patio, in partial shade. It usually grows to a height of five feet.

Note: If you have unidentified insects in your home or yard, bring some specimens to your County Cooperative Extension Service for proper identification.

Allergic Reactions To Insect Bites

If you have a mild allergic reaction to an insect bite, apply ice and then baking soda, meat tenderizer, or special ointments to the affected area. If there is more severe itching, swelling, bleeding or pain, contact a physician immediately.

If you are irresistible to our biting insect population, *Avon's Skin So Soft* (primarily a skin care lotion) may be your solution. It has become known as an effective repellent.

Caterpillars

There are several caterpillars that release a poison upon contact with the skin. Although they are called *stinging caterpillars*, they do not actually have a stinger. Poison is released through sharp spines which can break off and penetrate the skin. Some people experience severe reactions, while others have little more than itching and burning. They may be found on ixora, roses and hibiscus bushes.

Caution: Always wear heavy-duty gloves while gardening to protect yourself from stinging caterpillars, fire ants and thorny plants.

Lizards

They may at first appear to be pests as they dart around your patio or living space. In time, however, you will learn to enjoy their playful habits. These harmless little fellas are friends. They help maintain nature's balance by eating roaches, termites, beetles and caterpillars. You will see a variety of lizards, ranging from the little gecko (4") to the broad headed skink (10"-12"). If you do not want them playing in the house, place a dark towel over your guests and accompany them outside.

Frogs

At some time, you will either hear or see a tree frog. These harmless critters are not among nature's prettiest! But they are beneficial, preserving nature's balance by feeding on mosquitoes and insects. Their large toes (which look like long fingers) are used as suction cups to scale flat surfaces. Since they are nocturnal, you will probably not see them during the day.

Snakes

Of the 40 species of snakes in Florida, only the following six are poisonous: eastern diamondback rattlesnake, pigmy rattlesnake, cottonmouth (water moccasin), coral snake, canebreak rattler and copperhead. the canebreak and copperhead are more indigenous to Northern Florida.

All (except the coral snake) are pit vipers, so-called because of the small pit located between the eye and nostril on each side of the head. Other distinguishing characteristics include elliptical pupils and two large fangs in the upper front portion of mouth. Pit vipers usually coil before striking. If bitten, it is important to notice if two puncture marks have broken the skin; this is the signature of the pit viper.

The coral snake is the prettiest, but most dangerous of all. It has brightly colorful bands of red, yellow and black and a distinguishing black nose. Differing from the pit vipers, it has short fangs and a small face. It does not strike, but rather bites to inject its poison. The coral snake is slender, usually less than two feet in length and may look like a non-poisonous garden variety. Do not engage in any field study with these pretty little specimens.

If you want to increase the likelihood of never seeing a snake in your new Florida home, follow a simple plan of prevention. Close up small cracks or openings in exterior walls. Clean up dense areas of foliage close to your house. Shrubbery, brush and tall grass may be a habitat for snakes looking for rodents.

Snakes seek higher (drier) ground during periods of heavy rain. Be aware of this if you usually take long walks in grassy areas.

Alligators

Do not feed the alligators unless *you* want to become their dinner. They can be found along lakes, river banks and even marshy ponds near golf courses. You may not immediately see gators swimming in a body of water. They can stay submerged for about 3/4 of an hour. Don't allow your children or pets to play, wade or swim in an unfamiliar river, lake or pond.

People love to tell old war stories about snakes and alligators. The truth is that you may live in Florida for many years without ever seeing either a snake or an alligator. But, since they do live here, it is wise to become more familiar with them.

For more information, contact your County Cooperative Extension Service *or* the Florida Cooperative Extension Service:

Institute of Food and Agricultural Sciences
Entomology & Nematology Dept.
University of Florida, Gainesville, FL 32611

Home Security

Florida's carefree lifestyle often prompts people to become less careful in their living habits. We are more inclined to leave the front door unlocked while relaxing on the patio and gardening in the yard or to leave windows open while running a few errands.

Studies show that if the common burglar cannot gain entry within the first five minutes, he/she may become discouraged and move on to homes which are more inviting.

Don't Be Vulnerable!

Make your home less attractive to the thief by following these guidelines:

Contact Your Local Police Department for a safety survey of your home by a crime prevention officer.

Know Your Neighbors. Form a support network. Let your neighbors know when you are planning to be away from home. Ask them not to hesitate in contacting the police if they see anything unusual.

Landscape Your Property to maintain its visibility. Do not block doors and windows with shrubbery (which serves as an excellent hiding place). Keep bushes low, not exceeding three feet in height or six inches below window level.

Use Exterior Lighting To Discourage Intruders. Low voltage (12v) outdoor lighting will highlight your house and property at minimal cost. There are also outdoor security systems, such as motion detectors which work in conjunction with outdoor lighting.

Secure Your House With Good Quality Doors and Locks

Entry Doors: Door composition should be solid core wood or metal and at least 1 3/4 inches thick. Use a high security deadbolt lock to secure all entry doors. It should have a solid brass cylinder collar and a bolt that extends into the frame one inch. Experts also recommend the pin tumbler cylinder lock. If you have any other type of lock, a seam blocker plate is recommended in front of the door knob to prevent tampering.

Doors which are mounted within 40 inches of a window or doors with glass inserts should be protected with a double-cylinder deadbolt lock. These doors lock and unlock using a key on either side. Place the inside key in a secure but very accessible place to permit your own emergency exit.

Sliding Glass Doors and Windows: Use key locks for windows along with jimmy proof plates to secure the frame. If need be, insert an object, such as a wood dowel or steel rod in the channel.

Additional Precautions For Sliding Glass Doors:
- K.M. Locks are hinges which secure sliders.
- Drill in Tap Screws, placed in the headers, eliminate play in the door to prevent easy removal from the frame.

Note: Polycarbonate security film strengthens glass.

Jalousie Doors and Windows: Jalousies are generally easier for gaining entry. Fit interior of jalousie doors/windows with a #9 gauge carbon steel, diamond shaped grate or glue each window into its slot with heavy duty epoxy glue to prevent removal. If possible, replace jalousie windows totally.

Garage: Keep your garage door closed and locked – even while you are in the house or outside in the backyard.

Suggestion: Electronic keypads on garage doors provide keyless access using a designated code. This eliminates the need to carry keys.

Alarm System

Before installing a security system, contact your local police for their recommendations. Some insurance companies will discount your homeowner's premium if you have an approved alarm system.

Know whether or not your alarm has an outside siren. Many systems only sound inside and therefore will not alert your neighbors.

Once, but preferably twice a year, test your alarm system. Voltage, sensitivity of detectors, and window/door contacts should be professionally checked and serviced. If you are closing your residence for the summer, service your system prior to leaving town.

Find out whether or not your alarm system must be registered with your municipal or county law enforcement agency.

Most importantly, if you have an alarm system, use it! If you are going out during the day, even for a brief period of time, *activate it.* Develop the habit!

Remember! Any unfamiliar person who comes to your door, no matter how well-dressed or well-spoken, may be a potential burglar casing your house.

The Enhanced 911 Computer-Assisted Reporting System

This system features an immediate display of the calling party's phone number (listed or unlisted) and location. If there is silence after a 911 call is received, police are automatically dispatched to the indicated location. When calling 911 from a pay phone, no coins are necessary.

Personal Care

Time to Acclimatize

The opportunity to be outdoors year-round may be the very reason you are a newcomer. However, under the tropical sun and high levels of humidity, routine tasks may leave you short of breath, overheated and fatigued. Ease into any strenuous activity, even if it is a familiar one.

Sun Sense

Develop a healthy respect for Florida's tropical sun. Florida has one of the highest rates of skin cancer in the nation. Avoid lengthy exposure in the direct sun between 10 am and 2 pm. UVB (short) rays burn during this time. UVA (long) rays are concentrated during early morning and late afternoon hours.

Caution: Sand and water reflect more than 50% of the sun's rays onto the skin.

Protect Yourself! Use a sunscreen with a sun protection factor (SPF) of 15 which shields against both UVB and UVA rays adequately. Any sunscreen should be applied liberally at least 15 to 30 minutes before going into the sun, and thereafter every two hours of exposure time.

Any outdoor activity requires some protection from the sun. There are cosmetic products with sunscreen which should be applied routinely to the face, neck, forearms and hands.

PABA Alert: If you are allergic to sulpha medications, it is possible that you could be sensitive to PABA-based sunscreen. Check with your physician.

Protection should begin at birth. Keep newborns (to one year of age) out of the sun as much as possible. Always protect the head with a brimmed hat or cap. Begin using a doctor-suggested sunscreen at the age of 6 months. Skin damage accumulates over a lifetime. More than 1/2 of the sun's damaging UVB and UVA rays will be accumulated by age 18.

Hint: If you should overdose on sun, consider Aloe Vera Gel, a soothing and greaseless product. Keep it in the refrigerator until needed.

Eye damage can also occur without adequate protection. New prescription eye wear can be treated to screen out UV rays. Over-the-counter sunglasses should have a UV stamp to designate 100% ultraviolet protection.

Cancer Information Service Hotline: They provide information and free publications on the prevention and recognition of skin cancer. Ph. 800-422-6237.

Exercise

Care & Comfort

Before participating in any sports activity, dust your sneaks with corn starch; it is much more absorbent than talcum powder.

Before exercising, take five minutes to stretch the appropriate muscle groups.

Learn to love water! Drink plenty of it at least 30 minutes before vigorous exercise, drink during exercise, and replenish your body with water afterwards.

Water loss through perspiration is a cooling process. Wearing a wet shirt during strenuous exercise is actually cooler than replacing it with a dry garment. A wet cloth draped under a hat (safari style) or around the neck is refreshing.

Water Wise

Swimming is a refreshing exercise, but it can cause dry skin and green hair. Moisturize your skin with a lotion before swimming. After the moisturizer is absorbed, apply sun block. Salt water and chlorine should be washed and rinsed from your hair immediately. Rinses designed to "strip" chlorine and other chemicals from your hair should be used on a regular basis to prevent "green hair."

Keep Walking - Rain or Shine

Your stamina will build in time as your body acclimatizes to the heat and humidity levels of a tropical climate.

During the summer, walk in the cooler morning hours or late evening hours. Wear loose, absorbent clothing and cotton socks.

Several area malls open their doors prior to business hours, facilitating aerobic walking in a climate-controlled, air conditioned space. A number of medical centers have formed Mall Walker Clubs, offering the support and companionship of others. Contact any major medical center or mall business office for further information.

Heat Alert: Heat cramps/exhaustion/stroke can result from a loss of body fluids during strenuous activity or long term exposure to high temperatures (especially with high humidity). Children and elderly people are most susceptible.

Preventive Measures: Know the signs of each condition and the appropriate first aid measures. During hot/humid days, wear loose absorbent clothing and a hat or visor. Avoid over-exertion and drink plenty of fluids, especially before exercising.

Environmental Allergies

Welcome to the subtropics and a 12-month allergy season. Dust mites, mold and grasses are present year-round. Trees and flowers pollinate January through April; grasses pollinate April through July. Ragweed season begins early August and extends through December. Allergies to new environmental substances may take six months to a year to appear. Allergy testing is *usually* not considered effective until you have lived here for six months. However, if you are having a problem, consult a physician who is Board Certified in Allergy and Immunology.

Allergy Hotline: The American Academy Of Allergy And Immunology provides referrals and printed materials for allergy sufferers. *Ph. 800-822-2762.*

Pool and Spa Care

Pools are a part of Florida's tropical environment. They are a natural extension of the house where the teperature year-round is warm and the lifestyle is casual. Spas are becoming increasingly popular for their therapeutic value and smaller space requirements.

POOL CARE

Pool maintenance can be performed by one of the many reliable pool companies. The menu of services usually includes a biweekly or weekly visit and consists of chemical balancing *or* chemical balancing and cleaning. If you choose to maintain your pool or spa yourself, you may want to bring in a specimen of water for analysis to a pool supply dealer.

Spot Etching: An Undesirable Design

Many South Florida pools are concrete, with a gunnite base and marsite (marbleized dust) finish. Spot etching, pitting, discoloration and areas of blotching of pool plaster can create serious problems for pool owners. At worst, a hole or pit may develop in the plaster.

Ounces of prevention include maintaining a properly treated and well-balanced pool as well as knowing the water source and mineral content of your water supply. Depending upon the condition, some pools may be candidates for an acid wash to remove the stains. But acid washing an older pool (after five years) with existing staining and spotting may further etch the surface, allowing algae to attach to it more easily.

Chemical Balancing

Chemical balancing is recommended on a biweekly basis, year-round; consistent care is especially important during the summer. The intense sun, heavy summer rains, and frequent pool use promote the breakdown of chemicals, bacteria and algae growth.

Always run the filtration system when adding chemicals to pool water. A biweekly program permits using fewer chemicals, which is more comfortable for swimmers.

Chlorine: 3.0 - 4.0 ppm (Suggested)

Chlorine, by itself, is a powerful disinfectant which kills bacteria and algae. When chlorine combines with contaminants in the water, however, it forms combined chlorine (chloramines) which dilutes its power as a disinfectant. Organic waste from swimmers (perspiration, body oils, body hair and dead skin) as well as rain, windblown dust/dirt and leaves combine with chlorine to form combined chlorine. A strong odor of chlorine and eye irritation result from excess organic waste in the chlorine. It is never the result of too much chlorine, but rather too little free (pure) chlorine.

Shock Treatment: Superchlorination.

A shock treatment is used when there is a build-up of chloramines (organic wastes) or algae. It is usually necessary after a heavy rainstorm or heavy bather load. Do not swim until there is a proper chlorine reading.

An Ounce of Prevention: As part of a prevention program, some pool companies recommend superchlorinating once a month during the winter and every other week during the summer. It is usually best to apply the shock treatment in the morning. Remain out of the pool for a few hours, until there is a proper chlorine reading.

To prolong the life of chlorine, *Stabilizer* is necessary. Sunlight (UV light) rapidly dissipates the strength and effectiveness of chlorine.

Algae

Warm water and hot, humid climates are ideal for algae growth. Algae consumes chlorine, leaving less of it available for use as a disinfectant. There are three common varieties that may take up residence in your pool.

Black Algae: Black, slippery spots which appear on the walls and bottom of the pool.
Green Algae: A free floating variety. It gives a green, cloudy color to the water.
Mustard Algae: Usually yellow or mustard colored, it appears in corners and crevices.

Vigorously brush algae away from the walls and steps, and super-chlorinate the water. If algae is resistent to these measures, you might have to use a good algaecide until the problem disappears.

Water Balance

Water balance is important in the maintenance of your pool and the water quality. The balance depends upon the interaction of the pH, total alkalinity and calcium hardness.

pH Balance 7.4-7.6 ppm (Suggested)

The pH is a measure of the relative balance between acidity and bascity of water. The pH level affects chlorine efficiency. With a high pH, there is less chlorine available to sanitize the water; eyes burn. A low pH also causes eye irritation due to higher acidity. Scaling, an abrasive coral-like deposit on pool walls, occurs with a high pH. With a low pH, the acidity of the water will corrode the plaster and metal piping and fittings.

Total Alkalinity (TA) 80-140 ppm (Suggested)

This is a measure of the actual amount of alkaline chemicals in pool water. TA stabilizes the pH balance. If the TA is high, it will require persistence and frequent acid treatments to bring it down. If the TA is low, there will be sudden and rapid fluctuations in the pH and it will be difficult to control stability.

If the alkalinity is within the desired range, it is easy to establish and maintain the pH. If it is difficult to maintain a balanced pH, check the TA.

Calcium Hardness (CH) 200-350 ppm (Suggested)

CH measures the amount of calcium carbonate in your pool. If the level is high, scaling and cloudy water can occur. In the tropics, evaporation is a significant factor. If your source water is hard, a concentrated residue of minerals will remain after evaporation. When refilled, the water will have a higher CH. In soft water areas where there is a low CH, etching and corrosion can occur. Test for calcium every two-four weeks.

After balancing chemicals, wait 30 minutes for chemicals to circulate before using the pool.

Pool Mechanics

Pool filtration systems should run approximately 10-12 hours per day in the summer. In the winter, approximately six-eight hours per day is suggested.

Note: Moisture may accumulate in the electrical parts of your motor during high humidity seasons. Running the filtration system will dry out excess moisture. Contact a pool service if you plan to be away for a period of time.

SPA CARE

A spa contains approximately 1/50th the volume of pool water. The ratio of the small volume of water to the number of bathers, build-up of organic wastes, high water temperatures, and high evaporation rate can lead to rapid declines in the chemical balance. Chlorine quickly dissipates in its effectiveness as a sanitizer, leaving the spa user more vulnerable to bacterial growth. Heavy use of the spa increases the need for chlorination.

Maintenance Procedures

Bromine is often used as a spa sanitizer, instead of chlorine. Although it is more expensive than chlorine, it is very effective. In hot water, it does not break down as quickly as chlorine, nor does it cause eye irritation when it combines with organic matter in the water. Chlorine, however, is more effective in combating algae.

If a shock treatment is necessary due to heavy use or rains, a non-chlorine shock treatment is available.

With normal use and conditions, test pH and chlorine levels two-three times per week, alkalinity once per week, and calcium once per month. Speak to your spa dealer or supplier to establish the correct chemical balances for your spa.

If you and others are using your spa on a regular basis, drain the water and clean it every three months.

Hint: Put on a pair of old gym socks and use your toes to scrub those hard-to-get-to corners and crevices.

Resources: For more information on pools and spas, contact the National Spa and Pool Institute (NSPI), and request the brochure which lists their various publications:

2111 Eisenhower Avenue
Alexandria, VA 22314
Ph. 703-549-0493

Water Refreshers

Chemical Safety

Make sure that all your test solutions are current. Look for expiration dates. Test kits and chemicals should be kept in a cool place to preserve the freshness of the chemicals. Always read the test results in a shaded area.

Store chemicals away from other chemicals with adequate ventilation in a dry, cool place. Never store chlorine and acid next to each other.

Pool Plantings

Do not design plant areas too close to poolside. Frequent rains may cause a soil runoff into your pool water.

Do not place fragile plants, shrubs or trees where water splashes. Use high moisture tolerant landscape plantings. It's not the chlorine that kills the plants, it's the water!

Hurricane Precautions

Prior to the hurricane season, call your pool company and ask if they will give you poolside instruction on disengaging your pool equipment in the event of a hurricane.

- Know how to turn off all electricity to the motor, pump, lighting, and pool cleaners.
- Do not drain the pool or lower the water level. The rising water table and pressure may cause it to pop out of the ground.
- Superchlorinate the water prior to a hurricane.
- Do not throw any patio furniture into the pool. Chemicals will harm the furniture and the furniture can scratch the sides of the pool. Place your pool equipment in an inside storage area.

- If you have a screened enclosure or patio, remove the panels of screening on opposite sides to allow the wind to blow through the area. Most screens cannot sustain winds of 75 mph.

For more information, contact your County Division of Emergency Management.

Storage Solutions

Storage problems in tropical Florida are directly related to the six months of 24-hour excessive heat and humidity, ever-present mildew, mold and insects. Mildew grows in warm, damp, and airless places. It is a fungus which appears on fabrics, leather, wood, and paper. Humidity and moisture are particularly problematic with new construction and beach properties. Air conditioning, used moderately year-round, will reduce the amount of heat, humidity and mildew throughout your home.

Closet Storage

Ventilated shelving is very popular in warm climates. The open wire permits good air circulation and is suggested for use in any high humidity location, including bedroom closets, kitchen pantry or bathroom storage areas. It can be purchased at any of the home centers by the foot or in precut kits.

Look for sturdy wire with a heavy vinyl coating for long-term use; the vinyl coating on poor quality shelving will become tacky in time.

Climate Control

To minimize mildew, open closet doors and leave a closet light on for a few hours each day; air conditioning vents should remain open.

If electrical outlets are available, *Damp Chasers* (low voltage dehumidifier rods) can be mounted above the floor molding to reduce moisture; these heat rods were originally used to dry out the moisture in pianos.

Damp Rid, which contains granules of calcium chloride, is a dehumidifier found in most supermarkets. The granules draw humidity from the air, trapping the moisture in its container. The liquid must be emptied and granules replaced routinely for continued effectiveness.

Garment Protection

- Dry clean garments on a regular schedule to reduce climate stains; remove the plastic covering to prevent fabric discoloration and mildew.
- If using plastic garment bags, open the zipper. Separate the opening with a dowel-like rod to allow air circulation. Porous cloth garment bags are preferable.
- Mothballs and crystals should be placed above clothing since their vapors are heavier than air. An old sock or stocking stuffed with mothballs will serve the purpose.
- Clothes should not be laundered with starch or fabric finish if you are preparing them for storage.
- Unprinted, white, low-gloss or tissue paper can be used to protect stacked items. Paper is a natural absorbing agent.
- If closet moisture is a problem, loosely stuff your footwear with paper.
- White poster board can be used to eliminate grid marks if stacking items on wire shelving.
- If you live near the ocean, use plastic or wood hangers for long-term storage.

Insect Control

Cedar blocks and chips repel moths and other insects as well as adding a pleasant fragrance.

Bay leaves, scattered on shelving and along closet baseboards, deter palmetto bugs.

Kitchen Storage

Several varieties of food-infesting beetles, weevils, ants and palmettos can invade your pantry. Grain/flour beetles and rice weevils can be present in their unhatched state – even in sealed boxes and bags.

Prolonged storage, especially in hot, humid conditions, promotes the maturation process of these insects. They quickly spread from box to box, eating through cardboard, paper and plastic wraps. If noticed, check the entire cupboard.

Weevils may appear as black dots on the pantry ceiling. Roaches also enjoy high shelf corners, appearing at night to feed. They leave behind black seed-like excrement and an oily secretion.

Spices, such as hot peppers or chili powder are also pest prone. Spread spices onto a white paper napkin or plate before adding to the cooking pot.

Minute sugar ants (which scurry in different directions) love sweet, sugary foods, but are also at home under the sink.

Keeping these Pests at "Bay"

Bay leaves contain cineaol, an ingredient which repels roaches and other insects. Place bay leaves in liberal quantities throughout food storage areas. Use a leaf or two in flour, sugar and tea canisters. Replace them before the onset of summer for maximum protection.

Grain products, even those in unopened boxes, should be stored in plastic containers, heavy duty zip-lock bags, or in the freezer.

Anything left out overnight is potential bug food.

Garage Storage

Garage storage should be used only for replaceable or non-valuable items. Heat discoloration, fabric rot, mildew and rust can occur, even when there is some ventilation. If you need extra space to store your more valued possessions, check into air conditioned storage locker rentals.

Sports equipment with metal parts, bicycles, refrigerators/freezers, and washers/dryers should be waxed yearly if kept in the garage. Near the ocean, these metals should be rinsed to remove salt air residue. Dry thoroughly; salt and moisture create rust. Rubber seals on garaged refrigerator/freezer doors will mildew in spite of frequent washing. Cosmetic replacement may be necessary.

Books, important papers and fine clothing should not be stored in the garage or attic. They discolor and are susceptible to insects and mildew.

Suitcases also invite mildew if stored in a dark, humid garage or attic. There are commercial products available to remove mildew stains, but the odor seems to remain. Scented toilet tissue, placed in suitcases, absorbs moisture and provides a pleasant fragrance. You can also purchase a mildew-stop pouch made for suitcases and trunks.

Garbage containers, stored in the garage, should have tight fitting lids. Sprinkle a layer of baking soda around the bottom of the can before lining it. Before sealing your trash bag, add 1/4-1/2 cup of ammonia to discourage animals from partying. Scraps of food, which cannot go into your disposal, should be wrapped and stored in your freezer until trash is collected.

Water on Tap

Most of the drinking water in Florida comes from rain which seeps through to an aquifer, an underground cavern of porous limestone. City wells pump the water from the aquifer and send it through a purification process at a local treatment plant. Tampa is not served by an aquifer, but taps surface water which is purified at a treatment plant.

Is the Water Safe to Drink?

All water has "contaminants," but safety standards for maximum allowable levels have been established by the EPA and Florida's Dept. of Environmental Regulation (DER).

There are some concerns that pollutants may be finding their way into tap water after it leaves the water treatment plant. Many city water utility systems test the water at various distribution points en route to our taps.

Is Lead a Problem?

Lead contamination in drinking water can result from lead-based solder in the joints of your plumbing system. For a good many years, lead-based solder has not been permitted in any new construction. You may want to have your water tested for lead contamination since it is not recognizable in drinking water. Use a reputable testing lab which has been recommended by your utility company or local health department.

Safer Than It Looks!

Colorless rainwater passes through vegetative matter, which tinges it with color. Yellow/brown is the natural color of ground water as it enters the aquifer.

Chloramines (chlorine and ammonia) have replaced free (uncombined) chlorine as a disinfectant in order to maintain safety levels. Free chlorine gives water the appearance of being "clear as rainwater." Unfortunately, however, chloramines do not sufficiently bleach out the unattractive color of our natural ground water.

Tastier Tap Water

To improve the taste of tap water and remove chlorine, allow the water to stand in an open container at room temperature for several hours before refrigerating.

Refreshing cold tap water is as foreign to the tropics as polar bears! Our water pipes are relatively close to the ground surface. Tropical temperatures heat the ground, warming the water as it travels through the system.

Private Wells

If you are obtaining your water from private or community wells, it is important to find out about the water quality, how it is regulated, how often it is tested, and whether there is a need for additional treatment.

Home Water Treatment Units

If you are not satisfied with the quality or taste of your water, you might want to consider a home treatment unit. But first, have your water tested. Each system is designed to deal with specific problems, and each one has its pros and cons.

1. Activated Carbon Filters. Remove some organic contaminants which may be responsible for the undesirable taste, color or odor of tap water; reduce the odor of chlorine. Most will not, however, filter many of the inorganic chemicals such as salts or metals in the water. Some filters claim to remove lead; obtain printed assurance of this from the manufacturer.

Caution: The filter may become saturated with the impurities it was designed to remove. In addition, levels of bacteria can collect and multiply on the carbon filter, necessitating replacement. When purchasing the activated carbon filter system, ask about maintenance and replacement filters.

2. Reverse Osmosis (RO) Units. Remove some organic elements plus a considerable amount of inorganic chemicals, such as metals (including lead), salts, nitrates and asbestos. Minerals are also removed, depleting some important nutrients from our water supply. Tap water is filtered through a membrane and collected in a storage tank.

Caution: There is considerable water waste; four gallons of tap water may only yield one gallon of RO filtered water. It also flows through the system more slowly than tap water. Membranes need periodic replacement.

3. Distillation Units. In this two-step heating-and-cooling process, the water is first vaporized and then condensed. Most inorganic chemicals, such as minerals, metals, and nitrates are removed and harmful bacteria are destroyed. But, some chemical pollutants – such as radon, chloroform and PCBs – can slip through.

Caution: Heating the water adds to your energy costs.

Safeguards to Protect the Consumer

An EPA number on home treatment systems is only proof of registration. It does not signify EPA product endorsement or approval.

Free in-home tests of your drinking water by companies selling home water treatment units may only be a sales tool! Limited or unsophisticated tests may present only a partial profile of water contaminants, without revealing whether the levels are actually harmful.

Ensure that the manufacturer provides a warrantee for your home water treatment unit. Read the warrantee – prior to purchase (not afterwards)!

Contact the Florida Cooperative Extension Service for their booklet, *Home Water Quality and Safety.*

Bottled Water

Many people are purchasing bottled water as an alternative to the public water supply and home filtration systems. The bottled water industry is regulated here by the FDA and the Florida Dept. of Health.

Water junkies claim that bottled water smells purer, looks cleaner and tastes fresher. For many, the real plus of a home dispenser unit is *cold water on tap*. The cost of getting "hooked" is a monthly water bill.

Caution: Prior to entering into an agreement with a distributor of bottled water, contact the FDA to ensure that all safety standards have been satisfied. *Ph. 301-443-4166.*

Becoming a Part of the Community

Finding Your Way

Getting your feet wet in a new community is much easier if you know where to locate information and pinpoint services which are available to you. Contact the county public information desk, the office of the city clerk, the library reference desk or the chamber of commerce if you need assistance in accessing the appropriate person or agency that can help you.

The Chamber of Commerce has a wealth of information to provide, including maps, demographic information, community services (education, religion, healthcare), special events/attractions and business referrals. Many have printed listings of their community associations and clubs as well as monthly events. If there are newcomers clubs or groups in the area, the chamber can probably provide you with a contact number.

Note: If the Chamber does not have a full listing of organizations in your area, contact the main library for assistance. They may have printed materials or listings of local clubs and groups.

Retired Senior Volunteer Program (RSVP)

RSVP is just for seniors. If you are 60 years of age or older and not quite ready to dedicate yourself exclusively to a life of leisure, RSVP is waiting for you. You may be asked to complete a checklist of activities you enjoy which correspond to different types of volunteer positions and/or a personal interview may be arranged to assist you with some of your choices. It is an excellent way to meet new friends in the community, help others, and remain active and vital. You can donate as much or as little time as you wish. As a small perk, there are a few government benefits which are available to RSVP members.

Volunteer Bureaus

Many counties have a Volunteer Bureau which is actually a clearinghouse for a variety of volunteer positions in non-profit agencies and organizations. Volunteers may be involved in such diverse areas as social services; school programs; library assistance; health support; government programs; cultural institutions; and environmental causes. The placements are varied and may present some unique and interesting opportunities.

Place Yourself

There is a wealth of interesting positions in fields which need volunteers. If you enjoy animals, you might want to volunteer at the Humane Society; if exotic plants and flora have a strong appeal, consider volunteering at the nearest botanical garden; if you have always been a theater subscriber, check out the community theater for volunteer opportunities. You need to identify your passions and find creative outlets for them. On occasion, volunteer positions lead to paid employment.

Outreach for Meeting People

For many, one of the more difficult aspects of moving to a new community is meeting and developing satisfying relationships with other people. If you seek opportunities to meet others, consider volunteering your services to a special cause or joining one of the many groups. If you haven't already noticed, Florida communities have clubs to suit almost any interest. You may have to do some self-exploration prior to deciding which ones are most closely in sync with your own interests/values. Take the time to go through this introspective process, since you may lose enthusiasm and withdraw from the group if the activities are not stimulating and compatible with your own interests.

Agencies and Free Publications

Florida Dept. of Health & Rehabilitation Services
Ph. 800-342-0828
The Health Care Cost Containment Board publishes booklets on health care costs: *Diagnosis and Hospital Charges; Outpatient Surgery - Hospital Fees;* and *Guide to Nursing Home Charges in Florida.*

Florida Dept. of Insurance
Ph. 800-342-2762
They publish free consumers' guide books to assist you with your insurance needs: *Automobile Insurance Shoppers' Guide* (an excellent resource); *Health Insurance Shoppers' Guide; Homeowners' Insurance Shoppers' Guide; Medicare Supplement Insurance Shoppers' Guide; Life*

Insurance and Annuities; Long Term Care Insurance; Health Maintenance Organizations.

The Florida Dept. of Insurance has local consumer offices throughout the state. They provide assistance and answer questions regarding your insurance needs and problems. If you have a problem that has not been satisfactorily resolved by an insurance company, write to:

Insurance Commissioner
State Capitol, Plaza Level 11
Tallahassee, FL 32399-0300
If you would prefer to call the toll free number but cannot get through, call the Consumer Assistance Line *(Ph. 904-922-3131)* or the Commissioner's Office *(Ph. 904-488-3440).*

Florida Dept. of Agriculture and Consumer Affairs
Division of Consumer Services: *Ph. 800-327-3382*
Free pamphlets on Florida consumer protection and services: *New Residents' Brochure; Senior Services and Information; Rights and Responsibilities of Landlord and Tenant in Florida; Gotta Gripe* (lists toll free numbers of agencies which can help you with a problem); *Lemon Law* (lemon aid for new vehicles that are defective).

The Senior Consumer: Call and request this monthly newsletter (it's informative and easy to read).

County Cooperative Extension Service
They will send you a packet of information on Florida insects, horticulture, landscaping, and poisonous plants. Contact them if you have plant problems or need some gardening suggestions. They also provide information on food & nutrition, marine life and wildlife conservation.

IFSA Publications (Institute of Food & Agriculture Sciences - University of FL) are available through this office.

The County Cooperative Extension Office presents educational programs for the home gardener. Call for their Calendar of Events.

Hurricane Information: Division of Emergency Management
Publications on how to prepare for hurricanes and what to do are available on request through your county office.

Public Service Publications
Where To Turn: Published by the United Way, this resource guide lists and describes social service agencies and programs which are available in the community. The United Way provides a great network of referrals when you don't know where to turn for information or need to be directed to the appropriate agency.

Great Sources of Information

Telephone Directory

Use your telephone directory, which has invaluable information, especially for the newcomer. In the front section of the white pages, a *Consumer Guide* lists local calling zones, telephone exchanges and locations, as well as the U.S. and State of Florida legislators. In the front section of the yellow pages, a *Community Interest Guide* provides newcomer information, area zip codes, hurricane maps, area events and attractions, airport information, street maps and more.

Government Directories

State of Florida Telephone Directory
Division of Communications. *Ph. 904-488-9311*
The Florida Directory lists state, county and city agencies and resources. There is a purchase fee.

County Directories

Many counties also publish a *Directory of County Services*, which is usually free upon request. These "user friendly" guides are highly recommended as they describe government departments and the services they provide. To track down the publication, start with the Public Affairs Department.

Cultural Events & Attractions Hotlines

Cultural affairs councils, arts councils, arts alliances have gone to the hotlines. In many cities, a 24-hour recorded announcement provides a listing of current cultural events taking place during the week.

Weather Service

Southern Living Weatherphone provides current weather conditions and a seven-day forecast in 600 cities across the United States and 300 international cities. The average call is two minutes at a cost of

97¢ a minute. Weatherphone is easily accessible and especially convenient prior to travel. *Ph. 900-933-3397.*

Florida Vacation Information

If you are planning a vacation within Florida, the following numbers may be useful.

	Area Code 904	Area Code 305
Visitor Inquiry Services	487-1462	
Historical Sites	487-2333	
Hotels and Motels	224-2888	
State Parks	488-9872	
Camping	656-8878	
Diving	222-6000	
Golf	488-8347	
Tennis		652-2866
Pari-mutuels		470-5675